D1448381

OUT OF THE SHADOWS

A HISTORY OF WOMEN IN TWENTIETH-CENTURY WALES

OUT OF THE SHADOWS

A HISTORY OF WOMEN IN TWENTIETH-CENTURY WALES

DEIRDRE BEDDOE

UNIVERSITY OF WALES PRESS
CARDIFF
2000

First published 2000. Reprinted 2001.

British Library Cataloguing in Publication Data
A catalogue record for this book is available from the British Library.

ISBN 0-7083-1591-7

Typeset at the University of Wales Press
Printed in Wales by Cambrian Printers, Aberystwyth

To Chris

Contents

List of Illustrations

Acknowledgements

The author and publishers are grateful to the following for permission to include copyright material (numbers refer to the items in the *List of Illustrations*):

Anglesey County Archives Service 12; Butetown History and Arts Centre 3, 15; Gwynedd Archives Service 4; Hoover European Appliance Group 18; Imperial War Museum 7; Jenny Lynn 21; Jenny Matthews 22; Martin Shakeshaft 23; Marian Evans 10; National Library of Wales 16, 17, 19, 23, 24; Sonia Davies 20; The Hulton Getty Picture Collection 6; Ursula Masson 8.

Preface

It has taken me a long time to research and write this book and many people have helped me. I wish to thank them all. In particular, the following have given me practical help, advice and encouragement and my thanks go to Jane Aaron, Neil Evans, Angela John, Dot Jones, Sheila Owen Jones, Anne Jones, Janet King, Medwen Roberts, Ted Rowlands MP, Jenny Sabine, Catrin Stevens, Meic Stephens, Mari Williams and Jen Wilson. The help of Ursula Masson of the University of Glamorgan goes almost beyond the realm of thanks, as she read each chapter in this book before publication and was always ready to share her insights with me and to offer advice. Similarly my special thanks go to Pamela Michael, of the University College of North Wales, Bangor, and Avril Rolph, both of whom also kindly read sections of the text. I have relied greatly on the expertise, goodwill and assistance of the staff of many libraries, record offices and museums. I wish to thank the librarian and staff of the National Library of Wales, Aberystwyth, and in particular Kathie Hughes, Beti Jones and Ceridwen Lloyd-Morgan; the Learning Resources Centre at the University of Glamorgan, Pontypridd; Cardiff University Library; the Fawcett Library, London; the Local Studies Department of Cardiff Central Library and Marilyn Jones, Local Studies Librarian, and the staff of Swansea Library and Information Services. Similarly, I wish to thank Susan Edwards and the staff of Glamorgan Record Office and the archivists and staff of all the county record offices in Wales who have always been extremely helpful. My special thanks go too to the late Minwel Tibbott and to Beth Thomas of the Museum of Welsh Life, St Fagans. I am also grateful to Teresa Rees, Equal Opportunities Commissioner for Wales, and to Val Feld, former EOC Director for Wales. I would like to thank Kate Bennett, the current EOC Director for Wales, and her staff for the generous use of the EOC library and facilities.

I wish to record my sincere thanks to the Arts Council of Wales for awarding me a travel bursary, which enabled me to conduct my research.

It has been a pleasure to work with the staff of the University of Wales Press. My thanks go to Ned Thomas, who originally commissioned this book, and to Susan Jenkins, Janet Davies, Ceinwen Jones, Ruth Dennis-Jones and Liz Powell for their patience and professionalism. As always, I thank too my long-standing agent Mandy Little, of Watson Little Ltd, London.

I wish to thank my Aunt Kathleen Durbin, whose life has spanned almost the whole of the twentieth century, for her encouragement.

Finally, *Out of the Shadows* would not have been possible without the unfailing and unstinting help and support of Christine Lee. My greatest debt is to her.

Deirdre Beddoe

Introduction

I HAVE written this book for a wide audience. For most of us living in Wales today, it tells the story of the lives of our own mothers, grandmothers and, in some cases, great-grandmothers. It is a history common to us all, and, as such, belongs to us all. *Out of the Shadows* covers the period of our own lives too, and for women readers in particular will, I hope, help to explain not only how we have come to be where we are now, but how our own identities have been shaped by the times in which we live. I hope too that this book will be of use to students and teachers of Welsh women's history and Welsh women's studies on a wide range of courses and to those pursuing their own individual research. Finally, I hope that this study will be of service to those with a broader interest in the history of twentieth-century Wales. In recent years Welsh history, both as a formal academic subject and as presented in popular books and television programmes, has shown an increasing interest in both women's contribution to a whole range of movements and in women's everyday experiences of life. This book is intended as a contribution to the process, whereby the history of Wales will one day come to mean the history of all its people, both women and men.

I have been ambitious, perhaps over-ambitious, in what I set out to do. *Out of the Shadows* spans the whole of the twentieth century. I have taken the term twentieth century to mean what most people understand by it, that is the years from 1900 to 1999, and I have not followed the common practice of historical writing which begins the century in 1914. I have attempted to cover what I regard as the key areas of women's lives, namely education, waged work, home life, health, leisure, politics and other issues of special relevance to women. I have aimed to include the experiences of women of all social classes and I have tried to take into account how regional variations and differing linguistic and cultural traditions have affected the experiences of women in different parts of Wales. It is a tall order for a short book. I have made a genuine effort in all this, but I would be the first to admit that I have not always succeeded.

This book is concerned with the lives of all the women in Wales. I have used the terms 'women in Wales' and 'Welsh women' interchangeably and I have

Robert Street, Barry, VE Day party, May 1945. *Back row, left to right*: my grandmother, Nellie Beddoe, my Auntie Evelyn, Auntie Betty and my cousin Elizabeth. *Front row*: the author, aged three, in Union Jack dress.

done so advisedly. I have written about all the women who lived/live and made their homes in Wales, regardless of their place of birth, their linguistic or ethnic identity, and even how they regarded themselves in terms of nationality. I have not confined my notion of a Welsh woman to a narrow stereotype, for to do so would be misleading and exclusive. My own two grandmothers illustrate the point. My mother's mother, Kathleen Durbin (née John) was born in St Dogmaels (Llandudoch) on the Cardiganshire side. She was a Welsh-speaker, and identified herself both as a 'Cardi' and as a *Cymraes* (Welsh woman). In terms of any measure of *Cymreictod*, (Welshness) she scored high. My father's mother, on the other hand, Ellen (Nellie) Beddoe (née Brittain) was born in Cardiff, was monoglot English and I have no idea how she thought of herself in terms of national identity. (My only clue is that she ran me up a dress made from two union jacks for the VE Day street party in 1945, but the war put a great emphasis on Britishness and this might be misleading.) Both my grandmothers married sailors, who on marriage became home-based dock workers, and both young families moved to Barry at the turn of the century at the time when the town was being hastily built around the new dock. I did not know my grandmothers until the 1940s, when they were both old, and by the 1950s both had died. My memory is of two very different women. I recall my Cardiganshire grandmother, with whom we lived, sitting reading her big Welsh Bible by the fireside every evening. She was a very devout woman, but a church- and not a chapel-goer. She disapproved of drinking, smoking and gambling – to her cards were the 'devil's playthings'. A tiny woman, with her grey hair pulled into a bun, she was the personification of that icon of Welsh womanhood, the Mam. To me, as a little girl, she was somehow 'holy' and I venerated her in much the same way as I did the print of Holman Hunt's *Light of the World*, which hung on my bedroom wall. I do not recall her ever going out, except to church and to the cemetery to put flowers on someone's grave. My other grandmother, Nellie Beddoe, was quite a different case. She too was a practising Christian. Born a Catholic, she converted to Nonconformity and was a regular attender at the little tin Baptist Church at the top of Barry's Weston Hill, where her brother was superintendent. She had insisted that my father join the Band of Hope and that, at the age of ten, he sign the pledge. Her life-style was in marked contrast to that of my other grandmother. Whereas Nana Durbin was never out, Nana Beddoe was never in. She went on bus trips whenever she could and every night of the week (except on Sundays when she went to the 'tin Baptists'), she attended whist drives. She backed horses (but only in the big races like the Derby and the Grand National), she drank stout which she bought from the jug and bottle at the Bassett Hotel and she smoked Craven-A corked-tipped cigarettes. My point is this. Both my grandmothers were Welsh women and this book seeks to cover not only the diversity of their lives but a whole range of other wide and varied experiences of women who lived and live in twentieth-century Wales. Definitions of Welshness are not static. Whereas, perhaps in 1900, it was necessary to possess a list of attributes and beliefs to 'qualify' as Welsh, by the beginning of the twenty-first century many have begun to realize that 'the Welsh People' is a pluralist and inclusive term. I have applied such pluralism and inclusivity in my view of the whole century.

A century seems a vast entity to tackle. It spans three-to-four overlapping generations, with one generation of women passing their memories on to the next. In a way, *Out of the Shadows* tells the story of all our families, showing how the experiences and even life-choices of our immediate female forebears were shaped and conditioned by the times in which they lived. My maternal grandmother, tricked, according to family legend, out of her inheritance by a cruel step-father, fled to London at the age of fourteen. She took up the position of a domestic servant in a large, upper-class London house, a situation which was arranged for her by the house's cook who also came from Cardigan. She met my grandfather, a Bristol man, when his ship was docked in the Port of London. They married and set up home in Barry. She bore seven children over a period of some fifteen years. One son died in infancy and another, aged seventeen, was killed in the First World War when his ship was blown up in the Irish Sea: in the absence of a body, she never came to terms with his death. She devoted her whole life to raising her family and to her domestic work within the home. She was nearly forty-five years of age when she was allowed to cast her vote in a parliamentary election for the first time. My mother was born in 1912. She passed the scholarship examination to the county school, but there was no question of her taking up a place as the family could not afford the weekly fee, the uniform or books. She left school at fourteen and worked briefly in service in a local hotel before securing the job she loved most, that of cinema usherette at Barry's Theatre Royal: she got to see all the films free, over and over again. In the 1930s, she joined the army of young women who left Wales to seek work in England. 'Encouraged' by the Labour Exchange, she took a job at Huntley and Palmers biscuit factory in Reading but, unable to bear the home-sickness, returned home after a fortnight. She married my father, a dock-worker in 1939. In the war, she worked in the Fire Service and her older sister, who also lived with us, became a supervisor in the Bridgend Arsenal. My mother bore two children over four years, one of whom, my elder sister, died in infancy. As my father's work on the docks was neither well-paid nor secure, my mother took a range of part-time jobs in the post-war years. I was born in 1942, I passed the scholarship and actually went to what was by then Barry Girls' County Grammar School and was free. I went on to university, and was the first person in my family to do so: I was enabled to do this by the existence of student grants and the absence of any liability to pay fees. I graduated and entered first teaching and then lecturing. I have been able to make my own life choices, largely because of the existence of a free education system which put me on the road to economic independence. I have no daughters of my own but my nieces have almost all gone to university, married and combined careers with having families. Within the span of a century the change has been remarkable.

It would have been impossible to have written this book without the women's movement of the 1970s: women's history and women's studies are a direct product of that movement. My task has been made possible because of the work of many other people and because of the existence of a growing body of work on Welsh women's lives. I am particularly grateful to be able to draw on *Our Mother's Land: Chapters in Welsh Women's History 1830–1939* (1991) edited by Angela John, and on *Our Sister's Land: The Changing Identities of*

Women in Wales (1994) edited by Jane Aaron, Teresa Rees, Sandra Betts and Moira Vincentelli. The work of Neil Evans, Pamela Michael and Sydna Ann Williams in compiling the teaching and learning materials that constitute *Project Grace* (1994) is an enormous contribution to women's history in Wales. I am both indebted to them and encouraged by their path-breaking efforts. Many other individual scholars have written on specific topics within this field, and much of their work has been published in *Llafur: The Journal of the Society of Welsh Labour History*. The growth in recent years in the publication of auto-biographies of Welsh women and of oral history collections has also made my task easier. When embarking on my researches, I quickly realized the need to make extensive use of Welsh-language sources. I had been learning Welsh, in a somewhat desultory fashion, for years, but my overwhelming curiosity and need-to-know what lay within the *ffynonellau hanesyddol* (historical sources) focused my efforts remarkably. Learning Welsh has been not only an enriching experience for me personally, but has enabled me to access the experiences of whole groups of women, which would have otherwise remained a closed book.

I have also cast my net widely to embrace a range of contemporary printed, written and visual sources. This has often been very rewarding but, at other times, extremely frustrating. For example, there were nearly forty women's groups in Wales involved in the great pre-First World War campaign for 'Votes for Women', but only five collections of their papers have survived – those of the Bangor, Cardiff, Carmarthen and Llangollen National Union of Women's Suffrage Societies and those of the Swansea branch of the Women's Freedom League. Similarly, the records of the Women's Liberation Movement of the 1970s have already largely disappeared. Sources are vital and without them there can be no history. Archif Menywod Cymru/The Women's Archive of Wales was set up at the end of 1997 with the express purpose of locating sources and depositing them in existing archives and record offices for safe keeping. It is vital work. Fortunately, too, The South Wales Feminist History and Archive Project, established by Ursula Masson at the University of Glamorgan in 1996, has located many of the sources for feminist activity in the 1970s and 1980s and a wide-ranging oral interview programme run by Avril Rolph has rescued the experiences of some Welsh women. A database of these sources is now available. Far more such initiatives, for instance the large-scale interview programme planned for Merched y Wawr (Women of the Dawn) members, are essential to the recovery of women's largely hidden history. Wales lags behind in this. Scotland and England already have their own women's libraries and archive collections, and in Ireland a huge state-funded project to identify and locate sources has already been completed.

Women's history is new history and has only been in existence in Wales for some twenty years. It is not surprising, therefore, that a huge amount of research is still necessary to uncover the lives of women, who have for so long remained hidden from history. When I embarked on this study of women in the twentieth century, I soon realized that I was sailing into uncharted waters. This is particularly true of the period since 1945, where far more research is still required. But the need for more detailed investigations applies to the whole of the twentieth century. In researching this book I became aware of certain distinct gaps in our knowledge. While I have done my best to fill some of these and to give an overview of women's lives, I came up against whole fields of women's activities about which we know next to nothing. I have written, for example, on women's participation in local government in certain localities at various periods within the twentieth century, but a major research project is required to trace their involvement in the work of local councils throughout the whole country and over the whole century. I am also particularly aware that I have failed to do justice to women's role within the trade union movement in Wales. A large research project on this topic is crying out to be done. These are just two examples of areas in urgent need of investigation. There are many more, and throughout this book I have highlighted research projects which I hope others will pursue.

One of the great pleasures of researching this book has been finding out about the lives of individual women, some of whom were previously just names to me and others I had never heard of. Cranogwen, – Sarah Jane Rees (1839–1916), sailor, poet, preacher, editor, temperance leader and saviour of fallen women – remains my personal favourite but, since she died in 1916, she is more a nineteenth-, than a twentieth- century, woman. Mary Collin (1860–1955), the formidable first headmistress of Cardiff High School for Girls, was tireless in her efforts to give her girls the best education available, including in the sciences – not then considered suitable subjects for girls. She was Cardiff's leading suffrage campaigner and continued her work for women well into her old age in the 1940s. Elsie Chamberlain became Bangor's first woman mayor in the Second World War and was so good that she held the post for two consecutive years: she is a wonderful example of the good sense women can bring to local affairs. There are many others who stand out from our history including Edith Picton-Turbervill, Violet Douglas-Pennant, Margaret Lady Rhondda, Lady Juliet Rhys Williams and Megan Lloyd George. These were all aristocratic or very privileged women but they all contributed to the lives of a broad spectrum of Welsh women. Finally, Dorothy Rees was MP for Barry 1950–1 and a Glamorgan County Councillor. She was an 'ordinary' woman – her parents had lodged with my grandparents – and she was a passionate advocate of education for girls. She was the only one of this list whom I knew personally. But what all the women named here had in common was a sense of 'duty' to other women and to the whole community. It is, sadly, an unfashionable concept now.

I have singled out certain exceptional women, but this book is mainly concerned with the lives of all the 'ordinary' women of Wales.

I have made fairly wide use of statistical sources. I am much indebted to John Williams's *Digest of Welsh Historical Statistics* (1985). The decennial census as a source of information on women's work presents certain problems. It fails to record much of women's casual and seasonal work and, by using changing categories over the years, makes it difficult to chart change over time. There are difficulties too in establishing women's economic participation rates (i.e. the proportion of the female population who are economically occupied). I have based economic activity rate figures for 1901–61 on the *Digest of Welsh Historical Statistics* and from 1971 onwards on the figures provided in T. Rees, *Women and Work: Twenty Five Years of Gender Equality in Wales* (1999). My main aim has been to be as consistent as possible in providing figures.

Finally, this book is based on the belief that, without a knowledge of our past, we are always having to begin again. I have aimed to give a short account of the lives of our foremothers over the last hundred years. It has not been an uninterrupted tale of progress and, although clearly women in Wales have come a long way, there remains a long way to go. Our past is an important resource, not only for understanding the present, but also in helping to shape the future.

~ 1 ~
Good Wives and Respectable Rebels, 1900–1914

We know remarkably little about the lives of women in Wales in the years between the dawn of the twentieth century and the outbreak of the First World War in August 1914. Although for many of us this was the world of our grandmothers or great-grandmothers and, in generational terms, is not far removed from us, the period seems remote. It was an era in which women wore long skirts and large hats, travelled in horse-drawn vehicles, worked as live-in domestic servants (or employed them) and were still denied the basic rights of citizenship. Some view these years through a haze of nostalgia. They look back to an idyll of Welsh-speaking rural Wales, where farming was carried on in the age-old way and the farm wife boiled *cawl* above the open fire, or to a reassuring vision of tightly knit and supportive communities in the industrial valleys of south Wales, where the Welsh Mam, that icon of Welsh womanhood, ruled the home, keeping coal-dust, want and trouble out. Others use the period as a yardstick from which to measure progress and see how far we have come since then. They look back on the harshness of life – on mothers worn out by years of successive pregnancies, their hands reddened and sore from scrubbing – and mourn the wasted lives of young girls (and boys) whose talents and aspirations were thwarted by poverty. History is about neither of these things, neither about romanticizing the past nor about painting a picture of unrelieved gloom and hardship, at which we shudder and give thanks that we live in modern times.

History, by drawing on a wide range of evidence, be it from photographs, newspapers, statistical tables, autobiographies or record sources, seeks to reconstruct a picture of the past. Historians must determine, analyse and evaluate the factors which shape people's lives and chart change over time. There is a long tradition of historical writing in Wales about this period but it has focused on men's lives – on industry and industrial disputes between a male workforce and male coal-mine or slate-quarry owners; on the actions of male protagonists in male political parties and on conflicts between one patriarchal organization and another. Of course, all of these have a bearing on women's lives and should be taken into account, but women's history, rather than attempting to fit women into male-defined areas of what constitutes significant activity, must concentrate on issues which were central to women's lives. The selection process has to be women-centred.

This chapter locates women in the historical period 1900–14. It provides a brief survey of Wales in those years and assesses the impact of the major forces at work in shaping women's lives. It examines the single dominant factor which determined their existence – the doctrine and practice of separate spheres. Thereafter, I have selected the following topics – the legal status of women; home life; health; education; employment; and finally, politics and women's issues. In attempting to cover these aspects of women's lives, I have tried to bear in mind the diversity of their experiences, as determined by social class, cultural and linguistic identity and geographical location.

Wales 1900–1914

The Wales of 1900 was a very different place from the Wales of 1800. In 1800, Wales was primarily an agricultural country with a population of under 600,000. By 1900, Wales was industrialized with major coal, slate, metal and dock industries and a population of over two million people. Industry was heavily concentrated in the south, which acted as a magnet to people from other parts of Wales and, particularly after 1900, from England too. In 1801, less than 20 per cent of the population lived in Glamorgan and Monmouthshire; by 1911, 63 per cent of the total population of Wales lived in these two counties, whilst rural counties such as Brecon, Cardigan, Merioneth and Montgomery suffered population losses. Coalfield towns grew phenomenally. Between 1871 and 1911 the population of Pontypridd grew from 11,000 to 43,000 and the sprawling ribbon of townships snaking their way up the Rhondda valleys increased from under 2,000 in 1851 to over 152,000 in 1911. More people lived in the Rhondda Urban District than in the whole of Cardiganshire, Breconshire and Radnorshire put together.

By 1900, Wales was a dynamic country playing a major part in the world economy through coal, metal and slate exports. Her industrial towns had lost their shanty, frontier air and boasted rows of terraced stone houses, shops and emporia like the Co-op and Home and Colonial, town halls complete with mayor and corporation, towering chapels, monolithic miners' institutes, noisy music halls and silent cinemas. Cardiff was the jewel in the crown of newly industrialized Wales: it was an impressive metropolis with its civic centre, coal-exchange, railway station, department stores, banks, theatres, hotels, respectable villas and tree-lined avenues. Cardiff's wealth was based on coal exports and other south Wales ports, namely Swansea, Barry and Newport, thrived too. Country and market towns like Carmarthen or Denbigh enjoyed a relative degree of prosperity following the agricultural depression of the 1890s, whilst the railway network had opened up the resorts along the coastline of mid and north Wales.

But what did industrialization and demographic change mean for women? Whereas industrialization meant the creation of thousands of jobs for men and enabled Welshmen to find work in their own country and not to have to emigrate in search of it, for women its impact was totally different. It is arguable that, in the short term, industrialization destroyed women's jobs. John Williams and Dot Jones's comparison of census returns for rural Cardiganshire and industrialized Glamorgan shows that, whereas one in three Cardiganshire women was in paid employment in 1911, in Glamorgan the figure was only one in five. Industrialization in Wales took the form of heavy industries which employed men and created no comparable factory work like that of Lancashire for women. Similarly, the consequences of demographic change were different for men and women. Although some whole families moved into the coalfield, the Rhondda attracted large numbers of single men and some married men who left their families at home on the land. The result was the creation of mining communities which were, in the strictest sense, male-dominated. The 1891 census shows that in the Rhondda there were 167 males to every 100 females in the 15–34 age group. We see the peculiarly male nature of Welsh coalfield communities when we compare these figures with the proportion of men to women in England and Wales as a whole in 1891, 93 males to every 100 females. In the whole county of Glamorgan in 1901 there were 93.7 females per 100 males and 94.3 females per 100 males in Monmouthshire. But in some rural areas the picture was quite the reverse. In Cardiganshire, in 1901, there were 127.2 females to every 100 males and in Pembrokeshire 111 females to every 100 males. In practice, this meant that women living in the coalfield had very good marriage prospects but little hope of paid employment, whereas their rural sisters had reasonable job prospects but little hope of finding a husband.

The upheavals caused by industrialization and population movements had profound effects on the Welsh language and Welsh society. The proportion of Welsh speakers declined between 1900 and 1914. Whereas the census of 1891 recorded that 54.4 per cent could speak Welsh, by 1901 this figure had dropped to 49.9 per cent and, in 1911, to 43.5 per cent. By 1911, a clear linguistic divide had emerged chiefly between rural and industrial areas, with almost 90 per cent of the inhabitants of Anglesey and Cardiganshire recorded as Welsh speakers, but only 38 per cent in Glamorgan. Depending on where they lived, people conducted their lives either through the medium of English or Welsh.

Society was changing too. Although the old social structure still appeared intact, with wealthy landowners (like Lord Penrhyn in the north and Lord Bute in the south) at the top of the pyramid, the days of the great estates were numbered. Tenant farmers and day labourers and their families, though differentiated in terms of status, all lived hard lives of poverty or near poverty on the land. Change was most apparent in the urban areas. A clear industrial proletariat had emerged, conscious of its class position, and the small Welsh middle class was growing, its ranks swelled by commerce and the professions. Women's class and status were defined by that of their menfolk, fathers and husbands. In fact, women were subsumed by their husband's persona: such forms of address as 'The Reverend Mrs Griffiths' or 'Mrs Doctor Price' demonstrate this, while at the same time rendering the women invisible. But it is noteworthy that in the first decade of the century some single women, largely through their entry into the professions of teaching and medicine, were beginning to determine their own economic fortunes and to define their own class position.

In politics Wales was Liberal and in religion Nonconformist. Women's political aspirations are discussed later, so suffice it here to say that the Welsh Liberal hegemony was a mixed blessing for women. They profited from egalitarian Liberal views on, for example, education, but on the key issue of the day for women, women's suffrage, the Liberals proved false friends. Nonconformity dominated the religious scene with Calvinistic Methodists, Independents and Baptists being the largest denominations. The massive edifices of the chapels loomed over the rural and urban landscape as constant reminders of their influence. The chapels were patriarchal institutions, where power was concentrated in the hands of older men, who exerted rigid control over their congregations. Contemporary photographs of black-suited and bearded deacons and elders, stiffly posed in the high places of the chapel, call to mind Old Testament patriarchs and judges. Women (and young men) were excluded from these élite circles of power. Although several charismatic female revivalists, passionate and inspired speakers who drew vast audiences, had emerged in the second half of the nineteenth century, the chapel authorities regarded such women as threatening and subversive and often displayed open hostility towards them. Women played a prominent role in the brief but sensational religious Revival of 1904–5, led by Evan Roberts, an ex-collier from Loughor. Pushing the established chapel hierarchies aside, women and young men organized their own more democratic services with their outpourings of emotional fervour. Eight of Roberts's team of ten followers on his first missionary journey were women who, far from being besotted religious 'groupies', as male versions of history frequently depict them, in fact, played a key part in organizing meetings and preaching. But the Revival was short-lived and women were expected to keep to their divinely allotted role, espousing the virtues of obedience to male authority, godliness, cleanliness, sobriety and thrift. Those who strayed from the narrow path were cast out. Women 'taken in adultery' or hapless, unmarried pregnant girls were publicly shamed and expelled from chapels. There is no doubt that the chapel exerted enormous influence in some communities but we must be cautious in generalizing. Not all women paid heed to its stern moral codes because not all women were church or chapel members. In 1907 three quarters of a million people, out of a total population of some two million, were recorded as communicants in Noncon-formist chapels and the Church of England. Although this represents a high level of religious observance, it does show that the majority of the Welsh did not 'belong to' any church. Nevertheless, there were other means than attendance at services through which the values and codes of conduct imposed on women by the chapels were transmitted and policed, not least by women themselves.

But it would be wrong to regard the chapel as an entirely negative and disabling influence on women's lives. There were enabling and enjoyable features too like adult Sunday schools, Bible study groups, Sisterhood meetings, choir practices, temperance and missionary magic lantern shows, singing festivals, eisteddfodau, chapel teas and outings. Welsh religiosity, having shackled women in its narrow confines to the extent that the chapel was virtually the only public place outside the home a respectable woman could attend, did at least offer education, entertainment, confidence-building and a social space.

Separate spheres

The economic, social and political state of Wales had a direct bearing on women's lives, but one single factor exerted more influence than any of these – the doctrine of separate spheres. Originating in early nineteenth-century England, this notion was vigorously promoted in Wales, particularly after the attack on the morality of Welsh women in the 1847 *Report on the State of Education in Wales*. Separate spheres meant separate worlds for men and women. Man's sphere was the public domain of work and politics; woman's sphere was the private world of home and family. Man's duty was to provide financially for his wife and family through money earned in the outside world. Woman's duty was to be a wife and mother and to create a home which was a refuge from the forces of darkness outside its walls: under her care, home would be a centre of Christian virtue, moral purity and sobriety. These were the allotted spheres and there was no crossing over. A woman's work was to be entirely domestic – cooking, cleaning, sewing, bearing and tending children. The doctrine of separate spheres demanded that women, especially married women, should not be involved in the productive process, in the world of 'real work'. They should not work in industry, in commerce or on the farm.

These ideas were formulated originally for the middle class in large English industrial cities, but how appropriate were they for Wales? The wives of affluent businessmen in Cardiff or Swansea may happily have given up doing their husbands' books, but could a shopkeeper in Llandrindod Wells or Caernarfon afford to lose his wife's help behind the counter, as separate spheres demanded? The wives of great landowners lived leisured existences, but could small farmers do without their wives' work in the dairy? A great deal of research is needed to answer these questions, but it is unlikely that many Welsh households engaged in small businesses or in agriculture could have survived without women's contribution. But what women, whose productive labour was necessary to the family economy, could absorb from this ideology was the quasi-religious view of wife and mother, notions of respectability, temperance, godliness and cleanliness.

It is in the mining valleys of south Wales that we see the most complete adoption of separate spheres and women's absorption of the domestic ideology in the emergence of that archetypal stereotype – the Welsh Mam. The wife and mother of coal-miners and the custodian of the home, she waged an endless battle against dirt; she scrubbed the floors, the doorstep and her husband's coal-black back; she was devout, temperate, thrifty and respectable. That such a complete working-class incarnation of the doctrine of separate spheres should emerge in the coal-mining areas is no accident. The heavy burden of her labour within the house took up all her time and, even if she had wished to work outside the home, there was no waged work for women in these areas anyway.

By the 1870s and 1880s these ideas had taken firm root in Wales. When chapel member and mother of nine, Mrs Jones of Windmill Terrace, Swansea, died in 1879 an In Memoriam notice was printed. It extolled her virtues under three headings – Wife, Mother and Christian. The first of these sections succinctly encapsulates the ideal of Welsh womanhood:

> *As a wife*, she was noted for her cleanliness, and its place for everything and everything in its place; ability to fulfil the duties of her house with judgement in the best way. She possessed much wisdom in her transactions with all, but especially in her family. She was able to govern them without forgetting that the husband is 'head of the wife' and she was often heard to say to her husband when he would have been provoked, 'Tut, Hugh bach, never mind, things will come right again.'

Mrs Jones understood woman's mission and the ideal which she represented was to persist, with only a little dilution, until well into the twentieth
century. By 1900, however, progressive women in Wales were seriously
challenging this confined and restricted model of womanhood. They had a
long way to go.

The legal system

Welsh women live under the laws of England and Wales and, until 1918, those
laws were exclusively man-made and based on patriarchal assumptions which
legalized women's inferior status. Before the First World War, women were
entirely excluded from the law-making process. They could neither stand for
nor vote in elections to Parliament, the very body which makes the laws.

There had been a major gain for women through the Married Women's
Property Acts of 1870 and 1882, which gave married women the same rights as
single women and widows to own property. Until the passage of these acts a
married woman had no separate legal existence and on marriage, her property,
money in the bank, earnings and even the clothes on her back became the
property of her husband. In practice, the fathers of wealthy daughters had
protected their interests through marriage settlements. The Acts extended such
protection to middle- and working-class women. By the 1880s, the washer-
woman could at least call her mangle and her earnings her own.

But, in other areas, the law still worked in men's favour. Whereas a man
could divorce his wife, under an act of 1857, on the grounds of adultery alone,
this was insufficient ground for a woman to divorce her husband. Equal
divorce legislation was not passed until 1923. The husband remained the sole
legal guardian of children of the marriage until an act of 1925 brought in equal
rights to child custody. Until that time a husband, if he wished, could, for
example, remove a child from the marital home and send that child wherever
he wished. Edith Picton-Turbervill (1872–1960) of Ewenny Priory in the Vale of
Glamorgan, who was later to become one of the first Welsh women elected to
Parliament and an ardent reformer of women's legal rights, recalled such a
case. A woman from nearby Bridgend came to her in great distress and told
Edith that her husband had sent their six-year-old son to Canada to live with
his sister. The woman was perfectly sober and respectable, but as Edith,
looking into the case on her behalf, discovered, nothing could be done. The
mother had no legal rights in the matter.

Feminists agitated for legal reform and, indeed, in addition to the Married
Women's Property Acts, they secured certain improvements. In 1885, the age of

consent for sexual intercourse was raised from thirteen to sixteen and in 1908 incest, not hitherto a crime, was made illegal.

Legal advances were important but nothing would change fundamentally while women were economically dependent on men and confined to their own separate sphere.

Home life

Since a woman's place was in the home, the quality of housing available was of paramount importance to her. There were some substantial villas in places such as Cardiff, Swansea, Aberystwyth and Llandudno, but the general standard of housing stock in both industrial and rural areas was quite a different matter.

There were housing shortages in the coalfield, where building had failed to keep pace with the influx of immigrants and terraces had been thrown up by colliery owners and speculators. Much valley housing was of the two-up, two-down variety and overcrowding was severe with families and lodgers tightly packed in. Rhondda had one of the worst overcrowding rates in Britain: in 1911 there were 5.8 inhabitants per house. The demand for housing meant that people would take anything available. There were over five hundred cellar dwellings, without natural light and no through ventilation, in the Rhondda in 1899: the Medical Officer of Health (MOH) decreed them unfit for habitation, but the shortage of accommodation meant that they were not shut down. However, not all valley housing was bad. There were solid three- and even four-bedroomed, bay-windowed properties built for more affluent workers: the Lewis Merthyr Colliery Company built a new village at Llwyncelyn between 1890 and 1902, and in 1907 the Tredegar Iron and Coal Company began work on a village for its workers at Oakdale, Monmouthshire. When Alice Howell, then a little girl, moved with her family from the Forest of Dean into a new three-bedroomed terraced house, with parlour, living room and kitchen in Bargoed in *c*. 1905, her mother and the whole family were thrilled at the space and comfort after their cramped rural home.

The first decade of the twentieth century saw great improvements in the infrastructure of the Rhondda. Late nineteenth-century sanitation reports make grim reading, reporting, as they do, muddy water supplies with frogs coming down taps, ash closets and stinking privy pits and the River Rhondda littered with old beds and polluted with human excrement and the bodies of dead cats and dogs. But the implementation of the public health acts gradually cleaned up the piped water supply, ensured dry closets were replaced by water closets and connected houses to the newly built main sewer, which ran down to the coast.

Accommodation in rural areas was far worse. The one- and two-roomed cottages of stone or whitewashed mud, some earth-backed, were dark, damp and ill-ventilated. Some were unfit for human habitation and possessed no water supply, drainage or sanitation. The Caernarfonshire MOH in 1909 described dwellings in Abermarchnad near Cricieth, where ten houses had just five closets and one ash pit, had no windows and no back doors and their only ventilation came from skylights. Overcrowding was a rural problem too. In 1912, thirteen families of five and three of nine were living in two-roomed dwellings in Buckley, Flintshire. In the Holywell rural district, ninety-eight families of between five and ten people lived in two-roomed cottages. Writing in 1913 the Cardiganshire MOH summarized the plight of rural housing in his county. He wrote:

> a large percentage of so called 'houses' deserve no better term than 'hovel', as one so often finds them with leaky roofs, floors and walls saturated with damp, wall-paper peeling and mildewed, storm water flowing through living rooms, windows, small and never intended to be opened and in some localities, notably Cwmystwyth, 'back-to-earth' cottages abound.

It is hard to imagine how heavy the burden of housework was on Welsh women at the beginning of the century, lacking as they did all the basic amenities that we now take for granted – bathrooms, indoor lavatories, running water, hot water on tap, instant heating, cookers and electricity. Domestic work was solely the woman's responsibility and the weekly and daily round of chores – cleaning, cooking, washing and childcare – was exhausting. In the mining areas, where the housewife waged a continuous battle against the all-pervasive coal dust, women worked long days geared around the shifts of husbands, sons and lodgers. They cooked on open ranges, boiling pans and kettles on the hob and baking bread and roasting meat in the side oven. In some mining towns they still drew water from street taps and in the country from pumps, wells and rivers: it all had to be heated, in buckets on the fire or in copper boilers. They washed by hand, using soda or bars of soap, and rubbed each garment against a zinc rubbing-board. Workmen's clothes were dirty – thick with coal in the Rhondda, with slate dust in the north-west and with grease in the port towns. Author Kate Roberts described how her mother washed her quarryman husband's trousers:

> And it was a terrible day when she had to wash his working clothes. We had a saucepan to wash clothes. We had to do it all in the kitchen, in an egg-shaped saucepan which had a big handle across the top of it. She had to boil the working

clothes in water and soda. My mother – I don't know how she did it – would carry this big oval saucepan with the clothes inside it and put it under the water spout to rinse them in all kinds of weather.

Clothes were aired and dried in bad weather on wooden lines above the fireplace and on clothes-horses put in front of it, then ironed with a heavy flat iron heated on the fire.

The lack of a ready supply of hot water was one of the harshest trials of the miner's wife. In the absence of pit-head baths, miners had to bath at home every night. Mrs F. H. Smith, a Cardiff woman who had married a Rhondda miner in 1903, wrote to Margaret Llewelyn Davies of the Women's Co-operative Guild:

> I was very shocked that we had no convenience for our husbands to bath in. We had to bring a tub, or a tin bath, whichever we had, into the same room that we lived in, and heat the water over the living-room fire in a bucket or iron boiler, whichever we possessed. So you can imagine the life of a miner's wife is no bed of roses.

Carrying the hot water was not only heavy work, it was dangerous too. Mrs Smith remarked:

> No wonder so many children are scalded to death in Wales, as many people, unthinking, put the hot water in first, forgetful of the little ones toddling around them, and they stumble in. A little one, living close by me, five years old, died last week through falling in a bath of hot water.

Open fires were themselves hazardous and women in their long dresses and young girls in their voluminous pinafores were recorded as burning to death when stretching up to reach the mantel shelf.

But despite all the difficulties, or perhaps in defiance of them, women in the mining valleys took immense pride in keeping their houses spotlessly clean. They black-leaded grates, polished brass, white-stoned the front door step and washed the pavement outside. They were 'tidy' women who knew that cleanliness was next to godliness and they could say, 'We were poor but we were clean.'

Unlike coal or slate, we do not have the tonnage figures for sheets washed, dried and ironed, for potatoes peeled and boiled, or loaves of bread kneaded and baked in fire-side ovens. Women's work has passed unrecorded and, because it was unpaid, has not been technically recognized as work at all. But it was women's work which formed the bedrock of industrial production, servicing the needs of working men and reproducing the next generation of miners, quarrymen and dockers.

Housework was a class-specific activity: only working-class women and girls did it. Women of the upper classes never lifted a flat iron or a scrubbing brush and middle-class women, enjoying the help of domestic servants, avoided all the heavy work. Lady Rhondda was engagingly honest in declaring her ignorance of housework and childcare. When her mother-in-law suggested that she should teach the village women of Caerleon the domestic arts, she refused, saying, 'They know far more about these things than I do. I will not teach people things they know and I don't.' When in 1908 she married Sir Humphrey Mackworth, they kept three maids and a cook to look after the two of them. Edith Picton-Turbervill was even more candid. She was in her forties when she bought a weekend 'hut' and first tried her hand at cooking. 'Until I possessed my hut', she wrote, 'I had never – I am ashamed to say – boiled a potato or fried a sausage for myself.'

Class and income, as well as locality, had a direct influence on what people ate. In the rural areas the poor had a monotonous and inadequate diet. The Cardiganshire MOH wrote in 1910: 'The diet consists of tea, bread and butter, bread and milk, porridge, bacon, pork and broth (*cawl*). Butchers' meat is a 'rarity' as it is exceedingly difficult to obtain in most rural districts.' Fresh beef and lamb were beyond the budget of the farm labourer but bacon was a staple food and an essential ingredient to flavour and add substance to the *cawl*. Cottagers, especially the women, fattened up 'baconers' and salted the meat for the household's use. Better-off farmers' families had a more varied diet, including cheese, eggs and butter. Farm wives provided food for large numbers of people including farm workers and servants, so baking days were very busy and enough large round loaves of bread, slabs of cake and fruit and jam tarts to last a fortnight were cooked. Women in the industrial areas carried on what we have come to regard as a rural tradition of making jam, pickles and chutney and preserving soft fruit. Similarly, they made their own bread (often baked in the local bakery's ovens), pies, cakes and meat products such as brawn and faggots: making faggots in south Wales or pickling herrings in the north and selling them was one way for women to make a little money. In many parts of Wales it was the practice to cook a hot meal at midday and children carried their father's meal to his place of work. It is a feature of this period that women began to buy far more of their foodstuffs in shops or from traders passing along the street. But, however they acquired it, meals had to be prepared and cooked from basic ingredients.

It is now part of the folklore that in hard times women 'went without', denying themselves to feed their families. There were certainly hard times in these years with a long drawn-out strike in the slate quarries, frequent and lengthy coal disputes and a major dock strike. Women were also at the mercy of drunken husbands, who would spend their wages on drink and deprive their families of the barest necessities. The *Western Mail* of 12 January 1900 reported one such case in Grangetown, Cardiff, where a seven-month-old child died of starvation and the wife was discovered to have lived solely on tea and bread.

Health

Hard physical labour, poor diet, damp and overcrowded housing, together with the debilitating effect of frequent pregnancies, exacted a terrible toll on women's health. Margaret Llewelyn Davies, secretary of the Women's Co-operative Guild, in the introduction to *Maternity: Letters from Working Class Women* (1915), described the lives of even the more fortunate working-class mothers as characterized by 'perpetual over-work, illness and suffering'. Working-class women, in contrast to those of the middle class, received little medical attention. A visit to the doctor had to be paid for and women, who managed meagre family budgets, would not 'waste' money on themselves. The National Health Insurance Act of 1911 provided insured workers, male and female, with access to a general practitioner but very few Welsh women were insured workers and the Act did not cover dependants. In some industrial areas women (and children) benefited from their husbands' membership of a Medical Aid Society: metal workers in Llanelli and miners in Tredegar, for example, paid in weekly contributions for the doctor's services.

The consequences of poor living standards and state neglect of women's health are no more dramatically demonstrated than in the statistics for female mortality for the first decade of the century. In the Pontypridd Registration District, which included the Rhondda valleys, the mortality rate (deaths per 1,000 of population) in the period 1901–10 for women in the age group 20–24 was significantly higher than for men. This is in marked contrast to death rates for the same age group in England and Wales as a whole, where death rates for females were lower than those for males. As Dot Jones pointed out in 'Counting the cost of coal' (*Our Mothers' Land*, 1991), 'The unremitting toil of childbirth and domestic labour killed and debilitated Rhondda women as much as accident and conditions in the mining industry killed and maimed Rhondda men.' It is truly remarkable that such sacrifice has been allowed to pass unnoticed for so long.

Childbirth had a direct bearing on women's health and on the statistics of female mortality. Working-class families remained large throughout the period and families of six, seven, eight and more were common particularly in the mining districts. Michael Lieven's study of Senghennydd shows six families, all called Jones, and notes how many children each had in the years 1900–14:

> Hannah and Edward Jones had six children who survived until 1914; Margaret and Evan Jones had seven, Ann and William Jones had seven, Louisa and Thomas Jones had six, Mary and James Jones had eight and Polly and Thomas Jones had seven.

These figures refer to children who survived but not all children did. It was common practice for mothers, when asked how many children they had, to give two sets of figures – those who had survived and those who had died in infancy or at birth. In response to the detailed questioning of mothers for Margaret Llewelyn Davies's survey *Maternity* of 1915, women gave such answers as 'seven children, three still-births, four miscarriages' or 'nine children, six miscarriages'. Women at the turn of the century spent an *average* of fifteen years in childbearing and nursing, compared to four years in the period after the Second World War.

The great majority of births took place at home in bedrooms lit at best by oil lamps. There was no pain relief and the practice was for women to pull on a towel tied to the end of the bed when the pains came. Only in the direst circumstances were women given anaesthetic, as in the case told by a Swansea woman to Jeffrey Grenfell Hill:

> I was quite some time overdue and by this particular Saturday I had been in labour some time. On the Sunday morning my husband came to me and could see my distress. The midwife and my husband and my older brother were very concerned and so a doctor was called . . . By the Sunday night my mother told me that I had had the baby. I was so drugged up I could not take it in. On waking on the Monday the midwife told me that the baby was born dead. It was a breech birth, and the doctors had broken its neck and legs during delivery.

The letters to Margaret Llewelyn Davies tell horrific tales of miscarriages, still-births and medically mishandled deliveries, often followed by life-long disablement for the mother. One letter, entitled 'Struggles of a Miner's Wife', was from a woman who had borne seven children, only four of whom survived. Her letter is typical of the matter-of-fact tone in which such women recounted their experiences:

> I may say I had very good times at confinements except the first and the last. The youngest was born feet first, which was an awful experience, and her heart was

nearly stopped beating; so I think that left her heart weak; and she cut her teeth with bronchitis. I used to get up always by the ninth day until the last. I was between forty-one and forty-two when she was born, so I had to rest a little longer, but had to see to household duties as soon as possible.

Midwives had attended births since time immemorial. They had gained experience on the job and were trusted figures in the community, also often performing the necessary function of laying out the dead. The process of professionalization of the birth process and its relocation within the sphere of medical men advanced rapidly in these years. The Midwives Act of 1902 required that midwives should be trained, qualified and centrally registered; the untrained women, known as *bona fides*, were to be phased out. In practice, there were not enough registered midwives to meet community needs: as late as 1922 of the ninety-nine midwives practising in Flintshire, twenty-two were *bona fides*. Midwives and doctors had to be paid and the National Health Insurance Act of 1911 introduced a thirty-shilling maternity benefit to be paid to the husband: agitation by the Women's Co-operative Guild secured that this grant was paid to the mother from 1913.

The main concern of the state at this time, however, was not with the health of mothers but with that of infants, whose rising mortality rates were viewed with alarm, and with the physical condition of British youths. The Inter-Departmental Committee on Physical Deterioration, which had been set up in response to the poor quality of recruits to the Second Boer War, issued its report in 1904. The committee looked into the causes of what it called 'the annual sacrifice' of infants, but, instead of focusing on the obvious cause of poverty, it laid the blame on the fecklessness and ignorance of working-class mothers in matters of nutrition and hygiene. Its recommendations included educating mothers and young girls in cookery, infant care and cleanliness. This led to an even greater emphasis on domestic subjects in the education of working-class girls and to a number of measures to improve the health of the young. The Education Act of 1906 allowed local authorities to provide school meals and the medical inspection of school children began in 1907. The education of mothers was put in hand with the establishment of 'Schools for Mothers' or 'Babies' Welcomes', one of which was opened in Newport, Monmouthshire, in 1907. Mothers went along there seeking advice on how best to look after their babies but the health workers lectured them on personal hygiene and the need to eliminate dirt from their homes.

The blame for the infant mortality crisis was placed squarely on the mothers. The report of the Carmarthenshire MOH in 1908 is typical of many others:

In past years I have repeatedly drawn attention to the fact that the principal cause of infantile mortality in the District is due to the want of knowledge possessed by young mothers of the most elementary principles of feeding infants. In the absence of breast milk, their natural food, infants are fed on anything but what they should be, such as bread and water, tea, gruel etc.

In fact, infant mortality rates declined rapidly from 163 deaths per thousand births in 1893 to below 100 in 1914, but the problem of maternal mortality, which was set to rise from 1918 to the mid–1930s, continued to be largely ignored. In Wales, maternal mortality rates were consistently higher than for the rest of Britain. Between 1901 and 1910 the maternal death rate per 1,000 live births for England and Wales as a whole was 4.0; in rural Cardiganshire the figure was 5.7 and in the Pontypridd registration district it was 6.1. The situation in Wales became so bad that, by 1936, a special committee was set up to investigate maternal mortality in Wales: this is discussed in chapter 3.

Pregnancy and childbirth were not the only potentially life-threatening conditions for women. Tuberculosis (phthisis, commonly known as consumption, and other tubercular diseases) was the single leading cause of death for both males and females in the nineteenth century, and it remained the great scourge of the first half of the twentieth century. It was *y pla gwyn* – the white plague – and was more prevalent in rural Wales than in any other part of Britain. Between 1903 and 1907, of the fourteen worst hit counties, where the mortality rate from tuberculosis (TB) exceeded the mean figure for England and Wales, seven were Welsh. In fact, the top five counties in terms of deaths from TB were Cardigan (with a death rate of nearly double the average for England and Wales), Merioneth, Caernarfon, Carmarthen and Pembroke: Anglesey, which occupied seventh place, was soon to go to the top of the list. There were variations in the incidence of TB within counties. In the county of Caernarfon, for example, the coastal resorts of Llandudno, Conway and Penmaenmawr had much lower death rates than the rural districts. But while statistical tables of mortality rates help us to see the geography of the disease, they do not reveal the human story of whole families wiped out by it. D. Parry Jones, looking back to his youth in Carmarthenshire, recalled in *Welsh Country Upbringing* (1948), two families of his acquaintance:

> In one it carried off the father and five children in their middle twenties, leaving the mother, orphaned of her family to reach a ripe old age . . . In the other, four out of a big family of girls succumbed to it.

Doctors had only an incomplete understanding of the causes of the disease before the First World War, though clear links were made with damp housing, poor diet and tubercular cows' milk and its rapid transmission was related to overcrowded housing, where TB sufferers shared bedrooms with two or three other family members. There were attempts to raise awareness of the dangers and in Tregaron cards printed with information on 'How To Prevent Consumption' were sent to every household. Facilities for treatment were scarce and life-saving drugs had not yet been developed. Alltymynydd Sanatorium built in 1906 served the whole of the counties of Cardigan, Carmarthen and Pembroke. From 1910, the Welsh National Memorial Association focused on the problem and began to make inroads against the disease.

Mental illness and insanity, on the other hand, were largely regarded as intractable and insoluble conditions, from which there was no hope of recovery. Madness looms large in Welsh literature. Allen Raine (Mrs Anne Adaliza Puddicombe), the best-selling authoress of romantic fiction set in west Wales, supported her insane husband from her earnings and frequently touched on the subject. In *Torn Sails: A Tale of Welsh Village Life* (1908) she wrote:

> It is no uncommon thing to see in a small village containing two or three hundred inhabitants, two or three windows boarded and barred behind which are kept the unhappy sufferers from this terrible fate. The dread of the asylum hangs like a cloud over the scene that appears such a picture of rustic happiness.

In the same novel she traced the descent of one woman into madness, mirroring the stages of her decline by the gradual raising of her shawl from the normal position over the shoulders until eventually her whole head was covered by it as the woman shut out the world. Caradoc Evans, in his notorious and powerful short-story collection, *My People* (1915), also portrayed women in the same geographical area as Allen Raine. In his work, women were subdued into servitude and sometimes pushed into madness by the men in the family, who then proceed to treat them as beasts. The chapel elder in 'A Father in Sion' imprisoned his wife, the mother of his eight children, in a barred and padlocked loft, letting her out only at night when 'he threw a cow's halter over her shoulders and drove her into the fields for an airing'. Likewise Mathilda in 'Lamentations', the victim of incest by a self-righteous and Bible-punching father, was trapped like an animal and driven over twenty miles on foot by him, with hands bound 'in the manner a colt is driven, to the madhouse of the three shires which is in the town of Carmarthen'. It is interesting that both Allen Raine and Caradoc Evans wrote about the same small corner of rural Cardiganshire. Russell Davies's studies of the Carmarthen asylum, serving the counties of Cardigan, Carmarthen and Pembroke, would indicate that insanity was more prevalent in rural than in urban areas: whereas the industrial town of Llanelli recorded a rate of 2.3 certified insane per thousand population, the rural areas of Newcastle Emlyn, Llandovery and Narberth had rates in excess of 3.5. People in the rural areas were also more likely to send disturbed family members to the asylum – a fact which somewhat dents romantic notions of old and supportive kinship networks. But whether these unfortunates were confined at home or in the great gloomy edifices of the asylums, with their punitive regimes, restraints and uniforms for inmates, the recovery rate was abysmal. Despite the aspirations of medical staff, few recovered: in Carmarthen in the 1890s less than ten per cent of inmates were regarded as curable. The asylums – places rarely described by their full titles and usually denoted only by the name of the nearest town – were dumping grounds for the disturbed, the unbalanced and for problem family members. Their very names – Bridgend, Denbigh (serving five counties of north Wales) or Carmarthen struck a chill in people's bones and rightly so: few ever escaped their care.

Education

Life held few prospects for young Welsh girls in the years before the First World War. Their lives would follow the same pattern as their mothers – marriage, childbearing, house work and managing on a tight budget. They were prepared for such a future by the twin agencies of home and school. At home, girls helped with the washing, cleaning and cooking and acted as 'little mothers' to younger siblings. It was girls not boys who were kept at home on washdays and to mind the baby: truancy rates for girls were higher in many parts of Wales than those for boys. Many older women today, looking back on those years, say, 'I really wanted to be a nurse or a teacher, but it wasn't possible.' Their lives were determined by economic constraints and by the domestic ideology, which was promoted with vigour through the school system.

The only education available to the vast majority of working-class girls and boys was elementary. The Education Act of 1870 had established School Boards, locally elected bodies for which women were allowed to stand, to build and administer the new board schools. These schools, often towering edifices set in bleak asphalt playgrounds bounded by lavatory sheds, were erected with amazing rapidity after 1870. But the Boards did not cover all of Wales and in some areas children had to attend National schools (i.e. Church schools), much to the anger of Nonconformists. The Education Act of 1902 abolished School

Boards and placed responsibility for schools into the hands of county council education committees, bodies to which women could not be elected, only co-opted to fill token places. Attendance at elementary schools was made compulsory in 1880. The official school-leaving age, set at eleven in 1893, was raised to twelve in 1899 and to fourteen in 1918, though pupils often left before reaching the official leaving age.

Young girls with their long hair, ankle-length dresses, starched white pinafores and heavy laced boots, walked daily to school: in rural areas a four- or five-mile walk each way was common. Punctuality was important and late-comers were punished. Regular attendance was encouraged by attendance prizes and enforced by the truant officer – called variously the Boardie, the Whipper-in or *Plismon Plant*. The school day began in many places with an inspection of hands for cleanliness and there were regular inspections too of pupils' heads for lice, a problem which affected girls far more than boys, of teeth, hair, eyes, general health, boots and clothing.

Class sizes were large and several standards were frequently taught together. His Majesty's Inspector of Schools (HMI), visiting Mold Council in July 1908, reported that Miss Smith was teaching fifty-four girls from standards 3 and 4 in a small classroom in very hot weather. Discipline was generally strict. Joyce Leakey's mother kept her home from Brynhyfryd Infants School in Swansea because, 'they would slap and hit the children; even in the Babies' Class.' O. Wynne Hughes's Aunt Elsie recalled the woman teacher in Harlech grinding her knuckles into pupils' heads when they made a mistake. But discipline varied from school to school, as did the wider educational experience of pupils. Much depended on individual teachers, who had it in their power to make school a life-enhancing and stimulating experience or a living hell.

The evidence of school text and exercise books, together with local school records, conjures up long hours of dull lessons. Textbooks, invariably anthologies containing snippets of history (the kings and queens of England), geography (the rivers of France and the manufactures of England) and religion (the voyages of Saint Paul), sought not only to inform their young readers but to improve them morally. Poems, prose pieces and snappy mottoes urged members of the working class to know their place and stressed the virtues of honesty, cleanliness and hard work. 'It is a sin to steal a pin, much more to steal a greater thing' was advice with a particular resonance for young girls whose only career option was to work as a servant in the homes of the better-off. Teaching for both boys and girls focused heavily on the three Rs, but the curriculum was very clearly gender-differentiated.

Girls spent many hours sewing. They pinned and tacked and hemmed; they made pillowslips, pinafores and baby's clothes. Boys were spared this labour.

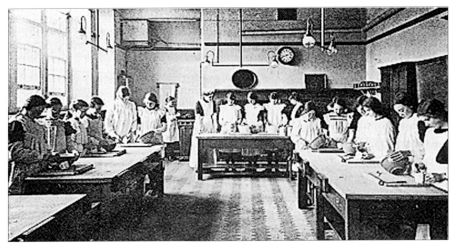

Cookery class, Caerphilly Higher Elementary School, 1914.

Emma Edmunds, headmistress of a Caerphilly infants' school in 1899, noted the syllabus for her young female charges for that year as:

1. Hemming, knitting, pin-drills.
2. To hem a pinafore or apron.
3. To knit a scarf, muff or pair of cuffs.

The infant boys, on the other hand, spent their time in learning how to draw 'twenty geometrical patterns and easy objects on chequered slates'. But gender differentiation of the curriculum went far beyond sewing.

Throughout the period from the 1870s to the First World War the emphasis on domestic subjects for elementary school girls expanded rapidly. From 1878, domestic economy became a compulsory subject and grants were made available to schools to teach first cookery (1882), laundry work (1889) and housewifery (1900). Specialist cookery and laundry centres were set up throughout Wales. By 1911 there were nine cookery and three laundry centres in Cardiff alone but even these did not meet the growing numbers of girl pupils, 'the future Home Makers of the City' as the Board of Education dubbed them. Accommodation was crowded and facilities were inadequate in south Wales. A lady inspector visiting one Cardiff centre reported:

The work was much hampered by the dirty condition of the stove and the lack of cooking utensils. The whole class had to wait for one teaspoon, which was much in demand for the measuring of sugar, spice, ginger and baking powder. Much time was lost in this way, and owing to the low temperature of the oven, the gingerbread scones had scarcely begun to cook when the class was dismissed.

Teachers tended to concentrate their pupils' efforts on making sweet things like cakes and buns, at the expense of wholesome fare such as meat pies and cooked dinners, for the simple reason that the former were more easily saleable. For years the centres had to recoup the costs of the ingredients by selling the food around the neighbourhood.

Parents were not altogether enthusiastic about their daughters spending so much time on domestic subjects, the general feeling being that they could learn that at home. Some Cardiff parents refused to allow their daughters to attend cookery lessons, so when the Cardiff School Board Cookery Sub-Committee planned to introduce laundry work in 1896 they polled the parents first. In whole areas of the city the parents declared against it, but washing, starching and ironing was nevertheless added to the schoolgirls' curriculum.

In fact, in the first decade of the twentieth century the domestic emphasis intensified. The Inter-Departmental Committee on Physical Deterioration Report of 1904, which had looked into the reasons for the poor health of recruits to the Boer War, blamed the ignorance of working-class wives for the poor state of British manhood and this led to an even greater concentration on domestic subjects in schools and in particular to the introduction of lessons in childcare. Albert Road Elementary School in Penarth was held up as a fine example to other schools. In December 1909, the magazine *School World* published an account stating that the older girls in that school spent five hundred hours a year on domestic subjects and (in addition to the usual cookery, laundry and housewifery classes) the girls learned practical childcare using 'live infants'. It reported, 'every week each little home-maker writes an account of the child under her charge. In this way, the girls gradually find out that there is no more interesting work than the care of children.'

There can be no doubt that the elementary education of working-class girls aimed primarily to produce good wives for working men and well-trained domestic servants for their betters. The history of girls' secondary education on the other hand is an inspiring tale and shows that public provision in Wales was in advance of England.

The Welsh Intermediate Education Act of 1889, one of the great achievements of Liberal Wales, was the product of long campaigning by influential Welsh men and women. Dr Frances Hoggan, Dilys Davies, Elizabeth Hughes and Margaret Hay Williams (Lady Verney) were vigorous and highly articulate advocates of both secondary education and higher education for girls in Wales and it was in large part due to their efforts that the 1889 Act enshrined the principle of equal opportunities. Under the Act a network of publicly funded intermediate schools was established throughout Wales, which made available an academic, as well as a practical and technical, education to girls and boys. By 1900, there were ninety-three intermediate schools in Wales erected in the counties and county boroughs and hence commonly called 'county schools'. Of these, twenty-two were boys' schools, twenty-one girls' schools, forty-three dual schools (that is schools with girls' and boys' sides) and seven mixed schools. The curriculum in them was soundly academic and, in the Welsh county schools, girls seem to have been regarded as of the same intellectual ability as boys and entitled to the same education as them, though some lingering prejudice remained against girls doing science.

The first generation of headmistresses of girls' schools was an impressive band, including Miss Mary Collin (Cardiff High), Miss Beatrice Holme (Carmarthen), Miss Catherine Davies (Llanelli), Miss Margaret Davies (Brecon) and Miss Annie Dobell (Blaenau Ffestiniog). Mary Collin was Cardiff's leading feminist and totally committed to equal opportunities. She inspired awe and affection in her pupils and sought to offer the very best education to her girls. She actively promoted the sciences and ensured that the school offered a whole range of extra-curricular activities such as debating and drama societies. Modelled on the schools of the Girls' Public Day School Trust, Cardiff High was characterized by an academic ethos and encouraged its girls to go on to university. The county schools were preparing the brightest girls for an increasing, though still limited, number of careers which were opening up to them.

Secondary education, however, was not free and not everyone who passed the scholarship examination could afford to take up a place at the county school or at one of the new municipal secondary schools opened after 1902. In 1907, under a reforming Liberal government, the number of free places was increased by 25 per cent and many municipal schools in south Wales were even more generous. Two-thirds of the girls at Dynevor Municipal School for Girls in Swansea in 1907 and nearly half of those at Cyfarthfa Castle Municipal School in Merthyr were exempt from paying fees. By 1913, Gareth Evans points out, 47.2 per cent of girls and 46.23 per cent of boys in Welsh secondary schools had free places. The doors of opportunity were opening and girls were taking advantage of this. By 1913, there were significantly more girls than boys in the secondary schools of Glamorgan and twice as many in Monmouthshire. This is an amazing fact and may perhaps be accounted for by boys finding secondary education 'sissy' or by parents not choosing to bother with secondary education for their sons as boys had to go out to work to bring in money for the household.

The contrast between girls' elementary and secondary education is striking, but secondary schools were not entirely immune from the mood in favour of a domestic education for girls. The Board of Education (Welsh Department) and the Central Welsh Board criticized the girls' schools for their neglect of domestic subjects and urged them to develop cookery and housecraft. In many cases this fell on deaf ears. The headmistress of Dr Williams School, Dolgellau (an older establishment brought into the new system) annoyed the HMI for domestic subjects by stating that she thought the subject was only for 'the most stupid girls in the school' and the 'last resort of incompetents'. Miss Vivian, headmistress at Newport Girls' School, thought domestic subjects fit only for the weakest intellects and described the pupils who did these subjects as the 'crocks'. Under such heads, the curriculum in girls' secondary schools remained firmly academic.

In higher education Wales lagged behind Scotland and England but by 1884 women were admitted to all three colleges in Wales – Aberystwyth, Cardiff and Bangor. The University of Wales Charter (1893) gave women a position of complete equality with men:

> Women shall be eligible equally with men for admittance to any degree which the University is, by this Charter, authorized to confer. Every office hereby created in the university, and the membership of every authority hereby constituted, shall be open to women equally with men.

These were very fine, liberal and democratic sentiments which were applauded by the Welsh women who had campaigned for equality in higher education, but it would be naïve to believe that in practice there was no distinction of sex in the University of Wales. However this open admission policy ensured high numbers of women students in the Welsh colleges.

Table 1.1 Numbers of full-time students (Wales)

| | 1900–1901 | | 1910–1911 | |
	Men	Women	Men	Women
Aberystwyth	266	208	262	192
Bangor	179	100	229	95
Cardiff	333	167	408	189

The record of the Welsh colleges in these years in admitting women stands in stark contrast to that of the ancient universities of Oxford and Cambridge, where only some 10 per cent of students were women, and is considerably better than that of English provincial universities such as Leeds, Liverpool and Manchester.

The higher education of women is closely linked with the teaching profession. The first teacher training college in Wales for women had been opened in Swansea in 1872, followed by St Mary's College, Bangor, an Anglican foundation originally training male students, in 1896. Bangor Normal College admitted its first women students in 1908 and, by 1909, approval had been given for the erection of a women's training college in Barry, which opened in 1914. These colleges, which produced certificated elementary school teachers, put a heavy emphasis on domestic subjects and the moral role of the teacher. Within the university the academic education of women was similarly yoked to teacher training. Cardiff (1890), Aberystwyth (1892) and Bangor (1894) all opened 'Day Training Centres', a misleading term since many students were residential, for the training of teachers. At first, students studied for their degree courses and trained as teachers at the same time, but after 1911 the pattern changed to a three-year degree course plus one year's teacher training. Teaching was the career most open to women in these years, and not surprisingly students regarded a degree as a passport to a teaching career in a girls' secondary school. There was also a financial incentive to following this route. From 1910 onwards, students who *pledged* themselves to a career in teaching were given a grant to cover their fees for all four years of their course. Women were 'locked-in' to teaching, but it was the teaching profession above all others that ensured Welsh women a career and with it economic independence.

In theory, by 1900, there existed a route whereby working-class Welsh girls could pass from elementary school to an intermediate or secondary school and hence go on to university. In practice, there were financial barriers and it was very largely the daughters of professional men, tradesmen and farmers who attended university. Of some seventy-six application forms for places in halls of residence in Aberystwyth surviving from 1905–6 and from 1913, only two were from the daughters of quarrymen and just one from a collier's daughter.

Discipline was strict for female students, and most modern accounts of the early days of Welsh university colleges concentrate on the restraints imposed on women. Although young men and women attended lectures together, they were not allowed to mix outside class. Cardiff frowned on 'mixed pic-nics' and joint drama productions; Bangor expelled two students spotted holding hands on Anglesey; and Aberystwyth banned conversations between male and female students except at sports meetings and social functions 'sanctioned by the warden of Alexandra Hall'. Female students in Cardiff and Aberystwyth, not living with their parents, were required to live in hall and indeed Miss Carpenter, first warden of Alexandra Hall in Aberystwyth, imposed harsh restrictions on her charges: she expelled a 'fast' student from hall for calling out of the window to a male student. Women students undoubtedly found all this oppressive: Alexandra Hall students revolted in 1907. But putting too much emphasis on these restrictions is to miss the point. The creation of halls of residence was a feminist initiative designed to create a secure space for women to live and work, free from domestic cares, and this they did admirably. Student rooms were comfortable and well furnished and servants did the cooking and cleaning. What appear now as ludicrous restrictions – for example students to be in by 6.30 p.m in winter and no entertaining men in rooms – were not at variance with Victorian and Edwardian codes of behaviour and offered parents the peace of mind to allow their daughters to go off to college.

Employment

Women's paid employment in Wales was characterized by three main features. Firstly, women's participation rates in the Welsh workforce were strikingly low. In both 1901 and 1911 only 23.6 per cent of women of working age in Wales were in employment, compared with 32 per cent and 32.8 per cent of women in England in 1901 and 1911 respectively. The chief explanation for this significant difference lies in the lack of any major manufacturing industry in Wales comparable to the Lancashire cotton and Yorkshire woollen industries, which employed large numbers of women, and the dominance of coal-mining in south Wales with its almost exclusively male workforce. Secondly, although the overall Welsh female participation rates are low, there was considerable regional variation within Wales. The rates for rural counties are higher than those for the industrialized counties. In 1911, for example, some 30 per cent of women in Cardiganshire and 27 per cent in both Anglesey and Caernarfonshire are recorded as in paid work. This contrasts starkly with the figures for Monmouthshire and Glamorgan of *c.*20 per cent and for the Rhondda, the heartland of coal-mining, of a staggeringly low 14.4 per cent. Thirdly, the Welsh female workforce was highly segregated, even more so than its English counterpart, with the majority concentrated in just three occupational groups as defined by the census as Domestic Offices or Services; Dress; and Food, Drink and Lodging. Significant numbers were also employed in agriculture and the census group of Professional Occupations had been for some time on a marked upward trend.

By far the largest group was employed in domestic service. The census of 1901 records that 50.7 per cent of the Welsh female workforce was in service, compared with 40.3 per cent in England. This is not surprising, given the doctrine of separate spheres, the domestic emphasis of elementary education and the lack of alternative job opportunities. Domestic service was regarded, right down to the Second World War, as the most fitting work for women and as the ideal training for future working-class wives.

Domestic servants were live-in workers, under the eye and control of their mistress twenty-four hours a day and seven days a week. The popular image of service derives from glamorized television series which show a large retinue of servants arranged in a hierarchy from housekeeper at the top down to scullery-maid and between-maid at the bottom. But there were few large houses in Wales where servants performed specialist tasks and enjoyed the company of below-stairs life. By far the most common experience of Welsh maids was working in a middle-class, or even a working-class, household where two girls, or frequently just one, did all the work.

The experience of the single maid-of-all-work was one of drudgery and loneliness. A young servant girl in Cardiff wrote to the *South Wales Daily News* in 1912 saying, 'I consider I am treated more like a slave than a human being . . . driven from 6.00 a.m. until eleven and twelve at night, eating my own meals while running about waiting on others.' Wages were low and justified as being so because the servant received board and lodging. In Cardiff a girl would be lucky to get a pound a month just before the First World War and from this she would have to buy her own uniform. Free time was very limited. Nineteenth-century servants had had just one Sunday a month off, but servants' expectations were rising by the first decade of the twentieth century. They wanted every Sunday off and a free evening a week so that they could see friends or have a night at the pictures. Unlike other jobs, there were no set hours of work: to be in the house was to be on the job. Small wonder domestic service was a deeply unpopular option for working-class girls and a shortage of servants was a perennial and ever-increasing problem.

Female domestic servants were a mobile group. Not only did these women move about Wales in search of work but Welsh maids, especially country girls who were regarded as hard working and god-fearing, were sought after by employers in England. Advertisements appearing in Welsh newspapers include many positions for 'Generals' and cooks in London and the Home Counties as well as in Liverpool and the north-west of England. Many women left Wales in response to such advertisements.

The other main options open to women were dressmaking and shop work. Dressmaking , while enjoying the status of respectable work, was extremely badly paid. Girls entering dressmaking had to pay their employer a premium of about two pounds a year during their two-year apprenticeship. When qualified, they would earn just five or six shillings a week. Miss Orme, assistant commissioner to the Royal Commission on Labour of 1893, analysed the wages of some 631 dressmakers in Wales and found that two-thirds of them earned under ten shillings a week and only eleven earned more than a pound. Dressmakers were employed in large drapers' stores and in workrooms; some worked from home and others, taking their sewing machines with them, travelled around the farms and outlying houses. There were opportunities for the enterprising and industrious. Elizabeth Andrews from Hirwaun, who later became the first Labour Party woman organizer for Wales, having served her apprenticeship, set up her own workroom when she was just nineteen. By 1908 she ran a large workshop in Ystrad Rhondda, where she earned £40 a year and received free board and lodging. She deserved her success, working a 68-hour week.

Shop work enjoyed a higher status than either domestic service or dressmaking. Working-class girls perceived it as chic and glamorous because assistants in department stores wore smart clothes and there was always the hope of meeting handsome and rich male customers. That was the fantasy; the reality was different. A distinct hierarchy of shop assistants existed, with the large emporia of Cardiff and Swansea at the top and the village or corner shop at the bottom. Even in the department stores the work was hard and the hours long. In south Wales, but not in the north, the living-in system was still the norm. Assistants lived above the store or in houses owned by it. They slept in cramped bedrooms – two to a bed, lived on weak urn-tea and badly cooked food and were given little time or indoor facilities for leisure. There were good employers, but in Wales Miss Orme singled out just one good draper, where comfortable bedrooms and a large sitting room were provided and the employer organized such recreation as a choir and a debating society. Assistants were kept in line by a system of fines. Margaret Bondfield, then an official of the shopworkers' union, noted the following in operation in Cardiff in 1907. Smoking on the landing incurred a massive fine of 2*s*. 6*d*., while wrongly addressing a parcel or putting the wrong date on a bill meant 3*d*. was deducted from wages. Wages were low and kept down by a reservoir of female labour anxious for shop work. Two-thirds of shop assistants in the 1893 Royal Commission earned less than £30 per annum, including board and lodging. In 1900, women shop assistants earned just 65 per cent of the male rate for doing the same job. Miss Orme herself attributed the low wages of women workers in Wales to the small number of openings available to them and to the large numbers of applicants for each job.

The shop workers' days were long as shops opened on weekdays from 8.15 a.m. until 7.15 p.m., with half-day closing on one day, and on Saturdays until 11 p.m. or midnight. The hours of standing took their toll on shop assistants' health – varicose veins, flat feet, menstrual and digestive problems were common.

Shop owners were not legally bound to provide chairs for assistants until 1900: large Cardiff stores such as David Morgan, James Howell and Seccombes and D. H. Evans in Swansea immediately complied. In the 1890s Miss Orme regarded the union (the National Amalgamated Union of Shop Assistants), with some two hundred women members, as strong in south Wales. The period from 1906, when Mary MacArthur founded the National Federation of Women Workers (NFWW), to 1914 saw a growth in women's trade union membership in Britain with numbers more than doubling, and a growing confidence among the women workers. We do not have the membership numbers for Wales but there are indications of a new found self-assurance in, for example, the strike of dressmakers employed in Ben Evans's Swansea store. In 1911, twenty-five women went on strike for better pay and conditions. There were mass demonstrations of more than 5,000 people in support of them: Mary MacArthur and Margaret Bondfield came down from London to organize them and industrialist Amy Dillwyn urged shoppers to boycott Ben Evans's shop.

Because Wales had no large-scale manufacturing industry and because the workforce of the south Wales coal industry was overwhelmingly male, it is easy to overlook the women who were employed in industry in these years. The numbers are not large but their experience is certainly worthy of further study. In 1911, the census records 3,525 women employed in the metal industry: these women were employed in the tinplate works centering on Llanelli and in iron and enamel works in south Wales. There was some degree of trade union membership amongst women tin workers. In July 1900, the *Swansea and District Workers' Journal* welcomed Miss M. M. Owen, one of two 'lady-delegates' from the Dock, Wharf and General Labourers' Union to Swansea Trades Council, 'to represent the organized women of Morriston'. Some 800 women were employed at coal mines, quarries and brickworks. Elizabeth Andrews had gladly taken up dressmaking as she dreaded being sent to the local brickworks, where women carted, or carried on their backs, loads of wet clay or performed the lighter work of moulding decorative bricks. At the slate-enamel works of north Wales, girls and women polished the wet stone: Miss Orme compared their work to housemaids polishing a stove. But by far the largest group of women factory workers in Wales was employed in the old woollen, tweed and hosiery industry, which in 1911 recorded 7,358 woollen workers, its highest number since records were kept. Women textile workers, spinners and weavers were employed in every county in Wales though the largest numbers were to be found in Glamorgan, Monmouthshire, Carmarthenshire, Flintshire and Montgomeryshire. Wages in the 1890s were usually between 9s. and 15s. per week, which compares favourably with other work. Workers in large establishments, such as the Pryce Jones Mills in Newtown with its large mail-order

Women unloading potatoes at Cardiff Docks, *c.* 1900.

business, enjoyed a programme of lectures, concerts and dances. Women worked too in a whole range of small factories making and bottling mineral water and jam, making and packing cakes, confectionery, clay tobacco pipes and fuses. Such jobs were popular and much in demand. Women also worked in steam laundries, dye-works and paper works. Perhaps the most surprising group of workers revealed by the sources are the women dockers. In the 1890s some 400–500 women, Welsh and Irish, were unloading potatoes at Cardiff docks, and at Swansea the female stevedores handled fruit and corn. We know little about these women, but they were still there in the early 1900s.

The hardest and heaviest work undertaken by women was in the countryside. Women had always worked on the land: given the small size of farm units and the near subsistence existence of many in the rural community, their labour was indispensable. The farm wife prepared the household's food, undertook responsibility for the poultry and the dairy (including caring for the milk cattle as well as butter- and cheese-making) and oversaw the work of her daughters and the female servants. Farm servants might work indoors and out. Outdoor women's work included tending cattle, cleaning out stables, loading dung carts, planting and digging potatoes, hoeing, taking up and topping and tailing turnips. These servants would obtain their positions at local hiring fairs

– such as the hiring which still ran at the top of Ship Street in Brecon up until the First World War. Girls would be taken on by farmers for the half year. Elizabeth Collet, a railwayman's daughter from Talgarth, took up a six-month position on a farm above Brecon, c.1910. There she assisted the mistress with the milking and butter-making, helped with the hay and corn harvests as well as doing indoor domestic chores. Other labour done by women on the land in some parts of Wales was not paid in cash, but formed part of a network of exchange dating back to medieval times. Farmers in Cardiganshire continued to allow local families living in cottages with no land attached (*pobl tai bach*), to plant rows of potatoes on their farms, for which they (the farmers) provided manure. In exchange for this the cottagers paid labour services to the farmer. It was frequently the cottage women who repaid this labour-debt by working at the corn harvest a day for each row of potatoes set. Similarly, women worked at the hay harvest in return for 'debt butter' (*menyn dyled*). Other women ran their own smallholdings: a fifth of the farmers and graziers in Cardiganshire recorded in the 1911 census were female. Such women might also undertake other work to supplement their income, ranging from collecting stones from hayfields to making quilts and dressmaking.

The contribution of women to the rural economy, whether paid in some way or unpaid, was important. In 1911, 9.4 per cent of occupied women in Wales were employed in agriculture but this is an average figure for the whole of Wales and is based on all thirteen Welsh counties. In some areas, agriculture was a significant strand of women's work. In the same year, 25.9 per cent of working women in Cardiganshire and 21.5 per cent in both Carmarthenshire and Montgomeryshire were employed in agriculture.

One other interesting category is women who ran their own businesses. At the top end of the scale were women like Amy Dillwyn, who owned and ran the Dillwyn Spelter Works in Swansea. Town or commercial directories are a rich source, as yet little tapped, which show the many other businesses in which women engaged. In towns throughout Wales they show women running private schools, owning dressmaking and millinery businesses as well as shops selling baby linen, ladies' underwear and clothing, wool and confectionery. In Rhyl and other north Wales resorts women kept boarding houses and teashops. The *Wales Trades' Directory* of 1903 for Cardiff, Barry and Penarth lists women pawnbrokers, several of whom including Mrs Fingelstone and Esther Levene came from Cardiff's Jewish community; publicans, of whom some such as Catherine Donovan of the Green Fields of Erin were Irish, as well as women who owned hotels, temperance hotels and restaurants. In Cardiff women had seen too the potential of running Registry Offices for Servants: at least three of the nine registries listed were owned by women.

Finally the growth in numbers of women in Wales engaged in the professions is clearly marked. In 1891, 5.3 per cent of occupied women are recorded under the census category of Professional Occupations; by 1901, the figure was 8.0 and by 1911, 8.6. The rise of this group was rapid, and the 1911 figure of 8.6 per cent for Wales is higher than the 7.2 per cent recorded for England. Such an increase is the result of women's admission to higher education. The figures include women in the medical profession, but their numbers were not large: of 1,253 doctors in Wales in 1911 only 11 were women and of the 451 dentists only 9 were women. It was the teachers, both in elementary schools and the graduate teachers in the new Welsh intermediate and secondary schools, who formed the core of the female professional class. It was necessarily so, since women were still not admitted to many professions notably the church, the law or accountancy.

Politics and issues

The doctrine of separate spheres had attempted to confine women to the private world of the home, but by the 1870s and 1880s Welsh women were entering the public arena. In Cardiff, Newport, Swansea, Caernarfon and elsewhere they campaigned for the repeal of the Contagious Diseases Acts (CD Acts), which had been passed in the 1860s to prevent the spread of venereal disease in the army and navy. The Acts gave police the powers to detain prostitutes, subject them to medical examination and confine them to lock hospitals: many women objected to these Acts because they appeared to legalize vice and because they operated a double standard – the prostitutes were medically examined but not their male clients. The CD Acts also raised fears that respectable women going about their business might be accosted and insulted by the police. The Acts applied only to certain named garrison towns in England and Ireland, but suggestions that they might be extended to towns in Wales, especially Cardiff, brought some Welsh women into this controversial campaign. In fact the Acts were never applied to Wales and were totally repealed in 1886. It was a victory for women's rights and Welsh women had played a part in securing it. In the same year, the Association for Promoting the Education of Girls in Wales came into existence and did sterling work in ensuring the entry of girls into secondary and higher education, before prematurely dissolving itself in 1901. But the first large-scale organization of women in Wales centred on a cause which was tailor-made for them – temperance, that is total abstinence from all alcoholic beverages.

Although women had been involved in subsidiary roles in mixed temperance societies since the 1830s, it was not until the 1890s that the first women's temperance organization was set up in Wales. Following a conference in 1892 at Blaenau Ffestiniog, called by Mrs Sarah Matthews of Amlwch, her sister Susannah Gee (both daughters of the publisher Thomas Gee) and Miss Parry of Bala, Undeb Dirwestol Merched Gogledd Cymru (UDMGC, the North Wales Women's Temperance Union) was formed. It expanded rapidly. Ceridwen Lloyd-Morgan, historian of the women's temperance movement in Wales, has shown that by 1896 UDMGC had 106 branches with 11,821 members. The success of women in the north encouraged women in the south but it was almost a decade later, in 1901, that Undeb Dirwestol Merched y De (UDMD, the South Wales Women's Temperance Union) was formed at the instigation of that most charismatic of Welsh women – Cranogwen. Sarah Jane Rees (1839–1916), sailor, teacher of navigation, poet, lecturer and preacher and first woman editor of a Welsh-language women's magazine, *Y Frythones*, was a long-time campaigner against the evils of drink. By the time of her death there were 140 branches of UDMD throughout south Wales in the counties of Pembroke, Cardigan, Carmarthen, Glamorgan, Brecon and Monmouth.

The temperance cause was respectable. Its members were middle class and included the wives of Nonconformist ministers and Liberal MPs: it met in chapels and its uncompromising opposition to alcohol, the cause of ruin to many a family, was perceived as falling within the ambit of woman's role as guardian of the home. But there was more to the movement than holding tea parties and magic lantern shows: women were encouraged to write pamphlets and stories, to learn organizational skills and to gain confidence in public speaking.

The temperance movement was linked to broader moral purity campaigns to rescue 'fallen women', hapless unmarried girls, who had become pregnant, and barmaids, the latter being regarded as not only exposed to moral danger but also as the victims of the brewers' greed: Cardiff barmaids worked fifteen-hour days in 1900 to earn just 10s. 0d. a week. Drink was seen as the first step on a maiden's road to ruin and the Wrexham branch of UDMGC ran a home for girls while Cranogwen took a particular interest in women brought before the courts on charges of drunkenness and 'associated evils'. Lletty Cranogwen was opened by the Rhondda branch of UDMD as a refuge for such women and as a memorial to its founder in 1922.

Women were also involved in the co-operative movement, through the Women's Co-operative Guild founded in 1883. Although members were recorded in Aberdare in the first year of its existence, the Guild took off rather late in Wales. Elizabeth Andrews set up the first Rhondda branch at Tonpentre in 1914. The Guild, initially formed to spread the message of co-operation among women, campaigned vigorously in the years before the First World War to bring about divorce law reform, improved maternity grants and conditions, equal pay for women and men in co-operative stores and to promote trade unionism. The Guild itself was widely referred to as 'the housewives' trade union' in this period.

Pit-head baths were also seen as a women's issue, and the women's campaign took off following a conference of the Women's Labour League in 1912 when Mrs Edward Edwards of Ogmore Vale placed baths firmly on the agenda.

In many ways, women's involvement in all the above movements can be viewed as attempts to improve women's lives within their allotted sphere rather than as any fundamental challenge to gender roles. But whether they sought to improve conditions of childbirth, to keep the home free of drink or coal dust, to gain admission for women to higher education or to improve their lives in any way, women had realized that they had to enter the public arena to agitate to achieve their ends.

The first appearance of women on elected bodies followed the creation of School Boards in 1870, to which propertied women could stand for election. The property qualification excluded many and, according to Ryland Wallace, only three women had been elected by 1886: Rose Crawshay, suffragist and iron master's wife (Merthyr and Vaynor Boards); Emily Higginson, campaigner against the CD Acts and wife of a Unitarian minister (Swansea) and Miss Margaret Marsh, a Montgomeryshire landowner (Llandinam). More research is needed to establish women's participation on School Boards after 1886, but in any case it was a short-lived opportunity as the Boards were abolished in 1902 and their function replaced by county council education committees, bodies to which at that time women could not be elected, only co-opted. Amy Dillwyn, having been elected to Swansea's School Board, declined an invitation to be co-opted to the new committee not wishing 'to be thrust down the ratepayers's throats without their being able to get rid of me if they wish'.

From 1875, women ratepayers could vote for and serve on Poor Law Boards of Guardians (the bodies which ran the workhouses), but few Welsh women served in this capacity until the property qualification was removed in 1894. By 1895, some eighty-eight women had been elected in Wales and Monmouthshire, though not until 1911 was the first woman elected as chairman [*sic*] of a Board of Guardians when Mrs Oldfield became chair of the Conway Board. Women had proved more willing to come forward for Poor Law, rather than School, Boards, perhaps because running workhouses or interviewing applicants for outdoor relief (benefits for those who remained in their own homes) drew more directly on their skills as homemakers. Mrs Rawlins of Rhyl wrote in the journal *Young Wales* in March 1896, 'The work of Women Guardians is essentially mothers' work, i.e. the management of the Workhouse, the children and the aged sick.' Indeed, the women guardians improved and humanized the system. The two elected in Pembroke Dock in 1894, for example, ensured that workhouse children were educated for the first time in local board schools instead of the workhouse school and abolished the hated uniform which marked them out as paupers. Mrs Trayler and her fellow woman guardian there bought the girl paupers 'bright coloured print pinafores and hats trimmed with different coloured ribbons so that no two are quite alike'. Nora Philipps (leading Liberal, suffragist and wife of Sir Wynford Philipps) saw this work as far more than just an opportunity for women to draw on their domestic skills and apply them to public administration. For her, their success in this field justified the claim that in order to fulfil their civic duties women should have civic rights.

But what civic rights did women have? By 1894, women ratepayers were allowed to vote in and stand for parish and district council elections. Nora Philipps, who was herself elected to Manorbier Parish Council, commented in *Young Wales* in 1895 on the numerous successes of women in parish council elections 'in many districts both in North and South Wales', but again research is necessary to chart the progress of women in local elections. Amy Dillwyn stood as a candidate in the first county election in which women were permitted to stand in 1907, but failed to win a seat on the Swansea County Council. In other parts of Wales some women enjoyed great success: Miss Gwenllian E. F. Morgan was the first woman in Wales to become a mayor, when she served as mayor of Brecon from 1910 to 1911. But the big issue in these years was women's right to vote in parliamentary elections. It was one thing to allow women to vote for and sit on local councils but quite another to allow them to vote for, let alone take a seat in, the mother of all parliaments at Westminster, the very hub of the British Empire. The only way women could ever gain the parliamentary franchise was for parliament itself, the very body which was excluding them, to pass legislation granting this right to them. It was to be a long hard job persuading parliament to do so.

Ironically, the political parties needed women's help. The Corrupt Practices Act of 1883, which forbade the payment of canvassers, together with the extension of the male franchise through the 1884 Reform Act, led party managers to encourage women to work for both the main parties – Conservatives and Liberals. The Conservative Party, which was never strong in Wales and whose support lay mainly along the Anglicized northern and southern coasts, admitted women to the Primrose League in 1884, where they were organized in the Ladies' Grand Council, became Primrose Dames and worked in local 'Habitations'. These were mainly, but not exclusively, in affluent areas. Habitations had been established in Llandudno and Bangor before 1900 and the Penarth Habitation was formed in 1909 with the earl of Plymouth as president and Mrs Forrest of St Fagans as dame president. Women were used for the essential work of fund-raising and canvassing, but the League did not promote women's suffrage and sought only vaguely to 'interest women in politics'. This is not to say that individual Conservative women did not support women's suffrage.

Spurred on by the success of the Primrose League, the Liberal Party began to organize its women from 1890. But Liberal women, not content to confine themselves to electioneering for male candidates, wanted a say in the big issues of the day like Welsh Home Rule and, above all, women's suffrage. By the mid 1890s, the Welsh Union of Women's Liberal Associations (WUWLA), with branches throughout Wales, was a dynamic organization with some 9,000 members. Its first two presidents were active suffrage campaigners with good contacts with the movement's London leaders. Nora Philipps was a woman of great intellect, an excellent organizer and superb public speaker. Her successor, Sybil Haig Thomas (1857–1941), wife of D. A. Thomas, Liberal MP and industrialist, was a quieter person but equally strong-minded and prepared to go to prison herself for 'the Cause'. But, by 1900, internal divisions within Welsh Liberalism over the Home Rule (Cymru Fydd) question had taken its toll on the women's organization: by that year there were only fifteen branches of WUWLA left in existence. Large branches such as Swansea, Cardiff and Holyhead kept going but it would seem that Liberal women in the early twentieth century transferred their efforts into non-party women's suffrage groups.

Women participated in Labour politics too. In theory, they were admitted as full members from the outset of the Independent Labour Party (ILP) but it would be naïve to overestimate the significance of this. As 'Matron', a regular columnist in the *Rhondda Socialist Newspaper*, wrote of the Rhondda ILP branches in the edition of 21 September 1912, 'These are conducted almost with a total disregard to the existence of women in the district or to matters in which women are interested.' Women may have felt more at home as members of the auxiliary Labour Party organization, the Women's Labour League (WLL) founded in 1906, which concentrated largely on 'women's issues' such as housing and childcare. Overt demands for women's suffrage – though many Labour women were suffrage campaigners – conflicted with socialist demands for full adult suffrage with no property qualification. This was resolved in 1912 when Labour became the first political party to back women's suffrage.

It is impossible to do justice to such a complex and important subject as the women's campaign for the vote in this short account. Here I can only give the broadest overview of the various groups active in Wales and their activities. But one aspect of the movement demands closer attention, and that is the membership of the suffrage societies in Wales.

The years 1900–14 marked the pinnacle of activity in the struggle for the parliamentary franchise. In particular, women pinned their hopes on the Liberal government, elected with a massive majority in 1906, but time after time their hopes were dashed. In fact, with the benefit of hindsight, we can see that it was unfortunate that the suffrage campaigners in Wales came up against a Liberal government. Given the passion with which Liberalism was embraced in Wales and the veneration of Welsh Liberal heroes, especially Lloyd George, the fact that the women dared to challenge him on his home ground partly accounts for the nastier episodes of violence against them. By 1912, after the failure of a number of Conciliation Bills (attempts to find a compromise solution to enfranchise some women), disillusionment with the Liberals was complete. Moderate suffragists reacted by forming an alliance with the Labour Party and the militants, no longer able to contain their frustration, went on the rampage with a spectacular campaign of law-breaking.

There were three main groupings of suffrage campaigners in Britain, all of which were active in varying degrees in Wales. The largest group, the National Union of Women's Suffrage Societies (NUWSS), founded in 1897 and led by Mrs Millicent Fawcett, was dedicated to achieving the vote by constitutional means. The first branch of the NUWSS in Wales was set up in Llandudno in 1907. In 1908, the Cardiff and District Women's Suffrage Society, which was affiliated to the NUWSS, was established as the first branch in south Wales. The NUWSS was by far the strongest of the suffrage groups in Wales and ran an active and well- supported campaign. By 1912–13, Cardiff was the largest women's suffrage society outside of London, a position which it sought to maintain in rivalry with Glasgow. By the same year, the *Suffrage Annual and Women's Who's Who* (1913) listed twenty-eight NUWSS local societies in Wales. These were Abergavenny, Aberystwyth, Bangor (plus a branch at Llanfair-fechan), Bargoed and District, Bethesda and District, Bridgend, Cardiff and District (plus a branch at Penarth), Carmarthen, Caernarfon (plus a branch at Pen-y-groes), Colwyn Bay, Cricieth, Dolgellau, Ffarmers District, Kidwelly and Ferryside, Lampeter, Llandudno, Llanelli, Llangollen, Merionethshire, Merthyr and District, Penmaenmawr, Pontypridd, Pwllheli, Rhondda Fach, Rhyl and District and Swansea. This list shows clearly that Wales was no back-water when it came to votes for women.

The NUWSS worked steadily to achieve its end, writing to and personally lobbying MPs, holding public meetings, organizing debates, raising funds through garden-parties and sales of work and by selling the NUWSS newspaper *Common Cause* and badges on street corners. The chance survival of the records of the Cardiff and Bangor societies shows the extent of this grass roots work. In Cardiff and District in 1913–14, sixty-seven public meetings were held, eighteen of which were for political groups, such as the ILP, the Women's Labour League and the Primrose League, and trade unions, including the Gas workers', Bricklayers', Co-operative Employees' and the Railwaymen's unions: all of the trade union groups passed resolutions in favour of women's suffrage. Cardiff also put on a course to train women in public speaking. In July 1913, two hundred women of the Cardiff and District Society marched through the city. This was not their usual style at all and the annual report for 1913–14 notes that many had misgivings about taking part in the procession but 'afterwards their enthusiasm was aroused and the desire to do something more in the future'. This local procession took place on the eve of the Great National Union Pilgrimage to London, in which women from Wales and all over Britain joined. Bangor's activities were very similar, including striking up links with trade unions and joining the Great Pilgrimage: women from Bangor, Caernarfon, Cricieth, Pen-y-groes, Pwllheli and Llandudno, cheered on by quarrymen, joined the Great Pilgrimage, linking up with the south Wales women to march on London.

The militant wing of the suffrage movement, the Women's Social and Political Union (WSPU), was founded in 1903 and led by the charismatic Emmeline Pankhurst. The WSPU was above all a brilliant publicity machine co-ordinating 'outrages' which ensured wide press coverage and thrust 'votes for women' to the forefront of public debate. Its members were prepared to smash plate-glass windows, blow up pillar-boxes, cut telegraph wires, attack places of male recreation such as cricket pavilions, golf-courses and boat-houses and leap out from concealed places to confront surprised cabinet ministers. They were prepared, indeed eager, to pay the price of imprisonment and even to endure the horrors of force feeding. Margaret Haig Mackworth, later Lady Rhondda (1883–1958), joined the WSPU after taking part in a suffrage march in London in 1908. Though a firm believer in the justice of the cause, her conversion to militancy was an emotional one. Militant suffrage, she wrote, 'was the very salt of life. The knowledge of it had come like a draft of fresh air into our padded, stifled lives.' She went on to help set up the Newport branch of the WSPU. She broke every taboo of her class – selling *Votes for Women* on Newport High Street, speaking on public platforms including that of Merthyr Liberal Club, where she was pelted with herrings and tomatoes, jumping on the running-board of Prime Minister Asquith's car and blowing up a pillar-box on Risca Road, Newport in 1913. For this last she was imprisoned and went on hunger-strike. The WSPU was not strong in Wales with only a

Policeman protecting a WSPU heckler, who interrupted a
speech by Lloyd George, from the angry mob at
Llanystumdwy, September 1912.

handful of branches – Newport, Pontypool and Griffithstown, Cardiff and
Barry in 1913 – but its activities grabbed the headlines. In north Wales, local
women and Welsh-born women who had joined the WSPU in England
attempted to organize events and met with hostility. Wales, however, was to
play centre stage in the militant years of 1912 and 1913 because it was the home
of prominent members of the government and attracted suffragettes from
outside. In June 1912 a London suffragette leapt out before home secretary and
Monmouthshire MP T. P. McKenna, who was accompanying the king and
queen on a visit to Llandaff cathedral. But it was Lloyd George, chancellor of
the exchequer, who drew English suffragettes like a magnet. They challenged
the great man in the Liberal heartland, confronting him at Caernarfon,
Wrexham and Llanystumdwy in 1912, provoking, especially in Llanystumdwy,
a vicious reaction from the crowd. In south Wales in 1913 the WSPU made

progress, conducting a series of meetings with railway workers and miners in the valleys: amongst these militant workers there was a certain admiration for the women's bravery.

Welsh women were also members of a whole range of other suffrage organizations. The Women's Freedom League (WFL), the third of the major organizations, was the strongest group in Swansea and in 1913 also had branches in Aberdare, Barry, Cardiff and Montgomery. Welsh women also joined the Church League for Women's Suffrage, the Progressive Liberal Women's Union and the Jewish Society for Women's Suffrage. Exiles in London could join the Forward Cymric Suffrage Union.

But who were the suffrage campaigners active in Wales in the run up to the First World War? In terms of class, the majority were middle class or even upper-middle class. We know that some individual working-class women were involved such as Labour Party activists Elizabeth Andrews and Rose Davies in the south Wales valleys and that working-class members of the Women's Labour League and the Women's Co-operative Guild also supported the cause, but little evidence survives. It is however not in the least surprising that the movement should be largely middle class. In Wales, there were no large industries employing women and therefore no opportunity for working women to organize. As for the working man's wife, with her large family and heavy domestic load, she had no time even to sit down at the end of the day, let alone to attend public meetings or sit on committees. One striking feature in Wales is the role played by educated women, particularly the teachers and head teachers. It was that new generation of intermediate and secondary school heads who were the main standard bearers of the revolution – Miss Collin in Cardiff, Miss Phipps and Miss Neal in Swansea, and Miss Holme in Carmarthen. All of these women were English-born and their prominence in the movement, taken together with suffragettes from England making sorties into north Wales to confront Lloyd George, would seem to confirm the idea mooted by contemporary Welsh opponents of women's suffrage, that the movement was an alien one, foisted on Wales by English women. This was emphatically not the case. Suffrage literature was produced in Welsh and prominent Welsh writers in both Welsh and English supported the cause: Cranogwen, Moelona (Elizabeth Mary Owen) and Allen Raine (born Anne Adaliza Evans) all wrote in its favour. Welsh women were prominent in the struggle, notably Amy Dillwyn, Margaret Haig Thomas and Sybil Haig Thomas. A great deal of work needs to be done to establish local membership of groups, a task rendered somewhat difficult by the convention of describing women by their husbands' names. Sybil Haig Thomas, for example, is invariably listed as Mrs D. A. Thomas. There are plenty of Davieses, Evanses,

Jenkinses, Joneses and Thomases on the Cardiff subscription lists. It is worth digging behind these to find the women. Mrs Edgar Jones, long-serving secretary to the Barry committee, was Annie Gwen Jones, a Welsh speaker, Aberystwyth graduate and a former governess in Hughesovska, and Mrs Aaron Thomas, vice-president of the Swansea NUWSS, was Carmarthen-born Eleanor Thomas. Welsh women were also active outside Wales. Miss Morrie Hughes, organizer of the WSPU in Harrogate and who had served time in Holloway Gaol, was the daughter of the Revd Thomas Hughes of Corwen. Admittedly, the organizer of the Cardiff WSPU just before the Great War was Cornish-born Annie Williams, but then Llanelli-born Edith Williams was a WSPU secretary in Cornwall.

Given the restrictions on women's lives – the lack of job opportunities, economic dependence on men and the male domination of the culture – women in Wales, of whatever origin, made a bold stand against the old order. But in August 1914 their campaigning came to an abrupt halt. The outbreak of the First World War was to change the focus of their lives.

~ 2 ~
Fur Coats and Widows' Weeds: the Great War, 1914–1918

THE First World War broke out in the summer of 1914. The assassination of Archduke Franz Ferdinand, heir to the throne of the Austro-Hungarian Empire, at Sarajevo on 28 June by a Serbian nationalist was the spark which was to set all Europe aflame. By 4 August, Britain, allied with France and Russia, was at war with Germany and Austria-Hungary. Most people in Wales, or in the rest of Britain, had never heard of the archduke and had no idea where Sarajevo was. The war took them completely by surprise and at first they failed to grasp its nature and its seriousness: they thought it would be all over by Christmas but already, before the year was out, it was being referred to as the Great War. This was a war far beyond anything they had ever experienced. It was the first 'total war', in which the state took for itself enormous powers and in which the scale of the slaughter was unprecedented. It was a war which was to have a profound effect on the lives of civilians, as well as the fighting men.

War, more than any other historical event, is clearly gender differentiated in its impact. For Welsh men the war meant the horrors of the trenches on the Western Front, the slaughter of the battlefields of Ypres and the Somme and far-flung campaigns, at Gallipoli or in Palestine and Mesopotamia. Some 774,000 British servicemen, of whom 40,000 were Welsh, were killed. These figures do not include merchant seamen: 1,000 black seamen from Cardiff's Butetown alone, and many other young men from Welsh ports, died in the war at sea. Of those fighting men who did return home, many were mutilated or seriously wounded. Existing historical accounts of Wales and the war have concentrated on the male experience or have assessed the wider effects of the war on the economy, social structure and political life of Wales, without noting the gender-specific consequences of the war on women's lives. To write on the impact of the Great War on the lives of women in Wales, is to write on a clean slate.

We must be wary, however, about bringing any prior assumptions to an examination of women's lives in Wales between 1914 and 1918. Many accounts of twentieth-century British history simply take as read the view that the war was a great turning-point along the road to women's emancipation – a view that does not accord with the evidence. The experiences of Welsh women in these years require careful scrutiny. In fact, far more research is necessary than I have been able to undertake into every area of Welsh women's lives in wartime, but with this clear proviso, I shall concentrate on the following: home life; the war-effort; paid employment; women in uniform; moral issues and a brief assessment of change brought about by the war, though we can only really evaluate any changes by looking at women's position in inter-war Wales.

At home

While the First World War brought gender barriers down in employment and offered excellent opportunities to those in a position to grasp them, the vast majority of women in Wales were in no doubt where they belonged: their place was in the home. They were there, in the words of Cardiff-born Ivor Novello's wartime hit song, to 'Keep the Home Fires Burning' and in several key ways their roles as home-based wives and mothers were strongly re-enforced during the war.

Although at the outbreak of war it was young, single men who had rushed to join the colours, many married men either volunteered or were later conscripted to meet the army's insatiable demand for men: by 1918 men in their mid-forties were being called up. Some benevolent employers quickly announced in the autumn of 1914 payments to wives of their workers who had gone off to fight: large companies such as the Ocean Coal Company in the Rhondda, Baldwins and Vivians in Swansea and major firms in Cardiff and Newport made arrangements to pay ten shillings a week to the wife and one shilling per child. But not all employers made such payments and the absence of the male breadwinner clearly meant that women faced grave financial hardship. The government introduced the payment of separation allowances for the support of wives and children of servicemen. The allowances – in part deducted from the men's service pay – show that in the absence of the male breadwinner, the state stepped in and assumed the duty of providing for his wife and family. It was an endorsement of the male role, which, at the same time, recognized the socially-useful part played by women.

There were administrative delays in making the payments in the early months of the war: wives had to send in their marriage licences and there were often hold-ups in processing these. Working men's organizations and civic leaders in south Wales demanded fairer rates of allowances and efficient methods of payment: the South Wales Miners' Federation (the Fed) called for a payment of one pound per week to the wife and five shillings for each child. In fact, by March 1915, the rates were set at 12*s*. 6*d*. for the wife of a private soldier, 17*s*. 6*d*. for the wife and one child, 21*s*. for the wife and two children, rising thereafter by two shillings per child. The rates were reviewed periodically and allowances cost the state the enormous sum of half a billion pounds between 1914 and 1918. There was a catch however. Payments were made conditional on the good behaviour of the women: this is discussed later under moral issues. Nor, given the rampant inflation of the war years, did the money stretch far.

For the housewife, the war meant rapidly rising prices and food shortages. By February 1915, the cost of flour had risen by 75 per cent since the outbreak of the war, meat by up to 12 per cent and sugar by 72 per cent. By June 1915, food prices in general were up some 65 per cent on August 1914, with the highest prices in the larger towns and cities, and the hardest hit groups those on fixed incomes, such as pensioners, and the families of unskilled men. The Board of Trade estimated an 81 per cent increase in the cost of living between 1914 and 1918 for the families of unskilled workmen and a 67 per cent increase for those of skilled workmen.

The war led to severe shortages throughout Wales, but particularly in the towns, of basic food stuffs – potatoes, bread, tea, sugar, butter, milk, meat and eggs. By early 1917, with the German U-Boats wreaking havoc on merchant shipping importing food supplies from abroad, the situation was grave. Bread and potatoes were staple foods of Welsh working people and both were in short supply. The severe winter of 1916–17, the worst for over twenty years in Wales, hit the potato crop hard. The *Western Mail*, 10 February 1917, reported talk of famine in south Wales and the *North Wales Chronicle*, 9 March 1917, observed, 'potatoes seem nowadays to be the very index of national well being' and noted that there were fears that supplies would run out altogether. Lloyd George, in a speech at Caernarfon, called upon, 'every man and woman who has a square yard of cultivable land . . . to grow a potato or a cabbage'. There were 'potato incidents' throughout the country as housewives fought to obtain supplies. In March 1917, a shopkeeper in Caernarfon had his scales smashed by angry women and the next week faced an enraged crowd of housewives, who fought over his two sacks of potatoes and refused to form a queue. A riot broke out in Wrexham, when women besieged a cartload of potatoes in the town square: some women fainted and the police were called in to quell the mob. By April, regulations governing meals in hotels and restaurants ordered one meatless and five potato-less days a week.

Some women responded positively to food shortages. By March 1917, the newly formed Women's Food Production League in Bangor had enrolled ninety women and taken on two plots of land for cultivation. Throughout Wales women became involved in the allotment movement and the Women's

Institute, founded on Anglesey in 1915, was spreading rapidly, encouraging as it did so, the production of home-grown food.

In 1917 posters urged people to 'EAT LESS BREAD', an alarming prospect for working people. To minimize shortages the percentage of flour extracted from wheat was increased and government bread, containing barley, maize, bean and potato flour was introduced. Women were exhorted to make cakes and scones from oatmeal, but the price of bread was a sensitive political issue. In June 1917, when Lord Rhondda was appointed as food controller, he made bringing down the price of bread his first priority . The standard quartern (4lb) loaf, which had cost 5*d*. in 1914, had risen to 1*s*. in 1917: he reduced it to 9*d*., at a cost of £50 million to the treasury. Queuing had become a feature of women's lives until he introduced rationing in the spring of 1917: meat, sugar, butter and margarine were put on ration.

It was men who made the supreme sacrifice in the war – laying down their lives for 'King and Country'. But the women at home paid a high price too, suffering months and years of anxiety, dreading the arrival of a War Office telegram and then facing the long, slow pain of loss – of loved ones, sons, sweethearts, husbands, brothers and friends. It is hard for us today to comprehend the scale of that loss: more than three times as many British fighting men were killed in the First World War than in the Second. Each passing month saw the death toll mount and the Rolls of Honour, printed in Welsh newspapers, lengthen. The records of Swansea Tipperary Club, a support organization founded in 1914 for 'The Women Who Wait', give a glimpse of the impact of war losses on one community. The organizer Mrs Annie Watkin Williams decided to carry on the club's activities after the war ended, 'for the sake of the 800 war widows not to mention the women who have lost their boys in the war'. As a historian researching the history of the Great War, it is impossible to remain unmoved by the physical historical evidence – the black-edged mourning notepaper, printed memorial services and the stone monuments, with their lists of fallen local men, erected throughout Wales at the war's end. But the sheer magnitude of the slaughter must not allow us to lose sight of the fact that each death was an individual loss to be borne by those who remained. By May 1915, the four Brooking sisters of Tenby had all suffered loss : the husbands of three of them had been killed in action and the husband of the fourth was a prisoner of war in Germany. Mr and Mrs Charles Lloyd of Maesycrugiau, Carmarthenshire lost their two sons, Duncan and Gwion, within one week at Gallipoli in August 1915. Mrs Mary Witts of Newport, Monmouthshire, had lost all three of her soldier sons by 1917. Women reacted to their losses in different ways. Mary Witts called for an end to the war. Winifred Coombe Tennant, 'Mam o Nedd' ('Mam from Neath'), whose nineteen-year-old son, Christopher, was killed near Ypres in August 1917, threw herself into public works and sought consolation in spiritualism. But it is the fictional character of Jane Gruffydd in Kate Roberts's *Traed Mewn Cyffion* (*Feet in Chains*), 1936, who best conveys the grief and anger that many Welsh women felt at the death of loved ones in a faraway war, whose causes they had never understood. Informed of the death of her adored son, Twm, by an official letter in English, which she had to have translated by the local shopkeeper, she was hurt and bewildered. Her anger and resentment, however, only exploded much later, when she was visited by a mean-minded official who came to assess her eligibility for a war pension following Twm's death. It was when this official boasted to her that he had just cut the pension of a neighbouring widow, who had also lost her son in the war, that she finally snapped:

Y munud hwnnw daeth rhyw deimlad rhyfedd dros Jane Gruffydd. Ers pymtheng mis o amser, bu rhyw deimladau yn crynhoi yn ei henaid yn erbyn pob dim oedd yn gyfrifol am y Rhyfel, yn erbyn dynion ac yn erbyn Duw; a phan welodd y dyn blonegog yma yn ei ddillad graenus yn gorfoleddu am dynnu pensiwn gwraig weddw dlawd i lawr, methodd ganddi ddal. Yr oedd fel casgliad yn torri, y dyn yma a gynrychiolai bob dim oedd tu ôl i'r Rhyfel ar y munud hwnnw, a dyma hi'n cipio'r peth nesaf i law – brws dillad oedd hwnnw – a tharo'r swyddog yn ei ben.

'Cerwch allan o'r tŷ yma, mewn munud,' meddai, ac yr oedd yn dda ganddo yntau ddiflannu.

'Fy hogyn bach i,' dolefodd, 'a rhyw hen beth fel yna'n cael byw.'

A thorrodd hi ac Owen i weiddi crio.

At that moment a strange feeling came over Jane Gruffydd. For fifteen long months, a deep resentment had been gathering in her very soul against everything that was responsible for the war, against man and God. And when she saw this plump man in his immaculate clothes preening himself on the fact that he had reduced a widow's pension, she lost control of herself. It was like a dam bursting. At that moment, the man standing before her represented all that was behind the War. She grabbed the nearest thing to hand – a clothes-brush – and struck him on the head with it.

'Get out of this house at once,' she shouted.

The man was glad to make his escape.

'My dear son,' she cried out, 'and something like you is allowed to live.'

Both she and Owen (her other son) broke down and wept.

(Translated John Idris Jones)

Other men did come back, some maimed or scarred in body and mind, and, in some cases, never able to work again. It was the womenfolk who nursed these war casualties for the rest of their lives.

Given the horrors of the war, the actions of women, usually the mothers, who protected and hid deserters from the police are easily understood. Women appeared before Welsh courts charged with harbouring deserters and were fined or imprisoned. A Cwmtillery woman jumped on the back of the police constable and struck him as he attempted to arrest her deserter sailor son. She was fined ten shillings. A Llanfairfechan mother was similarly fined for sheltering her soldier son who had deserted from the Royal Welch Fusiliers' camp at Oswestry: the young man, who had been 'wounded in the head by a bomb' on the Western Front, was clearly shell-shocked and disorientated but there was little official sympathy for such cases.

Welsh women threw themselves into the war effort. They organized accommodation and support for Belgian refugees in such places as Cardiff, Barry, Swansea, Aberystwyth and Carmarthen, raising funds through concerts and subscription lists: some like Mrs Gertrude Bailey of C. H. Bailey Dry Dock Company of Newport and Barry and Mrs M. Jenkin Lloyd of Llanelli received the *Medaille de la Reine Elizabeth* of Belgium for their efforts. Many put their energies into supporting and working for the Red Cross and St John's Ambulance: thousands of women in Wales worked as unpaid nurses. That there were a myriad opportunities for voluntary work became apparent within weeks of the outbreak of war. By October 1914, the south Wales branch of the Women's Emergency Corps was formed to co-ordinate such work and avoid wasteful 'overlapping'. Many organizations were set up to support the troops, especially Welsh troops, and to supply them with 'comforts' and necessities. The Tremadoc (Caerns.) Needlework Guild, set up in 1914 to supply clothing to Tremadoc men in the forces, had, by March 1918, produced and dispatched some 800 garments – shirts, socks, mittens, scarves and pyjamas. In Aberystwyth Miss Catherine Powell Evans organized a sewing circle at Penparcau: her surviving papers show her consulting lists printed in newspapers to see what articles were most needed at any particular time, using government-issued patterns and writing off to the Red Cross with queries such as, 'What size bandages are needed in the Dardanelles?' Bangor Women's Patriotic Guild, which attracted some 160 members within weeks of being registered for voluntary work early in 1917, knitted and sewed garments for the troops. Not only did they produce socks, mufflers and shirts, but they made mosquito nets and sun shields for the soldiers in Mesopotamia and Egypt. The wives of soldiers and sailors meeting in Tipperary Clubs also spent much time producing items for men at the front. Even schoolgirls did their bit. At Llandinam Council School, Montgomeryshire, where Glenys Orlando Jones's mother was a young teacher, the girls' contribution to the 1918 Christmas parcel for the troops consisted of fifty pairs of mitts, two scarves, thirty handbags and ten pairs of cuffs. Soldiers were rumoured to use such schoolgirl efforts as rags to clean their rifles. Boys and girls brought hard-boiled eggs to school which were collected and sent to wounded soldiers: actress Elen Roger Jones remembered giving in her egg at school at Marianglas, Anglesey, and later receiving a letter of thanks from a Yorkshire soldier.

Upper- and middle-class women in particular were tireless fund-raisers. They raised money through flag days, sales of work and public appeals in aid of the Prince of Wales Fund, the Welsh Red Cross, British and French troops, and prisoners of war. By June 1915, the Editor of the *Western Mail* estimated that nearly a quarter of a million pounds had been raised in Wales for war charities. One of the favourite Welsh charities was the Welsh Hospital at Netley in Hampshire, a newly built unit run by Welsh staff for Welsh troops. Local groups raised cash to fund beds at Netley at a cost of £250 each.

Of the hundreds of women's wartime organizations, the Women's Institute (WI) was to prove the most enduring and the most influential on women's lives. The first branch in Britain was set up in Llanfairpwll, Anglesey, in 1915 with the encouragement of Colonel Stapleton Cotton, chairman of the north Wales branch of the Agricultural Organization Society. Its original aims included promoting co-operation among women; bringing about improvements in women's work, especially in agriculture; increasing the home-grown food supply; and encouraging intelligent women to stay in rural areas by providing a greater range of interests for them. The WI spread rapidly. By 1917, the Institutes were taken over by the Women's Branch of the Board of Agriculture's Food Production Department and the emphasis was put on food production and domestic skills. In 1915–16 the Llanfairpwll branch, for example, heard talks on topics such as women's labour on the land and the government poultry scheme and viewed demonstrations on bread-making, fruit preservation and hay-box cookery. Local institutes set up food markets, selling produce wholesale to shopkeepers in Cricieth, Pwllheli, Porthmadoc, Caernarfon, Llanfairfechan and Llanbedr (Merioneth). These activities were directly related to solving the problem of wartime food shortages. There were also 'war comforts' classes, nursing and first-aid sections and, under the enthusiastic lead of Lady Anglesey, a Women's Home Defence Squad: the marchioness organized instruction for WI members in the use of firearms and hand grenades, but on the whole the WI concentrated on more traditional women's skills.

But what about the activities of the Welsh suffrage societies during the war? The NUWSS, putting its *raison d'être* of achieving the parliamentary franchise for women to one side – though never losing sight of it – co-operated fully in the war effort. The activities of the Cardiff and District Women's Suffrage

Society, as recorded in its annual report for 1914–15, show the contribution made by these able and intelligent women. They assisted the wives and dependants of servicemen through the Soldiers' and Sailors' Families Association; they helped to find and create work for women through the Queen Mary's Women's Workrooms Committee; in conjunction with other Welsh suffrage societies, they raised funds to endow a 'women's suffrage' bed in the Welsh Hospital at Netley; they worked with the Red Cross Society and the 3rd Western General Hospital; they helped the British-born wives of aliens through the Cardiff International Committee and assisted in the work of the Belgian Refugee Committee, the Belgian Soldiers Fund and the Belgian Relief Fund; they acted as translators to the Belgians and put on French classes for nurses and officers; they organized Women Patrols (that is the first women police), set up a club for 'Girls and Their Soldiers Friends'. But their most ambitious project, and one entirely in accord with their feminist aims, was to raise cash to set up a Welsh Hospital Unit for Serbia, staffed by women, and which was to work alongside the already established Scottish Women's Hospital (SWH). The Cardiff and Newport societies raised the then huge sum of £4,000 for this project, which is discussed further below. The much smaller Llangollen branch of the NUWSS also focused its activities on supporting the Scottish Women's Hospital and its Welsh unit and supported the work of a local nurse who went out to Serbia. The WSPU on the other hand threw its efforts into the recruiting campaign: Mrs Pankhurst herself came to south Wales to exhort miners to enlist. But this organization, despite being the most vocal and visible before the war, did not survive it, although individual Welsh WSPU members made a great contribution to the war effort.

The war afforded upper- and middle-class women with opportunities to show their true worth. For some it was a liberating experience. The immensely wealthy Davies sisters of Llandinam, who had led sheltered and restricted lives until the war, opened their own canteen near Troyes in France in 1916. Here, according to their biographer, Baroness White:

> They could scrub tables and sing songs and command and cajole their soldier customers. In other words, almost for the first time in their lives – each was now in her thirties – they could be themselves. They were also part of a team, with comrades on whose strength or weakness the fate of their enterprise depended.

Margaret Haig Mackworth, the WSPU activist daughter of Lord Rhondda, returning with her father from America in 1915, survived the sinking of the *Lusitania* when it was torpedoed off the Irish coast. Rescued after hours in the freezing water, the ordeal made her determined to play her part in the war

Margaret Haig Mackworth (née Thomas), Viscountess Rhondda of Llanwern.

The Hon. Violet Douglas-Pennant.

effort. She was appointed as commissioner of Women's National Service in Wales, controller of Women's Recruiting and as a member of the Women's Advisory Council of the Ministry of the Reconstruction. For the first time women were being appointed to government ministries. The most prestigious post held by any Welsh woman was that of Violet Douglas-Pennant, daughter of Lord Penrhyn: she became commandant of the Women's Royal Air Force (WRAF). Edith Picton-Turbervill worked tirelessly for the Young Women's Christian Association (YWCA), raising a quarter of a million pounds for its work in providing hostels and canteens for munition workers and members of the Women's Army Auxiliary Corps (WAAC): her twin sister Beatrice took charge of a large munition workers' hostel at Woolwich arsenal and her sister Violet was a controller in the WAAC.

But not all Welsh women supported the war. We know very little about Welsh women pacifists in these years, but in England, the leaders of the NUWSS, the largest suffrage organization, were split over the war, with some of its leading figures working for peace. English women pacifists linked up with other women in the international suffrage movement in Europe and America to try to end the war. Great obstacles were put in the way of delegates from Britain and from other European countries when they attempted to travel to the International Congress of Women held at the Hague in 1915. Only three women from Britain (from a delegation of 180) succeeded in reaching the conference; twenty-eight German women made it, but none from France or Russia. The congress was remarkable in that women from combatant nations sat down together and sought to bring an end to the war, and to all war, whilst the European conflict raged around them. They resolved to put pressure on politicians to reach a settlement and they set up a new organization, the Women's International League for Peace and Freedom (WILPF). There is evidence that some Welsh women adopted an anti-war position but far more research is required in this area. Following the Hague Congress, Gwenda Gruffydd of Rhiwbina, Cardiff wrote to the journal *Welsh Outlook* in September, 1915. She reported that deputations of women had met with leaders of both neutral and belligerent countries in an attempt to end the bloodshed. She argued that such action was possible for women, but not for men, in time of war and she appealed to the women of Wales to band together to work for peace. She wrote:

> I feel sure that there are thousands of my country-women ready to do all they can in this great cause, since it is we women who are so keenly alive to the damage to the race resulting from war, and the grief, the pain, and the misery it entails. I feel inclined to suggest that the names of sympathizers should be placed on record, and when we have a long list, we should decide what steps to take – whether we should affiliate ourselves to an English Society, or form ourselves into a separate Welsh one.

The only reply, published by *Welsh Outlook* the next month, came from a Welsh woman living in London who was totally opposed to 'sentimentally prating of peace' and urged women to play their part by making shells and doing men's jobs to release them to fight. We do not know if Gwenda Gruffydd was able to compile a 'long list' of sympathizers. However, Sydna Ann Williams in an article on north Wales women in the peace movement in the inter-war years, points out the existence of a branch of WILPF in Cardiff between 1915 and 1917 with some fifty members and one wonders if this was the result of Gwenda Gruffydd's appeal. The Women's Co-operative Guild, an organization which was growing in south Wales, also displayed strong anti-war feelings. At its annual congress in 1916, the guildswomen passed a resolution urging 'the Government to seek the earliest opportunity of promoting negotiations with the object of securing a just and lasting peace, and protests against the adoption of Conscription by this country'. The introduction of conscription in 1916 increased opposition to the war in Wales and there was concern about the excessively harsh treatment – imprisonment, hard labour and humiliation – of Conscientious Objectors. Agnes Hughes of Abercynon, Independent Labour Party member and friend of Keir Hardie, became organizer of the Aberdare No Conscription Fellowship and devoted herself to the work of trying to get war resisters, including her brother Emrys, transferred from military to civil prisons. Anti-war speakers visiting Wales in 1916, including Bertrand Russell,

Helena Swanwick and Philip and Ethel Snowden, spoke to huge, sympathetic audiences in south Wales: Helena Swanwick of the NUWSS addressed a crowd of over 2,000 in Cardiff in the autumn of 1916 but the meeting was broken up by 'patriots'. These audiences almost certainly included women as well as men but only detailed investigation will reveal the role played by Welsh women pacifists. However, they were unlikely to be a very large group. Most Welsh women, like Welsh men, though suffering increasingly from war-weariness by 1917–18, believed in the war. But when at last the war ended in November 1918, it was to leave a legacy of revulsion at the wholesale killing, which led to a far stronger and much more visible women's peace movement in Wales in the 1920s and 1930s.

Employment

The immediate effect of the outbreak of war was an increase in women's unemployment. In Wales, as in the rest of Britain, the well-to-do reined-in their expenditure on unnecessary luxuries. As economy measures, they dismissed servants, cancelled hotel holidays, cut back on the purchase of hats, dresses, jewellery and other luxuries, thereby throwing domestic servants, hotel chambermaids, milliners, dressmakers and shop assistants out of work or, at best, drastically cutting their hours. The *Western Mail*, 26 September 1914, reported that women and girls were being thrown out of work in Cardiff and that fourteen prominent firms in the city had put their women workers on half- or three-quarters-time. In Swansea, by December 1914, women's unemployment was double the rate it had been in December 1913. At this stage, no one foresaw the enormous demand for women workers which the war would create. They expected the situation to get worse and organized relief. The Queen Mary's Fund appealed for donations, in leaflets published in Welsh and in English, for the thousands of women thrown out of work. The Cardiff Central Relief Committee set up workshops and a toy-making class was opened in the city, to provide women with a means of livelihood in the face of what was expected to be a growing unemployment problem by the winter. But already before September 1914 was out, there were signs of growing opportunities, when the first big government orders began to come through. Ben Evans store, Swansea, won one of the largest orders ever previously placed in Wales, with a contract to provide 15,000 blankets and thousands of shirts, pants, vests and service-caps, and in October the West Wales Flannel Manufacturing Company gained an order to provide 150,000 shirts. The future of women in Wales's traditional flannel industry, centred on Newtown and

Llanidloes, was to be secure for the duration of the war. In early 1917, the Roumanian government ordered large quantities of Welsh grey flannel for its army and in October 1917 the government requisitioned the whole output of the principal Welsh mills. In north west Wales a sock industry was established with workshops at Blaenau Ffestiniog, Pen-y-groes and Talysarn, which produced some 300,000 pairs of socks for the allies.

The real turning-point in terms of job opportunities for women came in early 1915. In March, women between the ages of sixteen and sixty-five were urged to register at labour exchanges for war work. They were required to replace men in civilian jobs and, in the face of a growing shell shortage, in munitions factories. The need for female labour became even more acute after the introduction of conscription for men in January 1916 and by 1917, when 'substitution' (the practice of women replacing men) was already widespread, a further call was made on them in the Women's National Service Scheme (see next section).

The war opened up a wide variety of jobs, which had not previously been considered as women's work. They became shop assistants in grocery stores, shoe shops and even in butchers' shops in some Welsh towns. They drove delivery vans, both horse-drawn as in Talgarth in Breconshire and motor vehicles for the Penarth branch of the Co-operative stores. Cardiff even had women taxi drivers. Women made significant progress into office work, still at the outbreak of war a predominantly male stronghold: 'lady clerks' and bookkeepers were taken on in private, municipal and government offices. The Post Office took on large numbers of women. From August 1915 the Cardiff Telephone Exchange was staffed entirely by women: some women had worked at the exchange previously on day-shifts, but they now worked day- and night-shifts. By 5 September 1915, the *Western Mail* reported that 'Lady Postmen' were at work in Barry: here, as elsewhere in Wales, women sorted, delivered and collected the post. Perhaps an even more visible indication that women's role in the labour force was changing was the appearance of women on public transport. They were employed on the trams of Cardiff, Swansea and the Rhondda. Despite strong initial hostility from male workers, by November 1915 some sixty women conductors were employed by the Cardiff Corporation Tramways. Smartly turned-out conductresses in a uniform of double-breasted, knee-length coats, knickerbockers and long leggings, became a familiar sight. In Cardiff, some even became tram drivers. Women were also brought into industry in large numbers. At the Dowlais works, they served in the brickyards as machine hands, moulders and clay-grinders and in other departments as loaders, cleaners and messengers. At Cwmbrân, where some women had been previously employed, many more were taken on to make nuts, bolts and screws. In Cardiff women workers made airship and barrage balloons at the E. T. Willows works.

The women substitutes were not universally welcomed: there was outright opposition to them being taken on, mingled with fear and resentment and widespread disbelief that women could do a good job. At Cardiff Corporation Tramways the men at first refused to work with the women who were taken on as conductresses in 1915, and industrial workers often raised arguments that heavy work was damaging to women's health and to their future role as mothers. Some employers, particularly in small businesses, would not even consider taking on women, preferring to advertise for 'cripples and older men'. We have to remember that women were taken on to release men for the forces and some of the arguments put forward by men against women reflect their own unwillingness to take their place in the trenches. A Bridgend baker, for example, argued, in a case reported in the *Glamorgan Gazette* 16 February 1917, that his eighteen-year-old son should be exempted and could not be replaced by a woman: 'Women', he argued, 'are all right for pastry but it was impossible for a young lady to make a batch of bread.' Similarly, a Bangor grocery store manager, put his case for exemption from call-up, as reported in the *North Wales Chronicle*, 27 April 1917, by saying that whereas women are all right as shop assistants with a male manager to direct them, they were incapable of being managers. The most intransigent opposition to women workers came from Welsh farmers, as is discussed later.

We know very little of the composition of the Welsh wartime female work-force. Gail Braybon's study, *Women Workers in the First World War* (1981), is concerned with women employed in England but some of her conclusions may be adapted for Wales. In Wales, it is likely that many women war workers had been previously employed and that they transferred from domestic service or other women's jobs into substitution and munition work. But given the fact that far fewer women had been economically active in Wales before 1914 than in England, it is also likely that many new women workers were brought into employment. The majority were young, working class and single, though older married women of the same class worked too. Those employed on the trams and in factories were invariably working class. Few details are available on women's wage rates in Wales but they were very unlikely to have enjoyed equal pay with men. Cardiff male tramways workers had, as an act of self-interest rather than altruism, pressed for equal pay for the women, but there is no evidence that this was achieved: wartime bonuses (to meet rising living costs) paid to women on the trams, and to other women workers in Wales, were normally about half those paid to men. In general, women in Wales were pleased with their wartime wages, which were far higher than those they had earned before the war. Braybon estimated that the average pre-war pay for women in Britain was 13s. 6d. a week but by the end of the war this had risen to between 30s. and 35s. Even if these rates are scaled down for Wales, women were far better paid than they had been previously. The impression also emerges that Welsh women enjoyed their wartime experience of work. Emmy, a bus conductress, interviewed in the early 1980s by Swansea Women's History Group, thoroughly enjoyed her work: 'My mother didn't mind because it was a decent job and I needed the money, and anyway it was an exciting life! Plenty of friends, hard work but good times.' She worked all the routes and recalled the tramcars departing from the Swansea Empire being so jam-packed that people stood on the bumpers. Emmy married during the war but kept on working until the Armistice:

> I got married while working on the trams. My husband was in the navy. We had a reception in the house. All of my friends came and the people from my regular routes, including a lot of sailors who had heard about the wedding. All the conductresses who came to the wedding left with a sailor . . . When peace was declared I stopped work as my husband was coming home.

There were plenty of opportunities for educated women too. Former students from Cardiff's Aberdare Hall were working as doctors at home and abroad; employed in government offices in such departments as war pensions and separation allowances; serving as officers in the women's auxiliary services and gaining highly placed posts in private businesses. Those who stayed within the traditional sphere of teaching now found jobs in boys' schools open to them.

By far the greatest demand for women workers was in munitions. The process of dilution (the breaking down of a task previously done by a skilled man into a number of smaller operations), agreements admitting women to work 'customarily done by men' and large scale recruitment by the Ministry of Munitions led to the influx of thousands of women into the munitions factories from 1915 onwards. The state became an employer, operating National Shell and National Explosives Factories and Controlled Establishments (privately-owned factories brought under government control for the duration). National Shell Factories were set up in south Wales at Cardiff, Llanelli, Newport, Ukside and Swansea and in the north at Caernarfon, Porthmadoc and Wrexham. There were also explosives works like the huge HM Factory at Queensferry and Nobel's works at Pembrey, which was taken over by the government. It is difficult to obtain exact numbers of female employees, but as early as May 1916, Miss B. Strachan of the Board of Trade stated that there were 'fully 5,000 women and girls engaged in munition production in south Wales'. Of the shell factories, Newport was the largest in the south, with some 800 women employed at Maesglas and a further 200 at the Tyne Engine Works site, followed by Swansea and Llanelli, each with some 700 women workers. In the north, Wrexham provided work for large numbers both at the National Shell Factory and in other establishments. But by far the largest factories in the whole of Wales were the explosives works. Pembrey, 'the vast arsenal on the dunes', employed 11,000 men, women and boys. No detailed gender break-down is available for Pembrey, but on the evidence of other factories, some 70–80 per cent of production workers are likely to have been women. Detailed figures are available for the HM Factory at Queensferry, where, at its peak, 7,000 people were employed. Stripping out male labourers, construction and maintenance staff, this leaves a total of 3,418 production staff. Of these 2,492, or 72 per cent were women.

Workers travelled by tram and train to the munitions factories. A special station was built at Queensferry, serving workers coming in from Wrexham, Rhyl and the north Wales coast as well as the Wirral. Female munition workers were for the most part young and single but older married women were employed too: in Newport it was policy to take on soldiers' wives and widows. The length of shifts varied from works to works: at Uskside they worked twelve-hour shifts but in Swansea this practice was abandoned in favour of three eight-hour shifts a day. 'Protective' legislation, which had previously prevented women from working nights, was shelved during the war. Women made shell casings, with each factory tooled-up to produce a particular size and weight of shell: Swansea and Caernarfon, for example, produced eighteen-pounder high-explosive shells. At Pembrey and Queensferry, they manu-factured high explosives and filled shell casings. The latter factory was erected to produce guncotton (explosive cellulose nitrate) and TNT. There were health hazards in dealing with explosive substances. In 1917 and 1918 at Queensferry, 3,813 acid burns, 2,128 eye injuries, 763 cases of industrial dermatitis were treated and 12,778 accidents occurred. A report, published at the end of the war, noted that there had been only four deaths due to accident in the whole time the factory was open. But there were fatal accidents to women workers and the photograph of the funeral, one of two funerals of women munitions workers which took place in Swansea on August Bank Holiday Monday 1917, is testimony to the loss of women's lives. The two young women, Mildred Owen, aged eighteen, and Dorothy Watson, aged nineteen, were killed in an explosion, almost certainly at Pembrey, and their bodies transported by train to Swansea. It is a remarkable and poignant image, which shows the quasi-military tribute to the two dead girls with their coffins draped in the Union

Munition worker's funeral procession, Swansea, August Bank Holiday, 1917.

Jack and with their fellow female munition workers, in their uniforms, acting as pall-bearers. The *South Wales Daily Post*, 4 August 1917, describes the scene, with vast crowds assembled to pay their respects, all traffic stopped to allow the passing of the cortège and the procession led by 'the heroines' fellow workers.'

Munition wages were good. The best money, of six pounds a week, was paid at Woolwich Arsenal for boring and screwing and six guineas was paid to women tool-setters in fuse factories but this was not typical. The minimum wage was just one pound a week but it was possible to earn two to three times that amount. By Welsh standards, these were very high wages. However, Welsh girls who were earning even higher rates in English factories, notably in Coventry and Woolwich, found rising rent and food bills soon ate into their wages. Apart from the wages, there were other attractions. Women liked the camaraderie of factory work and groups of off-duty 'munitionettes' went around Welsh towns after work, dressed to the nines and looking for a good time. Factory conditions varied, with the very worst to be found in Controlled Establishments like Pembrey. There, the girls' 'danger clothes' were dirty and

Swansea National Shell Factory women's football team, 1918.

in rags; the changing rooms were overcrowded and instead of washbasins there was a long trough; the lavatories were dirty and full of rats and, since no lights were installed there for the most of the war, the women were afraid to go in. The National factories provided canteens, proper changing and washrooms, welfare and recreation facilities. Welfare officers, often women graduates, organized leisure activities. At Uskside there were women's hockey and football teams and a tennis club, while Newport had a mixed choir as well as a women's football team. Most munition factories had women's football teams, a remarkable development given contemporary notions of propriety and womanly conduct. The Swansea National Shell Factory team won three silver cups, were unbeaten champions for 1917–19 and raised over £700 for charity.

Women in Uniform

Before the outbreak of war, the only acceptable uniform for a woman to don was that of a nurse. There were already two organizations of military nurses, the Queen Alexandra's Imperial Military Nursing Service and the Territorial

Nursing Service, which between them could muster just over 3,000 trained women in 1914. Other professional nurses were also brought into military hospitals. Miss Emily Evans, matron of Aberystwyth Infirmary, who had already served in the Boer War and been decorated, became matron of the Welsh Hospital at Netley; Sister Wilkins from Cardiff Hamadryad Hospital served alongside the heroine Nurse Edith Cavell in Brussels, while other Welsh nurses were based at hospitals in France, Serbia and Egypt. Their numbers were vastly augmented by volunteers who served in the the First Aid Nursing Yeomanry (FANY), established in 1907 as a mounted nursing service but whose members acted mainly as ambulance drivers in the First World War, and the Voluntary Aid Detachments (VAD), formed in 1910, under the management of the Red Cross and St John's Ambulance Brigade. One Voluntary Aid Detachment consisted of twenty-three women, but in popular usage the initials VAD meant an individual nurse. The VADs were usually, but not exclusively, middle class and they worked in Britain and abroad. In Glamorgan alone 112 detachments were set up to staff forty-eight hospitals opened in the county during the war, in which 30,000 men were treated. Mrs M. Lucas was quarter master and assistant commandant to the Barry Island Hospital, the first VAD hospital opened in Wales. Women students at Aberystwyth formed their own VAD unit. Welsh VADs served widely overseas: Marjery Anwylyd Williams from Bridgend served as a VAD in military hospitals at Saumer, Rouen, Trouville, Camiers and Etaples from 1915–20. She was mentioned in despatches by General Haig and awarded the Royal Red Cross. Although in Wales we have no full-length account of life as a VAD to compare with Vera Brittain's *Testament of Youth* (1933), a young Welsh woman writing under the pseudonym 'Merch yr Ynys' in *Welsh Outlook* in October 1916 told of her experiences. In 'Dawn in a French hospital', she wrote of doing night-duty on a freezing ward, tending the wounded, making beds and steaming mugs of sugar-water and listening to French soldiers talk of their plans for *après la guerre*.

Welsh women served as doctors too and an increasing number of women medical students entered training during the war. When the Scottish Dr Elsie Inglis went to the War Office in London with a scheme for women's service abroad, she was famously told 'to go home and sit still' – advice which she ignored. She set up the Scottish Women's Hospital, under the auspices of the Scottish NUWSS, first in France and then in Serbia. In Serbia, her all-female unit won enormous respect. In March 1915, Elsie Inglis came to speak in Cardiff and in Newport and, at her suggestion, the two NUWSS branches launched an appeal to set up the Welsh Hospitals Unit for Serbia (later known as the Wales London Unit). London and Wales sent out to Serbia a unit of 200 beds and the female doctors and nurses to staff it. Dr Mary Eppynt-Phillips of Brecon, a former Cardiff student who had already served in Belgium, went out to Valjevo with the unit. Nurse Goodwin from Llangollen was another who joined it. The story of other women from Wales who went to Serbia remains to be researched.

While wearing a nurse's uniform was viewed as perfectly acceptable and indeed womanly, the appearance of women in other uniforms, masculine and militaristic in style, was a shock to contemporaries and led to taunts that women were aping men and to accusations of lesbianism.

Wartime conditions facilitated the fulfilment of a long-held feminist aim, the appointment of women police. The establishment near towns of huge army camps, which attracted prostitutes and local girls allegedly unable to resist so many uniforms, the employment of many thousands of women in munitions and the implementation of the Defence of the Realm Act (DORA) in 1914, meant that vastly increased numbers of police were required. Two distinctly different organizations seized the moment to gain approval for women police : both groups operated in Wales. Firstly, there were the Women's Patrols of the National Union of Women Workers (NUWW), which, despite the proletarian ring to its name, was a middle-class organization. The patrols were unpaid women volunteers, who worked locally for just a few hours a week and wore no uniform except 'dark and unobtrusive clothing', a NUWW armband and a numbered badge. In Cardiff, patrols were organized at the request of the Women's Advisory Committee, an umbrella organization of the city's many women's groups. There the patrols, many of whom were members of the middle-class Cardiff and District Women's Suffrage Society, worked at the railway station rescuing hapless girls who arrived with nowhere to stay, flushed out courting couples from shop doorways and the city's parks at night and cautioned and moved on prostitutes. In Swansea in 1916, Jennie Ross became Woman Patrol No: 2092. Her daughter, in an interview with Ursula Masson, recalled her mother's duties:

> She used to patrol about the docks and places where girls used to walk about. There was a very sinful place in Swansea at that time where respectable girls didn't walk along. That was the Prom . . . apparently there were goings-on of some mysterious kind, but no decent girls walked there.

The women patrols, with no powers of arrest and almost no official authority, performed a primarily moral function. The other group of women police, the Women's Police Service (WPS), was very different. The WPS was largely the brainchild of the wealthy and eccentric Englishwoman, Margaret Damer Dawson. She and the members of the WPS, drawn initially from the ranks of militant suffragettes, had great ambitions and they worked towards the day when women would become fully-fledged police officers with powers of arrest. WPS members were full-time, paid and prepared to serve wherever they were sent. They wore distinctive, military-style navy-blue uniforms with long skirts, belted jackets with silver buttons, black boots and large brimmed hats. They patrolled the perimeters of army camps and they worked at munitions factories. Forty WPS 'officers' were sent to the HM Factory at Queensferry in 1916 and others to Pembrey. They searched the women workers entering the factory for cigarettes and matches, investigated petty crimes and took calm control of the situation when explosions occurred. Inspector Guthrie, in charge of the WPS at Pembrey, survived three explosions and she and her team were commended for their courage. It would seem too they had a role to play in strike-breaking. Miss G. M. West, a policewoman at Pembrey early in the war, gives us a rare insight into the behaviour of Welsh women workers. Commenting on one segment of the workforce, she wrote:

> Then there are are the relatives of the miners from the Rhondda & other coal pits near. They are full of socialistic theories and very great on getting up strikes. But they are very easily influenced by a little oratory, & go back to work like lambs if you spout at them long enough.

Women were desperately needed to work on the land. The shortage of agricultural labourers, already beginning to be felt in 1915, became increasingly serious in 1916 and 1917, as conscription took its toll and food shortages began to bite. Appeals were made to women. In 1915 the Board of Agriculture set up Women's War Agricultural Committees to organize recruitment; in 1916 the Women's Land Army Service Corps was founded and training courses were laid on; in 1917 a women's branch, entirely staffed by women, was formed within the Ministry of Agriculture and the Women's Land Army (WLA) itself was set up.

Welsh farmers however were extremely reluctant to employ women. At a meeting of Vale of Glamorgan farmers held in Cowbridge, reported by the *Glamorgan Gazette*, 8 December 1916, the farmers made such statements as 'women are utterly unsuited to farm work' and 'only one woman in a thousand could do work on an arable farm'. Similarly in Denbigh, when a public meeting was called in the town hall to discuss organizing female labour, the *Denbighshire Free Press*, 24 June 1916, reported that although officials from the Board of Agriculture and the labour exchanges turned out in force, not a single farmer attended and the meeting had to be abandoned. Although in Wales at this period women – wives, daughters and outdoor female servants – participated in agriculture to a much greater degree than women in England, farmers were at first hostile to taking on young, often middle-class, town girls and questioned how these, after just a short training course, could replace skilled men. Training centres were laid on throughout Wales – on the Plymouth Estate at St Fagans, at Margam Park and at Cadoxton near Neath in the south and at Madryn and Llewenni Hall in the north, as well as in Chester. It was recognized that not all women needed training: on Anglesey, the county agricultural committee acknowledged that women were well used to farm work. There was a huge drive to recruit women both to work part-time locally and as full-time members of the WLA. Land Army recruitment meetings were high profile affairs. The novelist Berta Ruck attended one such event in Newtown. She described the parade of a hundred or so landgirls in their light drill uniforms and shady hats marching through the town to the music of a band and carrying a large banner which read 'ENGLAND MUST BE FED'. Girls atop hay wagons and older women driving dairy carts brought up the rear. Sir Williams Watkin awarded 'stripes' to successful landgirls and the recruiting officer, Miss Hilda Vaughan of Breconshire (also later to become known as a writer), stood in her elegant custom-made uniform and delivered a moving and persuasive speech to the young women of Newtown.

> I am putting before you the disadvantages of the life. Long hours! Hard work! Poor pay! After you get your board and lodge, a shilling a day perhaps. Very poor pay. But girls . . . The Royal Welch Fusiliers (the old Twenty-third) and the Welch Regiment are offering their lives for that. Will you not offer your services for that – for them?

She was certainly right about the pay and instead of monetary reward, she offered the girls good health, good sleep and good complexions. She stressed the urgency of the need for volunteers to work the land: 'My county was a green country. Now it is a red county. But must I look at the fields of crops and think, "These will rot in the ground because there are no hands to bring them in?".' Women undertook a whole range of tasks on Welsh farms. The first public competition for women land workers in north Wales, held at Rhuddlan in February 1918, included contests in milking, horse and tractor ploughing, thatching and digging. The levels of skill shown were high – though it was an elderly widow from Trefnant who had lost two sons in the war, and not a land girl, who won the milking competition. WLA members did many onerous tasks like shifting manure, cleaning out cowsheds, topping turnips and lifting potatoes. They worked with stock too, both sheep and cattle, and, rightly, regarded it as a triumph when the farmer allowed them to work with his horses. Others joined the Women's Forestry Corps. Young Jane Bickerton from

Rhes-y-cae worked alongside other Flintshire girls planting trees around Lake Vyrnwy, while in Breconshire Gertrude Painter was in charge of a contingent felling timber. It is difficult to establish the numbers of those serving in the WLA in Wales. Contemporary writers Ivor Nicholson and Lloyd Williams thought that the eastern counties employed more landgirls than the western, where farmers' wives and daughters took a more active share in farm work. Nevertheless, they estimated that some 150 WLA girls were employed in Cardiganshire, most of them coming from Glamorgan, Denbighshire and County Durham and that some of these stayed in the area after the war. Women proved their worth in agriculture and farmers who had reluctantly taken them on for the 1917 harvest retained them. They were still required after the Armistice, many staying on till 1919 and beyond: there were still eighty-five WLA girls in Caernarfonshire and twenty-three on Anglesey in January 1919.

By far the most startling innovation of the First World war was the creation of the women's auxiliary services and the appearance for the first time of women in military uniforms. In early 1917, National Service for Women was introduced and although it was just a voluntary scheme, Margaret Haig Mackworth stressed its importance. It was, she wrote in *Welsh Outlook*, July 1917, the first time the state had made an official demand on women: she saw this as the state saying directly to women, 'Your Country Needs You'. Through the National Service Scheme women were recruited to the WLA and to the newly founded Women's Army Auxiliary Corps (WAAC), the Women's Royal Naval Service (WRNS), both set up in 1917, and to the Women's Royal Air Force (WRAF), formed in 1918. Following her appointment as commissioner of Women's National Service in Wales, Margaret Haig Mackworth toured the country urging women to join up. At a huge meeting in Cardiff, reported in the *South Wales Daily News*, 17 July 1917, she called for women over twenty years of age to join the WAAC and serve as clerks in France and, in order to allay parents' fears, she quashed rumours of immoral goings-on in its ranks. Similar meetings were held throughout Wales. At both Bangor and Caernarfon, there were big public recruitment meetings, accompanied by exhibitions of women's war work, parades of VADs, WAACs and pitchfork-bearing landgirls, marching through the streets in step to the music of a women's band from Kinmel camp. All sorts of tactics were used to persuade women to enlist. Miss Collin of Cardiff High School held recruiting meetings in the school and, to set an example to others, released her own two domestic servants to join the WAAC. Rachel Ann Webb's older sister Emily joined the WAAC, after reading a newspaper advertisement calling for a Welsh girl, a Scottish girl, an English girl and an Irish girl to help form a women's army. Emily was sent back home to Abergwynfi with three rail warrants and orders to bring back three more girls with her. Margaret Haig Mackworth was in fact disappointed at the small number of Welsh girls who volunteered but by June 1917, the first contingent of some fifty girls left Cardiff for France.

Servicewomen acted as cooks, waitresses, storekeepers, car and motorcycle drivers, sailmakers, shoemakers and mechanics. Uniforms were provided and wages were quite good with clerks earning up to thirty-two shillings a week. But the treatment of the women's auxiliary services by the male military hierarchy was prejudiced and niggardly. Women were not integrated into the army and technically remained civilians. Nor were they allowed to hold the king's commission, so there were no officers in the WAAC, only 'controllers' and 'administrators' and, instead of NCOs, there were 'forewomen'. The women at the top of the auxiliary services came into frequent conflict with the male authorities and were greatly hampered by their restrictive attitudes. In Welsh terms, the greatest interest centred on the appointment of Violet Douglas-Pennant as first commandant of the WRAF on 18 June 1918. She faced constant obstructions from senior Air Force officers and was hindered at every turn by them. By 17 August, she handed in her resignation but this was refused. Instead, she was summarily dismissed on 27 August. There was widespread outrage in Wales, particularly in the north, that a woman who had done so much for the war effort and was Lord Penrhyn's daughter to boot, should be treated so shabbily. Her treatment became a *cause célèbre* and was to have very serious repercussions for Welsh women in the 1920s.

Moral issues

Moral issues have frequently surfaced in this brief account of women in the First World War. Women police patrolled the streets, public parks and the perimeters of army camps to prevent immoral liaisons, and speakers at recruitment meetings to the women's services had always to deny immoral conduct in their ranks. But the term ' moral issues' is open to interpretation. The military authorities considered the prime moral issue to be women preying on their men – leading the innocent Tommy astray and transmitting sexual diseases to the British fighting man. Yet another patriarchal interpretation of moral issues, which came to the forefront during the war, was rooted in fear of women's new-found freedom – both financial and freedom from direct control of their absent menfolk. Ministers of religion, magistrates, local councillors and other male pillars of the community condemned women's drinking and their dissolute behaviour. Women's groups were also concerned with moral issues but from a different standpoint: they saw women as victims who were in need of protection. In Wales we see examples of all three interpretations of moral issues – that of the military mind through the application of the Defence of the Realm Act of 1914; that of the civilian patriarchal outlook in the condemnation of the behaviour of soldiers' wives and threats to withdraw their living allowances; and that of the women's groups in their efforts to protect girls from moral dangers.

The Defence of the Realm Act 1914 (DORA) gave to the state and to the military authorities extraordinary powers, some of which were used directly against women. Probably the most extraordinary use of these powers in the whole of Britain occurred in Cardiff. Colonel East, commander of the Severn Defences, banned 'women of a certain character' from public houses between 7p.m. and 6a.m. and imposed a curfew on them, which forbade them to leave their houses between 7 p.m. and 8 a.m. Women who broke these rules were brought before a court martial. In November 1914 five women in Cardiff were tried under DORA and sentenced to two months imprisonment. One of the women, who had been picked up in Bute Street during the curfew and was clearly unbowed by her experience, told the court, 'I am very sorry. I will go to a convent after.' The whole affair was a staggering breach of civil liberties and was widely reported in the London Press. It provoked an outraged reaction from feminists who accused the military of bringing back the nineteenth-century Contagious Diseases Acts by another name.

Soldiers' wives, who were in receipt of separation allowances, came in for a great deal of criticism. In October 1914, the Army Council produced a memor-andum entitled, 'The Cessation of Separation Allowances to the Unworthy'; this asked the police to put women under surveillance and those *suspected* of drunkenness or consorting with men were to have their allowances stopped. This provoked an outcry from the Women's Co-operative Guild and other women's groups, which led to the modification of the measure, but still left the police with powers to enter a woman's home, give her 'a good talking to' and threaten her with the stoppage of her allowance if she did not mend her ways. It was eventually decided that only if a woman was convicted of drunken-ness would money be stopped. Welsh newspaper reports, in publishing prosecutions against women for drunkenness, always ominously noted if a convicted woman was in receipt of an allowance. Implicit in all of this was the assumption that women, with no husband around to keep them in check and with money in their pockets, would run wild. In Wales there were wide-ranging attacks on such women. The chairman of the bench in Tredegar, for example, as recorded in the *Caerphilly Journal* 4 January 1915, thought it was 'full time to make an example of some of the women whose husbands were at the front' and that 'it was a scandalous thing how some of these women misconducted themselves both as regards drink and misbehaviour.' In Cardiff a minister of religion stood outside a public house and counted the number of women going into the 'jug and bottle' (off-licence): he alleged that during his thirty-five minute vigil, 115 women came out carrying flagons of beer. It is as though, while the women's husbands were away, other men in the community felt they had the right to assume patriarchal authority over them. One Abertridwr woman put it very well in a letter to the *Caerphilly Journal*, 4 November 1915. It was, she wrote, as though the soldiers' wives had become public property:

> They are openly discussed in railway trains and public places of every description. One day I heard two ministers' wives discussing these women. Here at least I expected to hear them discussed with Christian charity, but no! You would have thought it was the qualities of a herd of cattle they were comparing in loud, coarse and strident terms . . .

One wonders what these two female moralists had to say, when in 1917, the government extended separation allowances to women who were not formally married to soldiers.

Women's groups took a different tack. They were concerned that young girls would be seduced by men, rather than the other way around. They proposed a twofold approach. Cardiff Women's Advisory Committee wanted to provide counter-attractions for young girls and at the same time to employ the NUWW patrols to keep an eye on any untoward behaviour on the streets. Their counter-attraction was a club for 'Girls and their Soldier Friends', which, from early 1915, opened every evening from 6–9pm and on Sundays from 2.30–9.15pm. The aim was to create a safe and congenial environment for girls to meet young servicemen. The YWCA also provided 'huts' and ran National Girls' Patriotic Clubs in Swansea, Cardiff and elsewhere to provide recreation for munition workers. These arrangements, taken together with all the leisure activities organized by the factories – the choirs and sports teams – indicate a desire to keep munitionettes out of trouble. They earned good wages, which some of them spent on make-up, silk stockings and fur coats, and this conspicuous consumption was regarded as a sign of unbridled female sexuality. They were seen as in need of control. As for illegitimacy, a rise in the numbers of children born out of wedlock was inevitable in the war. But the overall birth rate fell and there does not seem to have been a great public outcry against the birth of war babies.

Signs of things to come

There can be no doubt that in Wales, with its firmly held views on a woman's place, the war had spectacularly challenged gender-roles. Women had broken through into the male world of work – in engineering works and in munition factories, on the trams and on the railways, as policewomen, secretaries, clerks, civil servants, postwomen, farm workers and even as uniformed members of the women's services. Old notions of propriety and the conventions restricting women's behaviour had been shaken by the appearance of bare-kneed women footballers and flashily dressed munitionettes out for a good time in Welsh towns. Women had even succeeded in their aim, the vote. On 6 February 1918, the Representation of the People Act, enfranchising most women over thirty, became law. It was widely viewed at the time, and this truism is often repeated by historians, that women were given the vote as a reward for their wartime services. In fact, the winning of the franchise was the result of sixty years of campaigning. What their contribution to the war effort did was to make it impossible to deny them their rights any longer. Winifred Coombe Tennant of Neath accurately stated the position in *Welsh Outlook*, December 1916, when she wrote:

> Women do not admit their claim to the vote rests upon any services rendered to the state during the war. They regard the vote as an inalienable right of those among them who bear the burden of citizenship in such measure as would, had they been men, have entitled them to be voters. But it is idle to deny that the part played by women since the war began has profoundly affected public opinion in regard to their claims. It has brought sight to eyes that were blind and hearing to ears that were deaf.

The Act added six million British women to the parliamentary electorate, while at the same time admitting married women to the municipal franchise. The secretary of the small NUWSS society in Llangollen wrote with a great flourish in the minute book, 'The Winning of the Vote'. More good news followed. In November 1918, in time for the general election, women were allowed to stand as members of parliament. The Llangollen society was over the moon and 'rejoicing in the success which has attended its efforts' promptly, if prematurely, disbanded itself. Throughout the war the press and the government had lavished praise on women. Women had shown what they were made of and some feminists were optimistic that the war had laid the foundations for expanding women's opportunities in the workplace, consolidating their position in jobs newly-opened to them and taking their place in politics and public life. But were they right in 1918 to think that they were standing on the frontier of a brave new world? Or were they in for a rude awakening?

Women's wartime gains have to be viewed against the background of the enormous slaughter which had taken place on the Western Front and elsewhere. In view of the loss of life, there was a renewed emphasis on women as mothers, as the bearers of a new generation to replace those who had died. Concerns had been raised throughout the war about the impact of heavy work on women's health, particularly on their child-bearing capabilities and hence on their ability to reproduce 'the race'. In 1917, the National Baby Weeks Council, with Lloyd George as president and Lord Rhondda as chairman, launched the first Baby Week under the slogan, 'It is more dangerous to be a baby in England [*sic*] than to be a soldier of the line in France'. Baby weeks were held all over Wales. In Bridgend there was a bonny baby show and the film 'Motherhood', starring Mrs Lloyd George and Sybil Lady Rhondda, was shown at the Picture Palace. In Cardiff, in addition to all this, schoolchildren, both boys and girls, entered an essay competition with a choice of titles, either 'How I mind our baby' or 'Why I should kill that fly'. Emphasis had long been placed, as we have seen, on infant mortality and considerable improvements had been made, but the war made the authorities realize the close connection between maternal health and infant well-being and to pay attention for the first time to maternal mortality. A Local Government Board report on maternal mortality, published in 1916, brought home the full horror of the position in Wales. Eight Welsh counties headed the list of maternal death rates – Merioneth, Anglesey, Breconshire, Carmarthenshire and Denbighshire, with the first two of these having more than double the average maternal death rate for England and Wales. In 1918 the Maternal and Child Welfare Act, the brainchild of Lord Rhondda, was passed. It created powers for local authorities to provide health visitors and infant welfare centres. The emphasis remained primarily on the child but alongside this came provision for ante-natal, natal and post-natal care for women. Would the baby weeks and the passage of this Act prove more reliable indicators of what the future held for women than did the hopes and aspirations of feminists?

There is somehow a terrible irony in that the Great War, which had shattered and maimed men in body and mind, had allowed many women to stand tall for the first time in their lives. But what did the future hold? We cannot assess the impact of the war on women's lives from the standpoint of 1918 alone. Only by looking at what happened to women in Wales in the inter-war period, can we reach any conclusions about whether the war marked the dawn of a bright, new age for women or whether it had been merely an exceptional interlude.

~ 3 ~

Sacrifice and Solidarity,
1919–1939

THE period immediately following the Armistice of November 1918 was a confusing time for women. On the one hand, they still basked in the praise showered on them by a grateful nation and an over-exuberant wartime press and they benefited too from new legislation, which both enfranchised them and gave them entry into hitherto exclusively male professions. On the other hand, it quickly became apparent that old patriarchal attitudes had merely been put on ice for the duration of the war, and, with the coming of peace, life was to return to normal. Women were expected to resume their roles as wives, mothers and dutiful daughters. Newspapers and other media agencies, which in the war had celebrated the part played by 'our gallant girls' and 'our Amazons', changed almost overnight: before 1918 was out, they attacked 'women who stole men's jobs' and 'pin-money girls' and held up the role of the stay-at-home housewife and mother as the only desirable model of womanhood. Legislation restored jobs to men and the widespread introduction of marriage bars in the professions pushed women out of well-paid work. The national insurance scheme and the workings of labour exchanges made it not only difficult for women to claim unemployment benefit but even to gain recognition as unemployed persons. It was hard for contemporaries to accept the concept that a women could be unemployed. After all, there was always some man for her to look after, be it husband, son, father or brother. The only fit work for working-class women was regarded as in the home – her own or somebody else's – and labour exchanges operated what was essentially a policy of compulsory domestic service.

It was as though, in the immediate post-war period, women were seen as having got above themselves and had to be knocked back into shape and into a position of dependency on men. The back-to-the-home movement dominated women's lives from 1918 to 1939, but, in Wales, one other major factor, itself reinforcing this movement, must be taken into account and that is the all-pervasive effect of the long economic Depression, which lasted from the mid-1920s down to the late 1930s.

These were the years of mass unemployment, means-testing and crushing poverty, which remain deeply ingrained in the Welsh folk memory. In Wales the Depression was longer, harder, deeper, more intractable and more apparently hopeless than in any other part of Britain. Hardest hit of all were the coal-mining valleys of eastern Glamorgan and of Monmouthshire. Here and in many other parts of Wales, women suffered appalling poverty, with its attendant effects on their health, and they made great sacrifices for the sake of their husbands and children, but they were not just passive victims: they played a key role in bringing about improvements in their communities. It is in many ways tragic that the longed-for peace, after five years of war, should turn to dust and it is bitterly ironic that economic regeneration would only come about as a result of the impetus given by another world war. In order to make some sense of women's lives in the inter-war period, this chapter examines the dismissal of women from the workforce at the end of the First World War; women's paid employment in the 1920s and 1930s; the impact of the Depression on their lives; health; leisure; politics and issues of importance to women.

Demobilization

When the war ended, women were dismissed from the labour force en masse. Demand for munitions began winding down months before the Armistice and Welsh girls started to return home from munition factories in England, with just two weeks' pay in lieu of notice and a free rail warrant. Newport National Shell Factory closed down on 30 November 1918 but other Welsh factories remained open until January 1919. On 6 December the *North Wales Chronicle* reported that 'demobilization of women workers has not commenced to any great extent in North Wales', but stated that notice had been issued to the large majority of women workers in the various munition works. Queensferry, Wrexham, Uskside and Swansea all closed in January 1919. There was a strong sense that the women were reluctant to leave. The welfare officer at Uskside wrote in her final report: 'While everyone was thrilled and rejoiced exceedingly over the signing of the Armistice, the women were sorry to say good bye to Uskside on January 13 1919.' Wartime agreements and the Restoration of Pre-War Practices Act of 1918 ensured that jobs, where women had substituted for men, would revert to men in peacetime. Women were expected to step down in favour of ex-servicemen and, in many cases, in favour of men who had never been in the armed forces. A brief post-war boom enabled women to hold onto jobs a little longer, but economic depression in 1920 made it unacceptable for women to work while men were unemployed. In Swansea the last remaining 'lady railway clerk' left her post in

March 1920. Female tram drivers had realized that their work was strictly for the duration but the conductresses had hopes of staying on. A Cardiff woman tram driver told the *Western Mail*, 23 May 1917:

> all the women drivers I know are filling vacant places until the men come back from the front . . . we shall yield up the positions of women drivers (but) I do not think men will ever again take up conductorship.

In fact, although some of the Cardiff conductresses held on to their positions until about 1920, when the outcry about women stealing men's jobs intensified, in nearby Bristol ex-servicemen threw stones at trams demanding the dismissal of the conductresses. Similarly, women civil servants were sacked in large numbers and replaced by ex-servicemen. In 1914 the civil service employed just 66,000 women in the whole of Britain. By 1918 the number had risen to 235,000 but by 1928 was down to 74,000. Women, many of them well educated, had expected to stay on and develop careers in the higher grades of the civil service but, although the 1928 figures show a slight rise over 1914, most of the women were confined to subordinate grades.

The women's services were disbanded. By 1920, the WAAC (which had been renamed the Queen Mary's Army Auxiliary Corps), the WRNS and the WRAF had all ceased to exist. Women police had shown their usefulness during the war and several English and Scottish constabularies, including the Metro-politan Police, realized their value. By 1920, there were 400 women police in England, thirteen in Scotland and none in Wales. No woman police officer was appointed in Wales in the whole of the inter-war period, despite the efforts of women's groups, which are discussed later.

The end of the war created a huge problem of women's unemployment. By late January 1919, the Ministry of Labour stated that 425,000 women in Britain were unemployed and by March, the official figure was over 500,000. Lady Rhondda, as Margaret Haig Mackworth had become after the death of her father, distrusted these official pronouncements and believed that the true figure was nearer 1,500,000.

Insured women workers, including munition and other factory workers were entitled to claim 'out-of-work donations'. First payments were made to women on 6 December 1918 at the fairly generous rate of 25s. a week for thirteen weeks. In order to qualify for this benefit, women had to attend the labour exchange daily and be available for work, but the conflict came over what sort of work they were available for. Officials offered women jobs in the one sphere they did not want – domestic service – at wages as low as 8s.6d. a week. If a woman refused a job in service, she automatically lost her entitlement to out-of-work donation. If, on the other hand, she accepted such a low-paid situation and found after a few weeks that she could not live on the money, she could not reapply for benefit because as a domestic servant she was an uninsured worker and not entitled to benefit. The workings of this system drove women into service and made sure that they stayed there.

Domestic service was regarded as the most fitting work for women and in much of Wales it was indeed the only work available. On 6 December 1918, the first day payments were made, the *North Wales Chronicle* reported, 'the position in North Wales in the employment of demobilized women is not a good one as there is practically no known means of absorbing the labour.' The best solution was seen, of course, as domestic service. The mayoress of Wrexham instituted a survey of local householders who were looking for servants and similar surveys were conducted in Brymbo, Corwen, Bala, Dolgellau, Rhuthun, Ruabon and Denbigh. In Cardiff a reader wrote to the *Western Mail*, 29 March 1919, saying that she had advertised for six days for a servant to no avail. It seemed evident to her 'that most of the 2,000 women in Cardiff now in receipt of the unemployment donation prefer to remain as they are'. There was a press outcry that women should be receiving dole money at all and it was regarded as impertinent of them to turn up to collect it smartly dressed. Papers attacked them for having their hair curled and for wearing fur coats and kid boots.

The *Western Mail*, 20 January 1919, commenting on the thousands of women who had returned home to south Wales from English munition works, thought that it was high time they realized that:

> domestic service, which they were originally engaged in, must again be their main source of livelihood, that is if they want to do anything at all. Seaside places and other holiday centres throughout the country are said to be now reaping a harvest from young women who are out for a good time on their savings as munition workers and their donations.

Unemployed women were everyone's target. As late as 10 May 1920, when few women were still entitled to benefit, the *South Wales Daily Post* contrasted 'the lot of the boys who gave life and limb and health with that of the munition workers who could get a big balance and fur coats'.

Though loathe to return to hated domestic service, women could not hold out indefinitely. By the summer of 1919, the majority of women had capitulated and either entered service or simply returned home and stopped registering as unemployed. In March 1919, the number of women registered as unemployed in Britain was 500,000 but by November, it was down to 90,000, only 30,000 of whom were eligible for benefit.

Employment

Women's participation rates in the workforce were actually lower in inter-war Wales than they had been before the war. By 1921, only 21.2 per cent of women in Wales were recorded as economically active and, by 1931, the figure had slipped to 21 per cent. These figures are in contrast to the much higher female participation rates for England and Wales as a whole of 32.3 per cent in 1921 *increasing* to 34.2 per cent in 1931. Regional variations within Wales, which were evident in pre-war days, continued, with 27.4 per cent of women in paid work in Cardiganshire but only a staggeringly low 12.5 per cent in the Rhondda in 1921. In Cardiff, with a wider range of jobs for women, 29.2 per cent were employed in 1921 rising to 30.9 per cent in 1931. The First World War, as these figures show, cannot be seen as throwing open the gates of economic opportunity for women. Not only did participation rates for Wales as a whole fall from 1911 to 1921 and, again, from 1921 to 1931, but the nature of women's work did not fundamentally change. Domestic service remained the largest single occupation. In 1921 the newly created census category of 'Services, sport and recreation' (replacing 'Domestic offices or service') accounted for 44.5 per cent of women at work in Wales, and, by 1931, 47.7 per cent. As in pre-war days more women in Wales were employed in domestic service than in England: the figures for England and Wales were 33 per cent in 1921 and 35 per cent in 1931. In both countries there was an increase in the numbers going into service. This is not surprising given the middle-class outcry about lack of domestic help, the government drive to push women into service, lack of other work and the need to earn a living during the hard times of the 1920s and 1930s. By 1931, nearly 100,000 women *in* Wales were working in the census category of 'Services, sport and recreation – with the majority in domestic service – and thousands more had left to take up 'situations' in more prosperous regions of England.

In the 1920s and 1930s, the *only* training courses provided for girls and women were in domestic service. Courses were laid on by the Central Committee for Women's Employment (CCWE) in association with the Ministry of Labour. The CCWE wanted to offer courses in such subjects as horticulture and journalism, but the Ministry of Labour would only fund domestic courses. From 1921 homecraft courses of thirteen weeks' duration in residential centres were provided for trainees who gave a written undertaking to enter service. Between 1924 and 1939 the Ministry of Labour offered 'home training courses' in non-residential centres. It was quite clear that there would not be enough 'situations' to accommodate the numbers of young women seeking positions in service in their home areas. Councillor Rose Davies, JP of Aberdare in the *South Wales Daily Post*, 2 June 1923, stated that within the last year 503 girls had registered at the Aberdare Exchange, of whom 400 were prepared to take domestic service, but there were only 147 vacancies in the area. Aberdare at this time was putting on its second thirteen-week course for twenty girls under the age of eighteen. The depressed areas were targeted by the Industrial Transference Board, established in 1928 to retrain labour and to place people in work in more prosperous regions. South Wales had non-residential training centres for women in such places as Aberdare, Bargoed, Maesteg, Merthyr Tydfil, Neath, Pontypool, Swansea and Ystrad Rhondda. Girls were admitted first from the age of fifteen and later fourteen. On completion of the course, jobs were found for them. The Ystrad Rhondda Centre, for example, trained forty-two girls in the second half of 1928; of these, twenty found employment in Wales, thirteen went to London and the remainder to such places as Bath, Eastbourne and Weston-super-Mare. Many girls from south and mid-Wales attended residential courses in Sydenham and Leamington Spa, while girls from north Wales trained at Warrington, Market Harborough and Harrogate. By 1934, long courses of nine months' duration for fourteen-year-olds were introduced at certain centres. All these schemes trained 4–5000 girls each year, mainly from south Wales and the north-east of England: between 1920 and 1935 some 67,000 girls had been placed in situations. In addition to these official schemes, charitable and local authority homes, engaged in rescuing fallen women or sheltering girls in need of care and protection, also placed girls in service in distant places. The Barry Domestic Training Centre, which took in girls from broken homes, found jobs for them not only in private houses in Bristol, Reading and Bournemouth but, in the late 1930s, in large public institutions such as hospitals – a development reflecting the increasing 'publicization' of domestic service.

Girls went off to work in private homes, hotels and hospitals. Wages were between eight and fifteen shillings a week. The hours were long and the work heavy. One young woman, who took up a position in a nursing home in Bristol, where there were seventeen inmates but only two domestics (including herself), said of her work-load:

> I had to get up at 6.30 a.m. and clean the grates and lay fires, take early morning tea, help Cook prepare breakfasts, scrub the steps and all these kind of jobs had to be done before breakfast and then your cleaning came after breakfast.

Conditions were best in large houses with a retinue of servants, but usually the Welsh girl was the only one employed – the single maid-of-all-work-in a lower-middle-class household owned by a shopkeeper, tradesman or bank clerk.

Three Valleys girls in service in a large Penarth house,
1930s.

To a great extent domestic service was a matter of pot luck and everything
depended on the individual nature of the employer. One Rhondda girl,
interviewed by Hywel Francis, was employed by a Welsh family in a Clapham
Common dairy: she was made to feel part of the family, and even taken to the
theatre with them. But other girls came face to face with differences in class and
nationality – having to put up with employers who derided their Welsh accents
and ran the Welsh down. Many suffered physical deprivation and not getting
enough to eat was a common complaint. A Rhondda woman, interviewed by
Anne Jones, was put on starvation rations by her employer because the
daughter of the household was dieting:

> I was starved to death there. She locked everything up and gave me three lumps
> of sugar for one day and I had a small pat of margarine . . . and for my dinner
> every day I had half a bag of potato crisps for three weeks and yet I was cooking
> for them but being what-do-you-call slow, I suppose in those days I wouldn't
> think of taking anything. That's one thing that was always drummed into us –
> don't you ever take anything that doesn't belong to you.

The Welsh girls were young and naïve. Many arrived in London with no concept of the size of the city and expected to be able to walk to their employer's house. Very few had had the house checked out by the voluntary agencies and they worked for a pittance in places where no properly trained domestic worker would have stayed a day. Some, exploited and inhumanely treated, simply ran away and found themselves homeless, penniless and stranded. There were widespread fears that these girls were subject to 'moral dangers' – a euphemism for abuse by male employers, prostitution and 'white slavery'. The National Vigilance Association (NVA) and the Girls' Friendly Society (GFS) were particularly concerned about the innocent young Welsh girls. GFS workers met these girls at Paddington Station and escorted them to their new homes. On many occasions GFS workers prevented girls from being led off by strangers who hung around the station. The moral dangers were real enough, as Mr Semkins, secretary of the NVA, writing in the *Western Mail*, 17 February 1934, put it:

> Can you wonder that many get into trouble? If you spent your days working in a black slum and slept in a scullery, would you not accept brightness and gaiety if they were offered to you on your evening out by a plausible person, even though he were a stranger to you?

NVA records contain a heartbreaking collection of letters from mothers in the Valleys asking the organization to check up on their daughters, some as young as fifteen, who had not written home for weeks. This set in motion visits by social workers who attempted to deal with the problems. They dealt with girls who had been turned away by employers on arrival because they did not like the look of them, with employers who withheld wages and with runaways. The annual report of the NVA for 1929 contains such cases as that of an eighteen-year-old girl, found at Paddington, who had run away from a house in the East End where she had been mistreated and overworked looking after a family of eight and that of a 28-year-old married woman, mother of two and wife of an unemployed man, who had come to London to earn money to send home, but had been turned away by her employer on her arrival. A wide range of other organizations helped these girls, including the London Welsh Society and Welsh churches and chapels. When groups of girls from the same Welsh town travelled to the same area to work, they at least had a network of friends about them, such as girls from Aberfan in Sutton in Surrey and Barry girls in Kidderminster.

In Wales women continued to work in the tin industry in the Swansea and Llanelli areas, though their numbers declined dramatically, falling by two-thirds between 1921 and 1931. A similar decline took place in the Welsh woollen industry. Wales did not profit from the boom in light industries witnessed by the south-east of England and the Midlands, although some Welsh women migrated to these areas. These factories used new conveyor belt and assembly-line technology to produce electrical and other consumer goods – radios, light bulbs, refrigerators and packaged food – for the home market, but it tended to be less progressive English companies who recruited women from Wales and other depressed areas to work as cheap labour in unmodernized factories – making and packing such things as biscuits and toffees. Light industrial factories did not come to Wales until the mid–1930s. The first factory was opened on the Trefforest trading estate in 1938 and Polykoff's clothing factory was set up in the Rhondda in 1939. There were other small pockets of industry in Wales which employed women. In Flintshire, Courtaulds opened its new rayon factory at Greenfield in 1934 and by the late 1930s several light industrial works were established in Monmouthshire.

In other types of work the numbers of women employed increased. In both shop and office work women managed to hang on to the gains made in the First World War. The number of saleswomen in Wales doubled between 1911 and 1921 and again rose slightly by 1931. Shop work remained badly paid and with a large differential between male and female rates. Mrs Beatrice Hopkins of Abertillery recalled her sister getting a job at Thomas's China Shop at 7s. 6d. a week in the 1930s. That was regarded as a good wage, especially since the chic assistants in Bon Marché, who thought they were 'the cat's whiskers' in their smart black dresses, only earned five shillings. The spread of chain stores such as Woolworth and Marks and Spencer created more jobs: Pontypridd's Marks and Spencer opened in 1939. In Cardiff, black women from Butetown met with a wall of prejudice if they tried to get jobs in the city's smart stores: white shop girls, in their ignorance, refused to work alongside them. But the major development in women's work in inter-war Wales, as in the rest of Britain, was the growth in the number of women clerks and typists in offices. The numbers employed increased sixfold between 1911 and 1921 and continued to rise. It was respectable work but the wages were such that many 'business girls' could not afford two sets of office clothes or midday meals. The Depression actually brought wages down in this sector so that the British average wage (usually higher than the Welsh) in 1931 was 30s. for women clerks under twenty-five years of age and 50s. for older women; office girls started at 10s. to 12s. a week and typists earned between 20s. to 25s.

Women in the professions looked forward, at the war's end, to a bright new dawn of opportunities. The passage of the Sex Disqualification (Removal) Act (SD(R)A) of 1919 added to their optimism. It decreed that:

A person shall not be disqualified by sex or marriage from the exercise of any public function, or from being appointed to or holding any civil or judicial office or post, or from entering or assuming or carrying out any civil profession or vocation.

The Act opened the professions of the law, accountancy, engineering and any other career run by chartered bodies to women, though the Civil Service adroitly managed to exclude itself. But women's high hopes and expectations of the Act were quickly dashed. Professional women were victims of the economic depression, cuts in public expenditure, the backlash against women working and the widespread introduction of marriage bars, which meant that women automatically lost their jobs on marriage. Though the Act did admit women to professions which had previously been exclusively male preserves, by 1922 *Time and Tide*, the magazine owned by Lady Rhondda, declared, 'The Act means nothing, we have been hoaxed.'

Teachers formed the largest group of professional women. The production of teachers had already become something of a Welsh industry and from 1914 the new women's training college at Barry added to the numbers of teachers trained in Wales. The establishment of national salary scales by the newly formed Burnham committee in 1921 raised salaries and did away with such inequalities as Cardiganshire teachers receiving 20 per cent less in salary than those in Glamorgan, but Burnham did not introduce equal pay: women teachers were paid four-fifths of the male rate. Economies in public spending in 1922 actually cut teachers' salaries, and by 1930, the average salary paid to certificated teachers in elementary schools was £254 for women and £334 for men. Despite this differential, teaching was considered a well-paid job for women. Gareth Alban Davies, recalling boyhood Sundays spent in Bethesda chapel in the Rhondda, remembered the presence of schoolteachers in fur coats, that ubiquitous symbol of women's affluence. He noted, 'The fur coat itself set those teachers apart, but there was something else, too: they were unmarried.' The chief explanation for their single state was the widespread introduction of marriage bars in the early 1920s, though some women may have lost fiancés in the war. Some local authorities in England and Wales had operated marriage bars before 1914, many dropping them for the war's duration, but in the early 1920s marriage bars were widely introduced and by 1926, 75 per cent of local authorities in England and Wales operated them. Women teachers who were already married were dismissed and others were forced to resign on marriage. In July 1922, Rhondda Education Authority dismissed sixty-three married women teachers. Led by Mrs Elizabeth Price of Cwmclydach Infants School, who had been teaching since 1897, the women took the authority to court but lost their case. Public opinion was against married women working and, in this situation, some couples concealed their marriages and tales abound in south Wales of couples living in and teaching in separate valleys so the women could hold onto their jobs. Local authorities defended their actions in sacking married women on the grounds that there was wholesale unemployment of young teachers. There was some substance to this argument with 38 per cent of newly qualified women teachers and 32 per cent of men unemployed in Wales in 1924, but the real motivation was based on opposition to married women working while men were unemployed. Young Welsh teachers, like the servant girls, were compelled to leave Wales in search of work.

Nursing was the other main profession which attracted women. Indeed, it was an all female workforce. The Nurses Registration Act of 1919 put nursing on a professional footing, for the first time setting a national standard for State Registered Nurses. Nurses were subject to a very strict and restrictive regime, and did hard and heavy work for extremely low wages: as late as 1937 a qualified nurse earned just £65 per annum and a sister £125. Like teaching, nursing operated the marriage bar: in both professions women were expected to sacrifice a home and family for the sake of a higher vocation. Welsh girls trained both at hospitals in Wales and in large hospitals in England. Fflorins Roberts from Llanfaglan near Caernarfon went to Liverpool to train while many south Walian girls went to London: 20 per cent of the nursing staff at St Marks Hospital in the 1920s were from Wales.

During the war the number of women training to be doctors had risen but in the post-war period some of the large London hospitals banned their entry. In 1922 the London Hospital excluded women students because 'the staff have found difficulties in teaching to a mixed audience certain unpleasant subjects of medicine': St Mary's Paddington, Westminster and Charing Cross hospitals all closed their doors to women medical students in the 1920s. Training provision for doctors in Wales only fully commenced in 1921, with the opening of the Welsh National School of Medicine. Rose Griffiths from Cyfarthfa School, Merthyr was the first woman to enter and to graduate from Cardiff: she then spent her career as a GP in Merthyr. But the numbers of women doctors remained small with only some 2,500 qualified women in England and Wales by 1928. The history of women in medicine in Wales remains to be written, as does their involvement in the legal profession. The SD(R) Act allowed women to enter the legal profession but training as a barrister or solicitor was very lengthy and fees were expensive – £150 for the bar in 1927 and premiums of up to 300 guineas to enter a solicitor's office. By 1922, Irish and English women had been called to the bar and Scotland had its first woman advocate by 1926. Lists of 'women firsts' have yet to be compiled for Wales. In the University of

Wales a few outstanding women rose to professorships. In Cardiff, Barbara Foxley was the second woman professor of Education and Olive Wheeler the third; the newly opened University College of Swansea appointed Mary Williams as professor of French.

Hard times and home life

The single dominant factor affecting life in Wales in the inter-war years was the long economic depression, which brought in its wake mass unemployment on an unparalleled scale. Not only did this greatly damage women's job prospects, but it also had a devastating effect on the lives of women at home – the wives and daughters of unemployed men.

The economic depression, which was clearly evident by the mid–1920s, took Wales by surprise. Until 1914 the progress of Welsh industry had seemed unstoppable and the war had given agriculture as well as industry a further boost. The slump hit old heavy industries – coal, steel and shipbuilding – hardest and worst affected of all were the steam-coal producing central and eastern valleys of south Wales. There were early signs of trouble with a four month lockout in 1921. Decline in the demand for coal combined with the contraction of international trade and Britain's return to the Gold Standard in 1925, which made exports uncompetitive, meant disaster for the Welsh coal industry. In 1926 demands for longer hours and lower wages by the coal owners led to the nine day General Strike, 3–12 May 1926, followed by a six month lockout. Deprivation and an increasing burden of debt forced the miners to accept harsh terms on their return to work. From December 1926, south Wales miners worked an eight hour day (i.e. an extra hour on the day) for just about half the pay they had received in 1921. Some miners never regained their jobs after 1926 and unemployment began to soar. By 1928, the percentage of insured workers unemployed stood at 9.8 per cent for England and 21.9 per cent for Wales and by 1932, following the Wall Street Crash and the collapse of world trade, the figure for England had risen to 20.6 per cent and for Wales to 37.5 per cent. In certain coal and steel towns unemployment reached staggering heights: in 1934 74 per cent of the male workforce at Brynmawr, 73 per cent at Dowlais and 66 per cent at Merthyr were registered as unemployed. There was no hope for men to find work locally: they were long-term unemployed. In 1934, in south Wales 52 per cent of the unemployed had been unemployed for more than two years and 10.8 per cent for more than five years. The virtual collapse of the coal industry had knock-on effects for other industries. Shipping declined dramatically and by 1935 there was 25 per cent male unemployment in the Cardiff and Barry areas. Nor was the slump confined to industry. Welsh agriculture was, by the early 1930s (prior to the establishment of the Milk Marketing Board in 1933), struggling to survive: the average income of farming families in Wales was around £100 per annum. But the economic depression was not uniform in its impact. While the valleys of south-east Wales suffered appalling deprivation, Flintshire, with its rayon manufacturing, steel and building industries was relatively prosperous. Tourism and small businesses enabled the towns of the north Wales coast to expand and rows of new-style semi-detached houses were erected at Rhyl, Prestatyn and Llandudno. Commercial centres such as Cardiff and Swansea (which were not wholly dependent on coal and shipping) continued to enjoy a degree of relative prosperity and the anthracite coalfield and tinplate industry of the south west escaped the very worst of the Depression.

The most damaging result of the economic crisis in Wales, was the wholesale exodus of people, particularly from the valleys of south-east Wales. Between 1921 and 1940, 430,000 Welsh people left home to find work in the more prosperous regions of England: they went to such places as Hounslow, Dagenham, Oxford, Luton and Slough. Assisted by the Industrial Transfer Scheme (1928–37), it was the young and most energetic who left their close-knit communities to work in English factories and to live on suburban housing estates. Many never returned. An exodus occurred too from rural counties due to the agriculture depression. This had severe consequences for the Welsh language and the proportion of Welsh speakers continued to fall. Chapels, bastions of Welshness, declined too, affected by lack of money and shrinking congregations.

The years from 1926 to the late 1930s, with their abject poverty and appalling deprivation form the bleakest period in the history of twentieth-century Wales. Poor Relief was available only for the wives and children during the 1926 lockout: the men got nothing. Marion Phillips, chief woman organizer of the Labour Party, in *Women and the Miners' Lock-Out* (1927) painted a moving picture of women's lives:

> In the wretched little houses clustered round the silent pit-head, children are being born in houses which have been stripped of every saleable luxury. The mothers have been ill-nourished and living in continuous anxiety and face childbirth without any of the care and comfort they need.

But the worst was yet to come. 1926 was just the beginning for many in south Wales of long years of unemployment and left a legacy of debt on families that made it even harder to cope. It was almost impossible to live on the meagre unemployment benefit allowed in the early 1930s when a man with a wife and two children received just thirty shillings a week, which had to cover rent, heat and clothing as well as food. But the cost of maintaining the unemployed, even at these levels, was crippling the economy and in 1931 the new National (Coalition) Government cut benefits and introduced that most detested of measures, the Means Test. Workers who had been unemployed for more than six months were transferred from unemployment benefit to Public Assistance (in essence Poor Relief under another name), and every penny of income (in kind, as well as cash) had to be declared. This meant that if a son or daughter was working the father's benefit would be cut and this led to the break-up of families. Under this system, the *most* a man, wife and two children could receive was 27s. 3d. and benefit could be refused altogether. These new measures pauperized the unemployed.

It was women who managed the family budget. On their shoulders fell the burden of ensuring the survival of husbands and children through the skilled management of a meagre income. They bought only the cheapest and most filling foods – white bread, potatoes, sugar, butter and margarine, tinned milk, jam and tea, with the occasional treat of a bag of bacon pieces or broken biscuits. Official reports and letters to *The Times* criticized these housewives, urging them to bake wholemeal bread and feed their families on pulses and raw carrots, but these views take little account of the reality of working class life: sweet condensed milk or bread and jam were somehow 'cheerier' than a slice of brown bread and a glass of water. Women commonly stretched the family budget further by simply 'going without' themselves. At meal times, they said that they had already eaten or would have 'something' later. As Eli Ginsberg remarked, 'The children are hungry, the men are hungry, but most hungry of all are the women who deprive themselves so that their husbands and children can eat a little more.' Food was the woman's top priority but the budget had to stretch too to provide clothes and boots for the family. Women did their best – cutting down their old clothes for the children or dressing them in hand-me-downs. Eileen Warfield of Aberbeeg was thrilled when a wealthy lady gave her a lovely coat, but she did not hold on to it for long:

> It was gorgeous, with a lovely leather belt. I was quite tall and I could have carried it off. I took it home and I said to Mam, 'Look what Mrs Williams has given me,' and my father said to me, 'Lil's going to service next week, she needs that more than you.'

Boots might be got from a free boot distribution centre, set up by charitable bodies. The children had to be clothed and shod to go to school: if they could not get there they would miss out on free meals. Women made sacrifices to clothe the children, but even so contemporary commentators frequently remarked on the thinness of their clothes. Teachers were sympathetic, but not all local authorities were understanding and one can imagine the humiliation a mother would have felt on receiving the following notice from Monmouthshire Education Authority:

Notice of Ragged Clothing

The recent inspection of your child who attends Danycraig School shows that his (or her) clothing was in a ragged condition. There seems no valid reason why this condition should continue and in the interest of the child I trust you will see that he (or she) will henceforth be sent to school properly clad.

School Medical Officer

Women would not 'waste' money on new clothes for themselves. Out of doors they made an effort to appear respectable and tidy but at home their daily uniform was an old frock, covered by a wrap-around pinafore, bare legs and old, worn shoes. The appearance of these women, prematurely aged by poor diet and worry, was a world away from the chic images of the pert modern housewife in neat dress, pearls and frilly gingham apron pictured in the new-style women's magazines. The housewife of the magazines lived in a new suburban semi with a bathroom and hot water on tap, had a 'modern' kitchen with an electric cooker and cleaned her carpet squares with a vacuum cleaner. The wives of the Rhondda unemployed lived in terraced housing, lacking all basic amenities and still cooked on the open fire. Floors were bare, or at best covered by cheap linoleum, and the houses had been stripped of every saleable item of furniture, bed-linen and crockery – sold on the orders of the Means Test man. In many homes there were not enough chairs for everyone to sit on, pans to cook with or plates and cups from which to eat and drink: old coats served as blankets. Beatrice Wood's account of the three-roomed house in Dowlais where she lived with her parents, three brothers and one sister, shows the starkness of poverty. She described in *Wednesday's Child* the single living room-cum-kitchen where the whole family lived: it contained a Welsh dresser, a wooden table covered with a blanket, wooden chairs, an old couch, an enamel bowl placed on an orange box under the tap to act as the 'sink', a mirror on the wall above the tap and a shelf for their combs. The only cooking utensils were one kettle and one iron saucepan. But despite such poverty as this, or perhaps because of it, valleys women retained a pride in their housewifely role. They were 'tidy' women, who kept their homes spotlessly clean, scrubbing the front

Mrs Blodwen Williams washing the pavement in front of
her house in Ynysybwl, 1930s.

step and washing down the pavement outside: even on their reduced incomes
such women spent money weekly on polish (floor, boot and metal), soap and
washing powder. But not all women could keep up these standards and the
Pilgrim Trust's report, *Men Without Work* (1938), refers to the dispirited women,
who had 'lost all pride in personal appearance and the appearance of their
home': these were women 'whose outings extended little beyond the small shops
at the corner of the street', to which they slipped down without washing and
who saw little point in washing the children, because they only got dirty again.
Not every woman was a heroine, but neither were they all passive victims.

Survival strategies became more essential than ever. Beatrice Wood in
Dowlais scavenged for cabbage leaves from market stalls, took empty jam jars
back to the shop for the halfpenny deposit and she and her mother took in
work decorating braid, sewing on daisies at 1*s*.3*d*. for thirty-six yards. In
addition to selling food such as faggots and peas, women went out cleaning.
Ada Howells's mother in Abertillery used to decorate as well as clean houses –
'paper a house through for half a crown Mam would'. Women and girls, as well
as men, gathered coal from the slag heaps – a risky business for which they
could be prosecuted. Old potato sacks became sacking aprons and flour and
rice bags were bleached and sewn into pillowcases and tray cloths.

Outside bodies, notably the Quakers and the Salvation Army, established centres for the unemployed, where they could gainfully occupy their time and learn new skills. Women grouped together too, in some cases forming clubs on their own initiative, as at Senghennydd, and in others taking over the organization once a club had been set up by an outside agency. The South Wales and Monmouthshire Council of Social Service set up clubs for women in south Wales, under the Special Area scheme introduced in 1934. The clubs ran needlework and craft courses, which provided an opportunity for women to meet and talk together. Drama societies grew out of the clubs and these, like the keep fit classes, provided an interest and a much needed diversion. As ever, officialdom could not resist lecturing women on their domestic role: in 1935 an organizer of housecrafts was appointed and classes were run on the constituents of a balanced diet, food values and feeding the children. First aid and home nursing classes were also laid on. These groups were popular and increased rapidly. There were 109 women's clubs in south Wales by 1935 rising to 260 in 1939. Funding was also provided for girls' clubs and branches of the Girls' Life Brigade, Girls' Friendly Society, Girls' Guildry and the Girl Guides. Grants were given for uniforms and for camping holidays. In 1935–6 some 700 young girls from south Wales and Durham went on camping holidays. *The Second Report of the Commissioner for the Special Areas* (1935–6) stated that younger club members and girls 'who have had to mother a large family and on whose shoulders the main burden of housework has fallen' were given priority. Most had never had a holiday before and the report gives a glimpse of both the pleasure and the benefits such a break gave them. One club leader wrote: 'At the close of each week it was a pleasure to look at the girls' sunburnt faces and to feel that they had been strengthened in a small measure at least to meet the demands of the coming winter.'

Women also played an active part in fighting back against the system and the establishment which had brought them to such straits. In 1926 the women were involved not only in the traditional roles as cooks and organizers in communal kitchens and in sewing, altering and distributing clothes, but they took to the streets. They harassed and attacked blacklegs (strike-breakers) and the police who protected them. In October at Heolgwynt, near Cymmer, a crowd of 500 men and women attacked a lorry bringing in blacklegs under police escort, with sticks and jam jars. Sixteen women and twenty-three miners were charged: the women were all fined forty shillings, although one woman opted for imprisonment rather than paying the fine. Hywel Francis and David Smith in *The Fed* (1980) point out that women figured prominently in twelve major prosecutions in 1926, noting that these were mainly married women and older than the miners who were charged. The contemporary press commented on the women's involvement, finding it 'surprising' and 'strange' that they should be embroiled in these skirmishes. The *Western Mail*, 5 November 1926, noted, 'A strange feature of the disturbance is the surprisingly prominent part played by the women.' The courts clamped down hard on these women in an attempt to deter them from spurring others on. The stipendiary magistrate, in sentencing Mrs Elvira Bailey of Treorchy to two months imprisonment, was reported in the *South Wales Daily News*, 3 November 1926, as stating:

> You threw the first stone at the police constable and you set a very bad example to the women of the district. I find that the women have been taking too prominent a part in these disturbances and I must impose a penalty that will be a deterrent to others.

The events of 1926 show that women were prepared to break the law and attack strike-breakers in defence of their menfolk's claim to a living wage. But by the 1930s the main focus of their action was against unemployment. In 1934, when mass unemployment had taken on an alarming air of permanency and the ravages of the Means Test had taken their toll, the government introduced the Unemployment Insurance Act, which aimed to reduce expenditure on the unemployed. Under the Act, payment of benefit was henceforth to be made through the Unemployed Assistance Board and this new arrangement would mean cuts in benefit in south Wales: the Act also raised fears that the unemployed would be forced to work without wages in 'labour camps' and on public works.

In protest against the cuts and these schemes, a Hunger March left south Wales in 1934. There had been earlier marches but the 1934 march included a contingent of about a dozen women. Dora Cox, who walked from Tonypandy to London, recalled that the women headed the south Wales march: wearing bright red berets and with rucksacks on their backs, they walked the whole way. She explained:

> Well you couldn't not take part in any activity which would make people themselves feel that at least they were fighting back and also you felt it was absolutely essential to get other people to understand the enormity of the task.

En route the women received coaching in public speaking and addressed meetings on their overnight stops. But the march did not stop the progress of the Act, which was passed in December 1934 and was to come into full operation in February 1935. It was this Act, with its cuts in benefit, which was

Women hunger marchers taking a well-deserved break en route from Tonypandy to London, 1934. Dora Cox is second from the right and Ceridwen Brown of Aberdare sits to the far right of the picture.

to cause the eruption of the largest protests ever seen in the history of Wales and in which women played a leading part. On Sunday 3 February, sixty thousand people marched in the Rhondda, fifty thousand in the Cynon Valley and twenty thousand in Pontypool. Three hundred thousand people took to the streets in their 'Sunday best' in protest against the new unemployment bill. As Gwyn A. Williams put it, 'A whole community stood up and said No.' But it was on the next day, 4 February, that the women really made their mark. One thousand women and two thousand men, with Ceridwen Brown of Aberdare at the head, poured down the valley to Iscoed House, the Merthyr Unemployment Assistance Board (UAB) offices. They broke down the gates, smashed windows and surged into the building, where they ripped telephones from the walls and flung papers and records to the floor and tried to burn them. The crowd would listen only to Ceridwen Brown and her friend, the Dowlais Communist Jack Williams. The police were powerless.

Merthyr was the spark which set off demonstrations throughout south Wales, with women at the fore of the revolt. Their actions shook the government. On the very next day, a government spokesman rose in the House of Commons and announced that the new scales were to be put on hold. They did not come into effect for another eighteen months and then only in a modified form.

The events at Merthyr in February 1935 showed that women, as well as men, had reached breaking point. Their actions had ended in victory which gave a new sense of confidence to the people.

Health

Poor health continued to be a marked feature of women's lives and in many cases the economic depression led to a further deterioration in standards of physical and mental health. It was women themselves who drew attention to the appalling state of affairs in Wales and who vigorously campaigned to improve women's health and, indeed, to save lives.

Maternal mortality rates in Wales were far higher than in England. The Ministry of Health *Report on Maternal Mortality in Wales* (1937) revealed that the puerperal mortality rate (i.e. deaths directly related to childbirth) in Wales between 1924 and 1933 was 35 per cent in excess of the rate for England and the incidence of still births in Wales was 38 per cent above the English figure. Moreover, while maternal mortality rates in England and Wales as a whole *fell* between 1928 and 1935, in Wales, they *rose*, as Table 3.1 shows.

Table 3.1: Puerperal mortality rates: rates per 1,000 births

	Wales	England and Wales
1928	5.79	4.25
1929	5.58	4.16
1930	5.30	4.22
1931	5.13	3.94
1932	5.91	4.04
1933	5.75	4.32
1934	6.61	4.41
1935	5.89	3.93

Source: *Report on Maternal Mortality in Wales*, 1937

Maternal mortality was a problem affecting the whole of Wales. A death rate of over five per thousand births was regarded as extremely serious: in fact, in Wales between 1924–33, the rate was above this in all but two counties (Breconshire and Montgomeryshire) and two county boroughs (Cardiff and Swansea). In the rural counties of Anglesey, Cardigan, Carmarthen and Denbigh it exceeded six deaths per thousand. It was also a major cause for alarm that in the highly populated industrial counties of Glamorgan and

Monmouth, the situation was clearly deteriorating: the maternal mortality rates for 1929–33 showed an increase over the period 1924–8 of 14.2 per cent for Glamorgan and 42 per cent for Monmouthshire.

There were many causes for this state of affairs, ranging from lack of antenatal clinics and maternity beds in hospitals, infections in hospitals, the difficulties of midwives and doctors in attending births in remote areas, the general low standard of women's health and the obvious factor of poor diet and even malnutrition. The 1918 Maternity and Child Welfare Act had required local authorities to set up maternity and child welfare committees and permitted (but did not *require* them) to set up clinics and employ midwives and health visitors. The Act also permitted councils, in the absence of many women councillors, to co-opt two women representing women's organizations onto the local maternity and child welfare committee. Labour's Elizabeth Andrews campaigned throughout Wales urging local authorities to do this but was surprised at the hostile response from many county medical officers of health, one of them even dismissed her reasonable requests as ' wild, hysterical effusions'. The role of local women activists was therefore crucial and, as Pamela Michael notes in *Project Grace*, 'it was due to the campaigning efforts of Labour women such as Mrs David Williams and Lady Violet Mond in Swansea, and Alderman Rose Davies in Aberdare, that the early clinics came into being and helped to establish the principle and value of ante-natal care.' Six years after the passage of the Act, in 1924, there were only eight antenatal clinics in the whole of Wales, seven provided by local councils (i.e. two in Swansea, one each in Cardiff, Newport, Merthyr Tydfil, Aberdare and Llanelli) and one provided by a voluntary organization in Penarth. By 1934, the number of clinics had increased to 87, of which 78 were in Glamorgan and Monmouthshire, six in Flintshire, two in Denbighshire and one in Carmarthenshire. Eight counties still had no antenatal clinics to help expectant mothers. A system of home visits by health visitors was in place by 1934 in every county but the 1937 report noted that, 'Home visiting of expectant mothers was not done adequately or systematically.' The vast majority of births were home-births. Indeed women had little choice about this with only thirteen maternity homes in the whole of Wales: in 1934 these admitted some 2,200 women, out of a total of almost 40,000 live births in that year. The general poor state of women's health had an obvious bearing on their fitness for child bearing, but although the medical authorities realized this, they refused to admit that there was any link between poverty and maternal deaths. To have conceded this, would have been to admit that Welsh women were dying of malnutrition.

The most convincing evidence of the close links which existed between poverty, inadequate diet and maternal mortality came from the work of Lady

Juliet Rhys Williams of Miskin Manor, near Llantrisant. She devoted her energies to improving conditions for pregnant women in the Rhondda and to putting pressure on the authorities 'to save the mothers'. In an article in the journal *Public Health*, she describes how, in response to a maternal death rate of 7.2 in the Rhondda in 1933, the National Birthday Trust, in conjunction with the local authority took a number of steps to improve medical services to the women. They tried improving training for midwives, they laid on the services of a resident obstetrical specialist and they provided free disinfectant. This was all to no avail and the number of puerperal deaths continued to rise – reaching a death rate of 11.29 per thousand in 1934. In 1935, they made distributions of free food to the most undernourished mothers. The result of this simple action was that the death rate fell to 4.77 in 1935. The feeding scheme was then extended to Aberdare, Caerphilly, Gelligaer, Llantrisant and Pontypridd. But despite the dramatic nature of these results, the Ministry of Health refused to listen to 'Lady Williams's speculations'.

Whereas there was a widespread consensus on the need to save the lives of the mothers, the related issue of birth control was quite a different matter. It remained for many people a taboo subject and provoked opposition in some areas of Wales. There was certainly a dire need to help couples to limit the size of their families. The problem of unwanted pregnancies and having an extra mouth to feed was a serious one for women. One south Walian woman, who as the mother of ten had been awarded a willow pattern plate from the *News of the World*, wrote to Marie Stopes in 1921, 'What I would like to know is how can I save having more children as I think I have done my duty by my Country having 13 children.' When birth control campaigner Stella Browne toured south Wales and Monmouthshire in the early 1920s, she said that elderly women would come up to her at the end of her talks and say, 'You've come too late to help me Comrade, but give me some papers for my girls, I don't want them to have the life I've had.'

It is very difficult to assess how far 'mechanical' birth control methods (for example condoms and diaphragms) were used, as opposed to the practice of abstinence or coitus interruptus. In Merthyr condoms were widely available: a deputation complained to the chief constable about 'the wholesale distribution of and selling of contraceptives in the town by means of a slot machine and packing of sheaths in packages of cigarettes, sweets etc.'. Abortion, though illegal and very dangerous, was regarded as a method of birth control of last resort by working-class women and the 1937 *Report on Maternal Mortality* noted a marked increase in the number of abortions in Wales during the Depression. Family size actually fell significantly in south Wales during these hard times. The Rhondda UDC experienced a decline in the birth rate between 1911 and

1931 of 53.7 per cent compared with a decline of 38 per cent for England and Wales as a whole in those years. Birth control campaigners targeted south Wales, with their newspaper the *New Generation* running headlines such as 'Huge Miners' Families' and 'Teach the Miners Birth Control'. But what provision existed to provide advice to women? Kate Fisher's detailed study traces progress, or lack of it, in the counties of Glamorgan and Monmouth but research has yet to be done on other Welsh counties. In Glamorgan in the 1920s provision was limited to a clinic established in Cardiff in 1924 by Nurse Joyce Daniel, a hospital clinic in Abertillery (the first in Britain) which ran for a few years from 1925 and visits from Marie Stopes's touring caravan in 1929–30. In 1930 the government, through Memorandum 153/MCW, permitted (but did not compel) local authorities to provide birth control advice. This advice was confined to married women and only intended to help women in 'cases where further pregnancy would be detrimental to health'. By 1939, there were fourteen local authority clinics in Glamorgan mainly in the industrial areas. In Monmouthshire, on the other hand, where the Medical Officer of Health (MOH), Dr Rocyn Jones, was opposed to birth control, no local authority clinic was set up in any of the twenty-three districts under his control, until in 1935 he conceded to designate centres where advice would be given 'in cases of dire necessity'. In practice, when women did go to these clinics they were laughed at and turned away.

Medical Officers of Health could seriously hinder the process of providing advice to women. Not only Rocyn Jones in Monmouthshire, but Dr Morris of Neath was obstructive and others found excuses for not implementing Memorandum 153/MCW. Some wider opposition came from religious groups, notably from the sizeable Roman Catholic population of Merthyr and Cardiff and some Nonconformists and Anglicans. That progress was made in spite of opposition – though this may well have been exaggerated by birth control campaigners – and in spite of indifference or financial constraints by local authorities, owes much to individual campaigners. In south Wales the most influential figure was Joyce Daniel, a middle-class woman, who devoted all her energies, on humanitarian grounds, to spread the availability of advice to women. As an organizer for the National Birth Control Association she pestered MOH's, lobbied councillors and their wives, addressed women's groups and did everything in her power to get local authorities to implement Memorandum 153/MCW.

Poor housing and poor diet had a deleterious effect on women's general health. The Women's Health Enquiry of 1939, which was based on the evidence of 1,250 women in Britain, sixty-four of whom came from Wales, reveals a shocking and depressing picture of general ill health. When asked 'Do you feel fit and well?', almost a third of the respondents to the enquiry replied 'No' or 'Never'. In these days before the establishment of the National Health Service, clearly many of their problems – such as anaemia, bad teeth, eye defects and bronchitis – were the result of economic causes, chiefly inadequate diet and poor, damp housing.

The efforts of the Welsh National Memorial Association led to a 25 per cent drop in deaths from tuberculosis between 1920 and 1930, but in the 1930s the incidence of the disease began to rise again: between 1932–7, when the disease was in decline in Britain generally, there was a 30 per cent increase in deaths from the disease in the Rhondda. But in rural Wales the situation was far worse. Poor, damp housing and overcrowding – all factors linked with the spread of the disease – were particularly prevalent in north and west Wales and it was women who spent their days in these houses. Lady Megan Lloyd George, making her maiden speech in Parliament in 1930 as MP for Anglesey, spoke on the problem of women and tuberculosis: she was prompted by the publication of statistics showing that the death rate of women from TB on Anglesey was the highest but one of all the administrative counties of England and Wales. When a Ministry of Health Inquiry into the Anti-Tuberculosis Services in Wales and Monmouthshire was published in 1939, rural counties headed the table of deaths from the disease.

Leisure

Given the harsh realities of life, leisure was a concept which working-class married women barely understood. When a Caerphilly woman, the mother of five, was asked about her leisure time by the *Women's Health Inquiry* (1939), she responded that she was on her feet sixteen and a half hours a day and, 'After my children go to bed, I gets two hours rest, if you can call it rest, I am mending my children's clothes and tidying in those few hours I get.' But life was not all doom and gloom for everyone. The amount of leisure time they had and how they spent that time depended on a whole range of factors such as social class, location, age and marital status and how strict a moral code operated within a family. But cutting across all these factors, one clear point emerges. Women had far less freedom to enjoy themselves and 'to go about' than men.

Middle-class women, young and old, in affluent suburbs of Cardiff or Swansea and elsewhere, led a leisurely life of bridge-playing, tennis parties, teas at the Kardomah, theatre visits, dances at private functions, motor car excursions and holidays in hotels. It was a far cry from the life of a hard-pressed, married working-class woman. She would be lucky to get an annual day trip to the seaside. Even then, like Maggie fach, in Idris Davies's poem, she had to be coaxed to go:

> Let's go to Barry Island, Maggie fach,
> And give all the kids one day by the sea,
> And sherbet and buns and paper hats
> And a rattling ride on the Figure Eight,
> Leave the washing alone for today, Maggie fach
> And put on your best and come out to the sun
> And down to the holiday sea.

Many of the outings and treats for both young and old throughout Wales were organized by churches and chapels – tea parties, *eisteddfodau* and Sunday school outings in bone-shaking charabancs to nearby country spots, such as Iris Thomas's annual trip from Merthyr to Pontsarn Pavilion, six miles away, where all the children had a 'sit-down' meal and enjoyed the organized outdoor games. Holidays for the working class, unless staying with relatives in country areas or with family who had left home to work in England, were almost unknown. Only the fortunate few, who had husbands or fathers working on the railway, were able to travel. Because Eileen Baker from the Gurnos, in the upper Swansea Valley, had a father who was a signalman, her family received four free rail passes a year: the family went as far afield as Scotland – just straight there and back, stopping only for tea.

The most marked difference in the style of leisure available is seen in the rural and urban divide in Wales. In rural Wales, although the Women's Institute provided a friendly meeting place for older women, there were few opportunities for younger girls to socialize. Entertainment in these areas remained largely home-based, with in some areas the old *noson wau* (knitting night) surviving, and the home or hearth still being an important place for social gatherings. The radio enriched home entertainment. Chapels, and church and village halls, many of them newly erected War Memorial Halls, created a space for larger numbers to gather together. The Anglesey Union of Village Clubs and Societies, spurred on by its treasurer Miss Mathews, promoted literary clubs and drama groups – drama becoming more acceptable to the Nonconformist conscience – to rural communities. But for young women in the countryside, there were few opportunities for going out, let alone for meeting young men away from the watchful eyes of their elders. Alwyn D. Rees in *Life in a Welsh Countryside* (1950) made clear the restrictions imposed on their lives:

> It is unconventional for unmarried girls to go out unless they have some definite purpose, such as to attend a religious service or some other social gathering, or to

perform an errand to a neighbouring farm or to the shop – and to go out to keep an appointment with a lover is not normally included in the list of legitimate destinations.

He recalled that the girls of Llanfihangel-yng-Ngwynfa, in Montgomeryshire, asked the rector to arrange for *Urdd* meetings to continue throughout the summer months, 'so that we can come out'. In rural communities, courtship remained a very private affair – not conducted in public, but, in the age old Welsh way, in the girl's home at night. The suitor signalled the girl by throwing gravel at her window, then entered the house and sat in the kitchen with the girl while her parents slept upstairs. In some districts the old custom of 'courting in bed' may even have continued. In areas where there were economic grounds for girls marrying a suitable man from another farming family, girls' opportunities for meeting up with other young men were severely restricted.

The contrast with the range of entertainments open to young girls in urban Wales is striking. Although the leisure time of many girls was still entirely church- or chapel-based, it was the new lively secular entertainments, especially the cinema and the dance hall, which captured their imagination and enhanced their workaday lives. Whether they went to old fleapits like Swansea's Rialto and the 'sit and scratch' at the Cybi cinema in Holyhead, or to a plush modern palace of delights like the Odeon in Colwyn Bay or Cardiff's Capitol Cinema, they were transported to a world of Hollywood fantasy and romance. The cinema appealed particularly to women as an escape from reality: they swooned over Valentino and Bogart and plucked their eyebrows and dressed in cheap versions of Dietrich's and Garbo's raincoats and berets. Then there were the dance halls – the ritzy Locarno-style ballrooms like Barry's Savoy, the earnest dancing schools, where they learned to waltz, quickstep and foxtrot, and even the drill and church halls, where a Saturday night dance would be held. It was at dances, more than anywhere else, that young Welsh women met their future husbands. Unlike men, they never went alone either to the pictures or the dance hall, but went always in at least twos. Public houses remained male preserves in most of Wales but other 'public' areas too were closed to women. Men in the mining valleys had the rich resource of miners' libraries: a Resolven woman recalled that women were not even allowed into the parish reading room until a radio set was installed in the 1920s, and then they were specially invited in to listen to it. And even the most respectable and affluent of Welsh women would not have either been allowed, or certainly not been allowed to feel comfortable, to eat in a public restaurant alone at night. Women had made some advances in social emancipation, but compared to the freedom enjoyed by men, their lives still remained constricted.

Politics and Issues

Nearly seventy years of campaigning had led to the partial victory of 1918, when women over thirty, who met certain property and other qualifications, were granted the right to vote in parliamentary elections. It was to take another ten years before women were allowed to vote on the same terms as men, at the age of twenty-one. The huge pre-war feminist movement did not survive the war intact. The Women's Social and Political Union (WSPU), the most vibrant, volatile and headline-grabbing of the suffrage groups, disappeared. It was the lower profile societies – the Women's Freedom League (WFL) and The National Union of Women's Suffrage Societies (NUWSS) – which survived into the post-war world. The NUWSS changed its name to National Union of Societies for Equal Citizenship (NUSEC), but the new organization did not preserve a united front. British feminism, by the early 1920s, was broadly split into two main camps – new and old feminism. New feminism, under the leadership of Eleanor Rathbone, a woman with strong links to north Wales, centred on improved welfare for mothers: the central plank of its programme was family endowments, later known as family allowances. Old feminism, the leading advocate of which was Lady Rhondda, concentrated on achieving equal rights with men: the most prominent equal rights group was the Six Point Group, established in 1921. In addition to this ideological rift, feminism was fragmented into a whole range of single issue groups, such as the National Union of Women Teachers (NUWT) campaigning for equal pay and the Open Door Council, which fought against restrictive (i.e. protective) legislation against women. There was weakness in this disunity, and British feminism was ill equipped to deal with the post-war mood. Whereas there had been a broad consensus on the eve of the war in favour of votes for women, by the early 1920s, there was an anti-feminist backlash. Women were told that they should be content with their gains and, in a climate of growing male unemployment, they were expected to return home to their roles as wives and mothers. Feminism began to be perceived as old hat and dated. When a group of University of Wales women graduates wrote to the journal *Welsh Outlook* in March 1922 proposing that women should organize to ensure the selection of a female candidate for the university seat in the general election, they were dismissed as being 'pre-war' in their tone. In Wales women were aware of the dangers of fragmentation and in 1922 set up the Union of Welsh Women to ensure co-operation between a wide range of women's groups (not all feminist) – including the NUWT, NUSEC, the Women's Guild of Empire, and various housing and welfare groups. Far more research is required into this group and its activities. It is probably true to say of Wales, as of England, that feminism, though with depleted energies, soldiered on in the 1920s until at least the achievement of equal franchise in 1928, but thereafter dwindled and waned.

The early 1920s saw the passage of a series of Acts of Parliament for which women had long pressed. In addition to the Representation of the People Act (1918) came the Eligibility of Women Act (1918), which enabled women to become members of parliament from the age of twenty-one, i.e. a full nine years before they were permitted to vote and the Sex Disqualification (Removal) Act (1919), flawed though it was, opened up the professions to women. Other Acts improved women's position as wives, mothers and widows: in 1923 women were granted the right to divorce on equal grounds with men, in 1925 equal guardianship of children, also in 1925 widows' pensions and in 1927 the right to legitimize a child by marriage to the father. Finally the Equal Franchise Act was passed in 1928.

But what happened to the Welsh women's suffrage groups? The Llangollen NUWSS disbanded itself, as we have seen, in 1918 and no doubt others followed suit: it is unlikely that more than a handful of the thirty-odd Welsh groups which had existed in 1913 survived into the post-war world. South Wales however was exceptional in this. Active and well-organized Women's Citizens Associations, direct descendants of the suffrage campaign, and affiliated to NUSEC operated in Abertillery, Cardiff (including Barry and Penarth), Ebbw Vale, Newport and Swansea under the umbrella organization of the South Wales Area Group of Women's Citizens Associations. The pre-war suffragists continued to lead these local groups – Miss Vivian in Newport, Miss Margaret Kirkland and Mrs Mary Cleeves in Swansea, and Miss Mary Collin and Professor Barbara Foxley in Cardiff. It was entirely fitting that this should be so since down to 1928 equal suffrage was still the main item on the agenda for women's groups. These women were either businesswomen or well-qualified academics, employed in education in high status positions, and they enjoyed the wide respect of their communities. In fact it was the very respectability of the post-war women's groups in south Wales that ensured them a strong voice on a wide range of issues and enabled them to achieve certain successes.

Fortunately, the records of the Cardiff and District Women's Citizens Association (CDWCA) have survived, giving a picture of the group's activities throughout the inter-war years. Equality of opportunity, and the representation of women in government, were enshrined in their aims. With a membership of around 550, for most of the 1920s, they formed an effective pressure group. They campaigned on the whole raft of feminist issues which became law between 1918 and 1928, particularly on equal franchise. The passage of the Equal Franchise Act of 1928 put an additional 25,000 women, aged between twenty-one and thirty, on Cardiff's electoral register. They held public meetings before general elections in which all the (male) candidates were incisively questioned on their views on women's issues. They were particularly keen to promote the election of women to local councils: in the 1920s in Penarth they canvassed for Constance Maillard, a leading campaigner for the welfare of mothers and infants, and in Cardiff for Professor Barbara Foxley, both of whom were elected. Similarly, they pushed for more women Guardians (and later members of Public Assistance Committees) and women magistrates. They were incensed when in 1920 the Welsh Insurance Commission, which had comprised four members – three men and one woman (Violet Douglas-Pennant) – was replaced by the Board of Health for Wales with no women members. Dr Addison, the Minister of Health who made appointments to the Board, further provoked Welsh feminists by saying that he knew 'no woman in Wales fit for the job'. CDWCA sent him a list of suitable women. They worked to promote the cause of peace, supporting the Welsh Women's Memorial, Peace Pilgrimages and the League of Nations (see below) and they were involved in a whole range of other issues concerning women including the dismissal of married women teachers, 'protective' legislation, maternal mortality and the condition of housing in Wales, but there can be no doubt that, after equal franchise, the cause closest to their hearts was the employment of women police. They invited prestigious speakers on this issue to Cardiff including Margaret Damer Dawson and Lady Astor, who made several high profile visits to the city; they ceaselessly petitioned the city's Watch Committee and sought support from eminent public figures but, in the face of immovable chief constables, they failed in this and Wales remained without a single policewoman until the Second World War. The Cardiff group and others in the South Wales Association continued their activities into the Second World War. Given the climate of the times, theirs was a remarkable achievement.

The role of women in both national and local politics is a huge topic which has yet to be researched and my comments here must be tentative. It is certainly true that after the end of the war, women became involved in politics in large numbers. This is especially clear in the case of the Labour Party, which, by virtue of a new constitution of 1918, enabled women to become individual members of the Party for the first time. By 1933, there were 11,207 male and 9,160 female party members in Wales, with several constituencies having a majority of women members. Similarly, the numbers joining the Women's Co-operative Guild surged. Within the Labour Party, women opted to keep within their own women's sections and to concentrate on a women-centred programme of welfare reform for the benefit of their working-class sisters, but they had very little influence over party policy and had only token representation on the national executive committees. Their lack of influence was clearly demonstrated in the struggle that Labour women had in persuading their male colleagues to allow the maternity and child welfare committees to give birth control advice: only in 1930, did the minority Labour government relax the ban against the clinics giving out advice. In the Labour Party, as in the other political parties, women were marginalized and regarded for the most part as the 'help-meets' of men. Even the exceptional women, who did make a mark upon politics in Wales have been written out of the history books and their contribution ignored. Charlotte Aull Davies in 'Women, nationalism and feminism' showed how Mai Roberts from the Caernarfon area was a leading figure in the creation of the Welsh Nationalist Party in 1925, but it is a group of six men who are officially recognized as the party's founders. Other leading figures in the party, later renamed Plaid Cymru, such as Kate Roberts, Catrin Hughes and Mallt Williams deserve recognition for their contribution. Only by painstaking research can the role played by such women be established and evaluated.

Similarly, the part played by women in local government is in need of investigation. Dedicated women stood for and were sometimes elected to local councils throughout Wales but their activities remain hidden from history. Clearly it was difficult in such a gender-segregated society for women to make a substantial breakthrough in local government and indeed to hang on to hard-won seats. In Cardiff in 1924, Professor Barbara Foxley won the Cathays seat on the city council as the official Liberal candidate and, by 1927, Rhoda Parker is recorded as a councillor, but women could not count on steady progress. By 1928, there were fifty-two men on the Cardiff City Council and no women and only sixteen women Poor Law Guardians compared to eighty men. In north Wales, on the other hand, Mrs Elsie Chamberlain joined Bangor Council in 1930 and remained there, with only one year's break, until 1950: in 1941 she became Bangor's first woman mayor.

Getting into parliament was an even harder task, achieved by only two Welsh women in the inter-war period. The general election of December 1918 was the first in which women were able to stand. Seventeen women candidates stood throughout Britain, but only one in Wales – 55-year-old Professor Millicent MacKenzie, Cardiff's first woman professor of education (1904–15) and an active member of the Cardiff Suffrage Society: she stood unsuccessfully for the University of Wales seat as the Labour candidate. The general elections, which come thick and fast in 1922, 1923 and 1924 saw only five candidatures by women in Wales. In 1922 the Hon. Mrs L. Broderick, Conservative, contested Denbigh; Mrs D. Edmondes, Conservative, stood in Ogmore and Professor Olive Wheeler, Cardiff's third woman professor of education, stood as Labour candidate for the University seat. In 1923 Mrs L. Follard was the Liberal candidate for Gower and in 1924 Mrs Broderick stood again for the Conservatives in Denbigh and with 47 per cent of the vote came close to winning. But none succeeded. The number of women candidates selected to stand in Wales was consistently low – one in 1918 out of a total of seventeen women candidates for the whole of Britain, three in 1922 out of thirty-three, one in 1923 out of thirty-four, and one in 1924 out of forty-one. It was extremely difficult for women to win selection for parliamentary seats and when they were selected, it was usually in seats which were regarded by the party organizations as forlorn hopes. The 1929 election, known as the flapper election because women over twenty-one were allowed to vote for the first time, saw a record number of female candidates. Sixty-nine women stood in Britain, three of them in Wales. Rhuthun-born novelist Grace Roberts (1879–1962) stood unsuccessfully as a Liberal in the safe Labour seat of Caerphilly and a young Conservative candidate, Mrs May G. Williams, stood in almost equally unwinnable Pontypridd. But 1929 saw the great turning-point for the hopes of Welsh women with the election of Megan Lloyd George as Liberal MP for Anglesey. In the election of 1931 she held on to her seat with an increased share of the vote, while the Conservative Mrs C. Bowen Davies stood unsuccessfully in Caerphilly as did Labour candidate Miss F. Edwards for Flint. In 1935, the last general election of the inter-war period, Megan Lloyd George won Anglesey yet again, while two Conservative women, Mrs N. J. Stoneham in Caerphilly and Mrs F. E. Scarborough in Ebbw Vale stood hopelessly in these bastions of Labour power: Mrs Scarborough certainly had little chance against Aneurin Bevan. Lady Juliet Rhys Williams, the dedicated campaigner in the fight against maternal mortality, stood as a Liberal in a by-election in Pontypridd in 1938. Though failing to win, she achieved a very creditable 40 per cent of the vote.

Perhaps because of the difficulty of getting selected for winnable Welsh seats, some Welsh women and women with strong Welsh connections stood in constituencies outside Wales. Emily Phipps, former Swansea headmistress and leading feminist, stood in Chelsea for the Labour Party in 1918; backed by the Federation of Women Teachers, of which she was president, she ran an all women campaign with a female election agent and campaign manager. Winifred Coombe Tennant, 'Mam o Nedd', a leading feminist and eisteddfodic figure, contested the Forest of Dean for the Liberals in 1922. She was also the first British woman delegate to the League of Nations. Edith Picton-Turbervill of Ewenny Priory stood unsuccessfully as Labour candidate in North Islington in 1922 and in Stroud in 1924, before winning the Conservative stronghold of the Wrekin division of Shropshire in 1929 and becoming the first south Walian

Megan Lloyd George campaigning on Anglesey in 1931.

woman MP. She was a devout and caring woman, whose great interest was the church: she spent much of her life campaigning for women's admission to the ministry and priesthood. As an MP, she gained wide respect through her Parliamentary bill, the Sentence of Death (Expectant Mothers) Bill, which became law in 1931 and banned the barbaric practice of sentencing pregnant women to death. Her parliamentary career was, however, short lived and she lost her seat in 1931, following Ramsay MacDonald's formation of a National Government. 1929 saw the election of two Welsh women to parliament, albeit only one of them for a Welsh seat. Throughout the inter-war years Megan Lloyd George was the only woman to represent Wales in the House of Commons. The House of Lords was an entirely male stronghold, where peeresses were not permitted to take their seats. Lady Rhondda challenged this in a high profile campaign and in 1922 it looked as though she had won when the Committee of Privileges recommended that her claim should be accepted. But a piece of skulduggery by the lord chancellor led to the rescinding of this decision and, despite her continued efforts, women were not admitted to the House of Lords until 1958, the very year in which Lady Rhondda died.

Megan Lloyd George (1902–66), the youngest child of David and Margaret Lloyd George, had grown up in the heart of the political world, living from the age of six to fourteen at No. 11 Downing Street and then moving to No. 10. She was a lively, intelligent and fun loving woman, who was politically committed to a radical social agenda and an ardent nationalist. Her abilities were evident, but there can be no doubt that without her father's intervention she would never have been selected as Liberal candidate for the safe seat of Anglesey. Both within and outside parliament she was a powerful and scintillating public speaker and as a chic and attractive young woman, just twenty-seven years old at the time of her first election, she was very much in the public eye. In the inter-war years she campaigned against fascism, working with the Welsh Ambulance Fund for Republican Spain and the Save the Bilbao Children Movement. Closer to home she worked to improve rural housing, to cut unemployment and she supported women's rights.

Women campaigned on a whole range of issues in inter-war Wales – against unemployment, means testing and cuts in benefit and for birth control, women police and increased numbers of women in public life. Housing was also very much a woman's issue. Elizabeth Andrews had given evidence on the poor state of Valleys' housing to the Sankey Commission on coalmining in 1919 and Mrs Alwyn T. Lloyd and Miss M. D. Jones, of the Welsh Housing and Development Association, made available 'a huge mass of information' to the Ministry of Reconstruction on housing conditions in Wales and the improvements which women wanted. But poor housing continued to dog Wales throughout the inter-war period. Overcrowding was a problem not only in urban Wales but in the rural counties. In 1936, Anglesey figured as the third worst county in the whole of England and Wales, while Caernarfon, Denbigh, Flint, Montgomery, Pembroke, Glamorgan and Merioneth were all in the top twenty on the table of overcrowding. There was a desperate need for new houses, particularly council houses. The 1919 Housing and Town Planning Act placed responsibility for remedying housing shortages on local authorities and the first Labour Government gave a great boost to council house building. Conservative governments however discouraged local authority building, preferring to rely on the private sector, and in 1932 the National Government abolished all subsidies for council building. Between 1919 and 1940, 146,471 new houses were built in Wales, 50,061, or just over a third, by local authorities: most of these were erected in the counties of Glamorgan, Monmouth and Denbighshire. Lady Megan Lloyd George spoke of poor housing and its link with tuberculosis in women in parliament in 1930. She had good cause to complain: on Anglesey only 84 council houses had been built between 1919 and 1929 and in the year of her speech only twelve were built. Poor housing was to be a continuing Welsh problem.

But it was not only domestic issues which commanded women's attention. The First World War had shaped the thoughts of a whole generation of Welsh women and, above all else, they wanted to ensure continuing peace. Their commitment to world peace is clearly demonstrated by the Women's Peace Memorial of 1924. 'The Memorial from the women of Wales and Monmouthshire to the women of America' was a vast project: 390,296 women in Wales signed the memorial – a figure in excess of 60 per cent of the female population over eighteen. Conferences were held throughout Wales on the theme of peace. By 1926, drawing on the old suffrage tradition of long marches or pilgrimages, women from all corners of Wales took part in the Peacemakers Pilgrimage to London. The north Wales march, drawing on women from over fifty towns and villages from Pwllheli to Prestatyn, went first to Chester, before joining up with the English marchers. Peace was the seminal political issue for the north Walian women. Sydna Ann Williams's study of women in the north Wales peace movement points out that whereas the old suffrage movements in south Wales, and especially in Cardiff, carried on after the war, in the north, women's organizations were less overtly feminist but incorporated a feminist agenda within a broader set of objectives: peace was seen as a natural aim for women, the moral custodians of the nation. The North Wales Women's Peace Council (NWWPC), formed in 1928, was a very active body, which campaigned for disarmament and the peaceful resolution of potential conflicts, but its position became increasingly difficult with the rise of European fascism in the 1930s and the drift towards war. It had finally to reconcile itself to the Second World War on the grounds that they believed 'war in defence of freedom to be a lesser evil than surrendering the whole of Europe, and especially its youth, to slavery to Nazi principles'. The NWWPC had a radical agenda, but through acting in the role of women as guardians of the race, managed not to alienate the dominant forces in north Wales – the chapels and the Liberal Party.

Left-wing women were active in opposing Franco's fascists in Spain and a very broad spectrum of women gave direct help to the Basque children, who were brought to Wales. They helped run homes for the children in Brechfa (Carmarthenshire); Sketty Park, Swansea; at Old Colwyn in north Wales and in Caerleon, where Mrs Fernandez, a Dowlais-Spaniard, ran the home.

Conclusion

The inter-war period as a whole saw little change in the lives of women in Wales. It is true that women made certain advances with regard to the law, parliamentary enfranchisement and employment in the professions and in offices, but fundamentally the lives of the vast majority of Welsh women remained much the same as in the days before the First World War. The old doctrine of separate spheres remained almost intact. In practice, women made little headway in politics and those women who entered the male world of the professions did so at the cost of sacrificing home and family life. Education for girls in elementary schools continued to focus on domestic subjects and secondary education, which was still not available to all, remained beyond the reach of many clever girls whose families could not afford to pay for school uniforms and books. Mass male unemployment made these inauspicious times for women to make gains in the world of work, and domestic service remained the largest sector of employment for Welsh women. Myths persist that the 1920s in particular was a time of female 'emancipation' and sexual freedom but there is little truth in this beyond a small group of 'flappers' in London's high society. Emancipation for Welsh women was confined to wearing shorter skirts and having their hair bobbed, though even then no respectable woman would be seen out without a hat. Similarly, there is little evidence of sexual freedom and unmarried mothers or 'friendless girls', as they were called, suffered social ostracism. Welsh women continued to live their lives within the confines of a narrow code of respectability and within the boundaries of their allotted sphere. If many of them had believed that the First World War would be the gateway to new opportunities, by the late 1930s, they knew better. When the Second World War broke out, they had no such high hopes.

~ 4 ~
Tipping the Scales against Hitler: the Second World War, 1939–1945

B Y 1939, just twenty-one years after the Armistice of 1918, Britain was once again at war. At 11a.m. on Sunday 3 September, families throughout Wales gathered around their wireless sets and heard Prime Minister Chamberlain announce, 'We are now at war with Germany.' These were chilling, though not unexpected, words. War had seemed inevitable since the mid-1930s as Hitler pursued his menacing policy of annexing neighbouring states. In 1938 Chamberlain had returned from a meeting with Hitler in Munich, waving an agreement and declaring 'Peace in Our Time', but although there was relief that war had been averted for the time being, few people put any reliance on Hitler's word and Britain used the breathing space after Munich to prepare for war. Given their usefulness in the First World War, women figured in government planning for the Second War. The Women's Voluntary Service for Air Raid Precautions (WVS) was set up in 1938 to provide support for Civil Defence and the women's services were revived. The Auxiliary Territorial Service (ATS), modelled on the First World War Women's Auxiliary Army Corps, was created in 1938, and by 1939, the Women's Land Army, another First World War organization, was resurrected. Construction began too of major munitions factories at an early date: work began on the Bridgend Royal Ordnance Factory, the largest filling factory in Britain, in 1938. The coming of war finally jerked Wales out of the economic depression which had paralysed its heavy industry and demoralized its workforce since the mid–1920s. It is a bitter irony that a war was needed to regenerate Welsh industry. In Wales there was widespread support for the Second World War. Although there was not the jingoism of 1914, when young men had set out to give the Kaiser a bloody nose and thought it would be all over by Christmas, there was a widespread recognition that this was a just and necessary war against fascism, and that this was a war that had to be won or else Britain would be invaded and ground under the Nazi boot. Not everyone agreed with the war however. The Welsh Nationalist Party, founded in 1925, believed that the British state had no right to declare war on Wales's behalf.

The Second World War was to have a profound effect on life in Wales and made a far greater impact on the civilian population than had the First World

War. The First World War had seen massive casualties amongst the fighting men: some 40,000 Welsh troops lost their lives between 1914 and 1918 whereas the comparable figure for 1939–1945 was 15,000. In the Second World War the civilian population of Britain was in far greater danger than in the First and some 60,000 people in Britain, with almost equal numbers of men and women, were killed in air raids. Welsh towns and cities, particularly the south Wales ports, were for the first time subject to aerial bombardment. Submarines blockaded Britain in both wars and meant shortages, but the disruption to trade was more severe in the Second War and women were called on for even greater ingenuity to 'make do and mend' and to use their domestic skills to compensate for the lack of basic foodstuffs. Many women had to do this as well as working full time. There was a real danger of invasion in 1940 between the expulsion of the British Expeditionary Force from Dunkirk in June and the air Battle of Britain in September 1940. Leaflets were issued in English and Welsh telling civilians how to act 'Os Daw'r Germans' (If the Germans Come). There was a significant population movement with Welsh men and women leaving Wales to join the forces and to work in English factories and a movement of people in from England, including those moving westward under their own steam and many thousands of evacuees, women and children, sent from large English cities. There was a large military presence too with American GIs stationed in Welsh towns and remote country areas: in the countryside, the arrival of the US troops marked the first occasion on which many Welsh people had ever seen a black face. The military also took over large tracts of land. The community of Mynydd Epynt, consisting of 54 homes and 219 people, was expelled to make way for a training ground in 1940. Iorwerth Peate, visiting Epynt in the last days before the evacuation, recalled seeing an 82-year-old woman, sitting on a chair at the furthest end of her yard gazing over the mountain with tears streaming down her cheeks. She had been born there, and her father and grandfather before her: 'It is the end of the world here', she told him. The appropriation of this land meant the destruction of one of the last bastions of Welsh culture and language in Breconshire. The war, with its influx of people from outside and the dominance of the English news media, brought further pressure to bear on the Welsh language. But perhaps the single largest challenge to the traditional Welsh way of life brought about by the war was the absorption of thousands of women into the industrial workforce. The sight of hordes of women, wearing slacks and with their hair in turbans, striding down the streets of Valleys towns to catch their early morning trains and buses to the great munitions factories, was regarded as an affront to Welsh manhood and a challenge not only to traditional family life but to the whole social order. It is certainly true that the women's wartime work in industry put a major dent into the notion of separate spheres, but whether this would prove to be a permanent inroad into the strict division of life and labour, or, as we have seen following the First World War, merely a temporary state of affairs, is a question which must be addressed. This chapter looks at women's work in wartime; the issue of equal pay; women's role in the services; women as conscientious objectors; life on the home front; the impact of the war on female sexuality; demobilization; and the wider effects of the war on women's lives in Wales.

Women's work

Although the establishment of the women's services before war was declared suggested that the government was going to make immediate use of the country's woman power, this was not, in fact, the case. Women who volunteered to work in 1939 and 1940 were told to go home and wait and some 10,000 women who had joined the Women's Land Army in 1939 were still unemployed by Christmas 1941. In fact, the outbreak of war in 1939, as in 1914, led to an increase in women's unemployment as milliners, maids, shop assistants and others in luxury trades were laid off. Both government and industry were slow to avail themselves of women's labour and employers needed convincing all over again that women were up to the job. However by early 1941, when Britain was fighting alone, without Russia or America, labour shortages led to hold-ups in production. At this point the government acted decisively and mobilized women. The first step was compulsory registration and in March 1941 all women aged nineteen to forty had to register at employment exchanges, thereby giving the Ministry of Labour a record of what they were all doing and enabling it to direct them into war work. Single women could be directed to work anywhere in Britain. At the same time the Essential Work Order compelled employers to take women on. Appeals were launched for women workers in the summer of 1941 and in December the government, through the National Service (No 2) Act, conscripted single women aged twenty to thirty (extended to include nineteen year olds in 1943). This was an unprecedented step, which meant that women were compelled to enter the services or industry. There was great reluctance to call on married women: this, it was feared, would upset the troops. One Cardiff woman stated, 'My husband said he'd come out of the Army if I go into war work.' But married women without young children could be directed to work locally, either full- or part-time, and the raising of the registration age to fifty in 1944 brought more women into the labour pool.

In addition to all these directives, recruitment meetings were held throughout Wales and newspaper advertisements urged women to join the services or to work in munitions factories. In Bangor in December 1941 a rally was held with all the razzmatazz of First World War recruitment drives. An ATS bugle band played and a Women's Munitions Choir sang 'There'll Always be a Britain' [*sic*]; speakers, including a 'radio star' and an ATS officer, urged girls to come forward and the mayor, Mrs Elsie Chamberlain, stated that there were 'a good many buxom young women in Caernarfonshire' who could be doing their bit. Newspapers ran articles with headings such as 'Happy Munitions Girls', *North Wales Chronicle*, 26 December 1941, reporting the high wages available and extolling the canteen, welfare and entertainment facilities. Happy workers were quoted, saying such things as 'I wouldn't go back behind the counter for anything', and trying to lay to rest any misgivings others might have had about entering munitions factories, such as:

> My mother told me how her face and hands had turned yellow while working in a munitions works . . . and I was afraid to venture. But now I know that modern methods of working have wiped all that sort of thing out of factory life.

It was a good piece of propaganda, but not strictly true. By late 1941, north Wales newspapers called for 10,000 women to 'tip the scales' against Hitler.

Women once again took over civilian jobs vacated by men on the buses (but only as conductresses and not as drivers this time around) and on the railways, in banks, in offices and in factories. Married women teachers were once again taken on. When the man who held the post of official gas tester at Pontypridd Municipal Gas Works was called up, Mavis Mitchell, a junior clerk, took over his post. Her new job included testing the calorific value of the gas four times a day as well as climbing the huge gas holder to check the plates for pressure. But it was only after a prolonged struggle, and with the help of the Municipal and General Workers Union, that she was awarded the full male rate for the job of £5 per week. Hilda Price, from Barry, who had worked at Sherman's football pools before the war, trained and qualified as an airframe fitter at RAF St Athan but only after a struggle did she win the right to check and service her own aircraft, rather than act as an assistant to a man.

Factories, which were converted to wartime production, brought job opportunities for women in many parts of Wales. In north-west Wales NECACO (North East Coast Aircraft Company), based in Llanberis and with a site in Caernarfon, employed some 3,000 staff, many of them women, manufacturing parts for bombers, while at Beaumaris the Saunders Roe Company, employing some 200 people, made seaplanes. Miss Winifred Brown, one of the staff there, had had a pilot's licence since 1927 and was a winner of the Royal Aero Club King's Cup for flying. In north-east Wales the aircraft factory at Broughton, set up in 1937, was engaged in the mass production of bombers producing 5,540 Wellingtons during the course of the war. Over 6,000 workers, half of them women, were employed and the 1944 propaganda film, in which a Wellington bomber was built in twenty-four hours, was shot at Broughton. In south Wales former unemployment black spots benefited from war factories, which created employment for many women, as well as men. In Merthyr Tydfil, Halls Telephone Factory was converted to the production of light engineering components, employing 845 men, 657 women and 40 juveniles by 1940, and at the Rotax works (formerly the British Sewing Machine factory) 150 women worked, together with 1200 men, making magnets. Other Valleys workers, female and male, travelled to wartime factories on the Trefforest Estate, where some twenty-four factories had been requisitioned by the Ministry of Aircraft Production, and in Cardiff, in addition to several large engineering works, other factories manufactured such items as barrage balloons. In Swansea, the Cwmfelin plant employed 3,000 workers, of whom 2,000 were women, turning out jerrycans at the rate of 7,500 a week and at Waunarlwydd some 2,000 workers, mainly women, produced sheet and strip aluminium for aircraft production. But the largest numbers of all were employed in munitions factories.

Ordnance factories fall into three categories – engineering (where guns and shell casings are made), explosive and filling factories. All three types of factory were located in Wales with six major works in the south. The largest was ROF Bridgend, on which work began in 1938 and where at its peak over 35,000 workers, the vast majority of them women, were employed. Another filling factory was located at Glasgoed in Monmouthshire. At Hirwaun small arms were manufactured by a workforce of 14,000. There were engineering establishments at Llanishen in Cardiff and in Newport and a naval propellant factory near Pontypool. As in the First War, Pembrey was an explosives factory, producing TNT. In north Wales Marchwiel, near Wrexham, was a very large explosives factory, ROF Valley at Rhyd y mwyn a filling factory, the old gaol at Rhuthun made shell parts and at Gresford Lodge women workers produced delayed-action fuses.

Women travelled from all over south Wales – from as far afield as Carmarthen, Swansea, Merthyr and Barry to work in the vast Bridgend Arsenal, leaving on trains and buses as early as 4 a.m. for the morning shift. The factory worked twenty-four hours a day, 365 days a year, and operated on a three shift basis. The shifts were colour-coded – red, blue and green – and women were employed in various sectors such as High Explosives, Detonators, Yellow Powder, Black Powder and Testing. The factory was divided into 'clean' and 'dirty' areas. Women, inside the clean area, wore overalls fastened with ties or rubber buttons,

Both English- and Welsh-language versions of this recruitment advertisement appeared in north Wales newspapers.

rubber-soled shoes and dust caps: no jewellery, rings or hair clips could be worn inside the area. Certain sectors were extremely dangerous, particularly the Detonator section as a single detonator, though only the size of an aspirin, could blow all the fingers off a woman's hand. Gwen Obern from Aberdare was in her first week at work in Bridgend, when an exploding box of detonators blinded her and blew off both her hands: several others were killed outright by the explosion. Women did not like working on the pellets section, where the powder turned the skin and hair bright yellow: blonde hair turned green. Despite government propaganda and the use of barrier creams, munitions workers in the Second World War once again won the nickname 'canaries' that they had in the First World War. The wages were good. In 1941 the minimum wage for a new process worker aged over twenty-one, was £2 9s. Most earned well over £3 10s for a 60-hour week at that time, rising to over £6 towards the end of the war. A survey of the work previously done by women munition workers at an Ordnance Factory 'somewhere in Wales', published by the *Western Mail*, 6 June 1941, showed that the women came mainly from low paid-work in shops, domestic service, clerical and luxury trades and that only 5 per cent had any previous experience of factory work and 10 per cent had no work experience of any kind. Margaret Plummer of Swansea, for example, had been earning 15s. 11d. a week in a laundry in 1939 before becoming an inspector of armaments at Bridgend at £4 10s. 0d. The other factor which women enjoyed, apart from the wages was the companionship and the organized entertainments, with workers forming their own choirs and bands and big stars visiting the factory.

But it is easy to exaggerate the benefits of war work. Apart from the dangers, factory work with its long hours was extremely tiring for women, who had to go home to cook and clean for their families. Childcare presented particular problems. The authorities in south Wales were slow and somewhat grudging about opening nurseries. There were complaints that those that were open were underutilized. In response to an assertion in the *South Wales Echo*, 13 January 1943, that in some south Wales nurseries 'the staff outnumber the children', a nursery matron responded that women were not using nurseries because they were not open long enough. Many women made their own private childcare arrangements and families, particularly grandmothers, were encouraged to take on children to free young women for war work as the advertisement 'Mother Finds a Way' shows. Shopping was also difficult as the shops were closed by the time women finished work. Hilda Price, at RAF St Athan, along with other married women, had at one point enjoyed the benefit of 'shopping time', but this was withdrawn and Hilda was sacked for continuing to take it. Some women were forced to take time off to catch up with work at home or to look after sick family members, but the penalties for

BEVIN'S BREAKFAST

4,000 Welsh girls, conscripted and sent to England by Bevin's Ministry cf Labour, will never return *(according to the New Wales Union)*

Ernest Bevin, minister of labour, eating Welsh girls for breakfast.

persistent absenteeism were harsh. The *Glamorgan Gazette*, 19 January 1945, records the case of a 21-year-old woman, who had twice been previously fined for absenteeism, receiving a two-month prison sentence.

Mobile Welsh women could be directed to work anywhere in Britain. Olwen Hughes Jones from a Welsh-speaking community on Anglesey, for example, was conscripted into industry, sent to a training centre in Chester and then on to Napiers Engineering Works in Liverpool. Before this, apart from the occasional Sunday school trip to Rhyl, she had never left the island. When she first arrived in Chester it struck her forcibly that she had moved from a place where she knew everyone, to one where she knew no one. Overcoming her *hiraeth*, but continuing to miss the language, she settled down in Liverpool and made good friends, before returning home at the end of the war. Plaid Genedlaethol Cymru protested against the tyrannical transference of girls from Wales, painting a vivid and alarming picture of trainloads of Welsh girls being deported as slave labour to work in English factories, and was concerned these young women would not return after the war. The cartoon printed in the *Welsh Nationalist* July, 1945 depicted Ernest Bevin, minister of labour, as a grotesque glutton devouring Welsh girls. The state did indeed possess draconian wartime powers and appeals from young Welsh women on nationalist grounds against transference to England were not well received. Kathleen Foley of Plasmarl,

Swansea, was fined £25, with an alternative of one-month's imprisonment, by Swansea Police Court in November 1943, for refusing on nationalist grounds to go to work in a factory in Birmingham. Whereas unemployment and means-testing had driven young girls away from Wales in the inter-war years, in wartime the transference of conscripted labour continued the process.

Within Wales, the war had a dramatic impact on women's place within the Welsh labour force. In Britain as a whole, the number of insured women workers increased by just 30 per cent between 1939 and 1945. In Wales, where so few women had been employed before the war, the number of insured women workers rose by 134 per cent. This novel role for Welsh women, as industrial workers, was plain for all to see and came as a culture shock to many in the south Wales valleys. The *Aberdare Leader*, 9 October 1943, commented on the daily spectacle of:

> Women and girls of all ages, married and unmarried, wearing turbans and 'slacks', smoking, laughing, haversacks slung on their shoulders, or little attaché cases in their hands – contrasting rather incongruously with 'permed' hair and lipstick – hurrying in large numbers to the bus or railway station, or, at the end of their day, pouring out of them in a swarm, tired, work-stained, but still laughing and cracking a joke. An unfamiliar sight surely in Wales, where women's place was always regarded as being in the home.

Indeed, it seemed to some that with the wartime abandonment of male and female traditional roles, the world had been turned upside down. Miners felt resentful that their wives and daughters in munitions factories were bringing home higher wages than they were, and were fed up with hearing their womenfolk praising the quality of their canteen meals and telling them how much they enjoyed 'Workers' Playtime' relayed over the work's wireless system. Peggy Inman noted in her study of the munitions industries that the Ministry of Labour received many letters from ex-miners who could not get work but whose daughters were being taken on at Bridgend. (By mid-1942, 3,000 ex-miners were already employed on light work in the factory but between 1943 and 1944 many more of these men were taken on and hundreds of women were transferred from Bridgend to the Midlands and elsewhere.) Mari Williams in *Where Is Mrs Jones Going?* points out that the long-term social implications of the women's new-found freedom and economic independence were viewed with grave apprehension. Chief constables and magistrates ranted against young women drinking in public houses, and newspapers printed letters and ran articles deploring the decline of domestic skills amongst factory workers who were accused of feeding their children on tinned food and failing to teach them cleanliness and discipline. But the fundamental fear of men in the mining communities, who felt an affront to their masculinity by their wives and daughters earning high wages, was that women were usurping the rights of men to employment and that this situation would continue after the war.

Whether their fears were justified or not, or whether patriarchal attitudes would prevail in the shaping of the post-war work force, is discussed in chapter 5.

Equal pay and equal compensation

Many women workers in wartime were well paid but only a few had equal pay with men. The group which pressed most ardently for equal pay were the women MPs. Women MPs from all parties, drawing on the tradition of inter-war feminism, formed a caucus called the Women Power Committee (WPC) in May 1940. They strongly criticized the government for its failure to recruit women in 1940–1 and demanded that there should be no conscription of women without equal pay. Leading parliamentary members of this group, which soon expanded to include representatives of trade unions and women's business organizations, included Lady Astor and Irene Ward (both Conservative) and Edith Summerskill, Labour: Megan Lloyd George, the sole Liberal woman in the House, also played an active role. Ernest Bevin, minister of labour and a trade-unionist himself, was firmly against equal pay and was reluctant to create an official body to advise the government on issues concerning women's recruitment and employment. The persistence of the WPC however forced a parliamentary debate in March 1941. Megan Lloyd George criticized the government's failure to recruit women:

> Women have been registered for months past and are still without work. They finally lost heart because they felt there was no place for them in the war machine . . . It makes one despair a little to think that we have again to go through the dreary process of convincing employers and managers that women are capable of doing skilled work.

She demonstrated the inequality in the treatment of women:

> Here you have a man and a woman, both without any knowledge of engineering, starting out from scratch in a training centre. They may have been a waiter and a waitress. From the very first week they arrive at the training centre, the man receives 60 shillings and the woman 38 shillings . . . What is the minister's justification for such unequal conditions?

But not only did women not receive equal pay, they were also unequally compensated for injury. The women MPs pressed home the unfairness of this situation. They failed to win the issues of either equal pay or equal compensation in 1941 but did spur the government into creating an official body, the Women's Consultative Committee, to advise on the recruitment and treatment of women war workers. They pressed on with the matter of unequal compensation, until finally, in April 1943, the Ministry of Labour gave in and introduced a single compensation scale for injured males and females. It was an important gain.

In 1944, partly as a result of pressure from women's groups and partly because the government expected a post-war shortage of teachers, the marriage bar for women teachers was lifted as part of the 1944 Education Act. An amendment to the Education Bill proposed equal pay for women teachers but, despite being approved by the House of Commons by a majority of one, this amendment did not form part of the final Act. Churchill sent the amendment back to the Commons and turned it into a motion of no-confidence in his wartime government. Thus, under the threat of resignation of the whole government, the issue of equal pay was defeated.

The women's services

A distinct hierarchy existed within the women's services. The Women's Royal Naval Service (WRNS), established in 1939, attracted many public school girls and projected an exclusive and superior image: would-be Wrens required references to join and, even then, there was a waiting list. The Women's Auxiliary Air Force (WAAF), with its blue uniform and its close association with the dashing pilots of the RAF, was perceived as glamorous, but the poor old ATS, the 'women's army', was the Cinderella of the services and was often, unfairly, the subject of bad publicity. The ATS, the least selective of the services, was regarded as 'common' and mothers did not want their daughters to join it, but conscripted women were invariably sent to the ATS. Officers within the ATS, the WAAF, the RAMC (Royal Army Medical Corps) and the Army and Air Force nursing services received the King's Commission in the Second World War, unlike the First, when their status was more ambivalent: women in the WRNS, however, were not given equivalent navy rank with men.

Many servicewomen worked in traditional women's jobs as cooks, store-keepers, telephonists and office workers, and driving was also widely regarded as suitable work for women. But the war also saw a great increase in the number of technical jobs allotted to women – in radar, communications and

ATS women on parade. *Front row, far right*: Vera Johnson from Butetown, Cardiff.

radio. Rhona Elias from Cardiff, a radar operator in the WAAF, was posted variously to Pembrokeshire, Devon and Cornwall. Betty Howard did the same job in the ATS, heading up a radar team at anti-aircraft batteries first in Penarth and then in Swansea. Daphne Price of Cowbridge and Olwen Landin of Rhyl both trained as kine theodolite operators – filming anti-aircraft guns firing at targets and calculating the accuracy of their aim. Lisbeth David of Llandaff, Cardiff, joined the WRNS and trained first as a 'sparks' (radio telegraphist), sending and receiving messages in morse code, and later, on being commissioned, became a cipher officer, serving in Northern Ireland, Portsmouth and Ceylon. Another distinctive feature of women's role in the Second World War was that some women were brought much closer to the actual fighting and into real danger. It was a major departure from tradition when in 1941 ATS members were empowered by the Army Act to participate as combatants. Manpower shortages led to the formation of mixed-sex anti-aircraft units (in which women predominated by two to one): women performed every operation, except actually firing the guns, though they gave the order to fire. Ruth Newmarch (née Harris) from Barry joined the ATS and as a member of the Royal Artillery Regiment served on an anti-aircraft battery in an area of southern England known as doodlebug alley, where the German V1s flew in incessantly overhead.

Being in the forces took many young Welsh women away from home for the first time. For some it was a great adventure but for others it was, at least at first, a frightening experience. Barbara Buchanan of Penrhyndeudraeth, Gwynedd, enlisted in the ATS as early as 1938 and, when conscription was introduced in 1941, she 'fought tooth and nail' for a posting to a centre to train conscripts. Along with other instructors, every six weeks, she trained a batch of 400 girls and women. In *Parachutes and Petticoats* she wrote:

We always felt so sorry for them. There were some with suitcases, some with carriers and parcels, some crying, some silent and fearful and some bravely hostile. But often within five weeks' training these timorous, homesick and crying girls were transformed into immaculate, confident female soldiers.

Barbara Buchanan and fellow instructors believed, 'No one could ever know how proud we were of these girls and what we had achieved. We had turned pieces of glass into diamonds.' Over and over again, when I have spoken to older women who joined the services they mention the new-found confidence their training and wartime experiences gave them. Those women who 'joined up' undoubtedly profited from the experience, but it was lack of confidence which drove many other young Welsh women to opt for work in industry, rather than the services, in the belief that they would not have to leave home.

Welsh women were also involved as doctors and nurses in the conflict. Rhona Price Davies, who had worked as doctor in both north and south Wales, became a captain in the RAMC and served in India. Although there were still some Voluntary Aid Detachment (VAD) and Red Cross nurses in the Second World War, nursing had become much more professionalized since the introduction of State Registration in 1925. Members of the military nursing services served on all fronts in the global war of 1939–45. Hilda Howells of Llanelli, for example, was a Queen Alexandra nurse (QA) serving in north Africa and Mary Morris of Llandogo, Monmouthshire, landed with the first unit of QAs in Normandy following the D-Day landings of 1944. The wartime experiences of these and many other women are printed in *Parachutes and Petticoats* (1995). Encouraging autobiographical writing by women in Wales is an important way of preserving their experiences and rescuing information which would otherwise be lost. By far the most moving account in *Parachutes and Petticoats* is that of another nurse, a genuine, quiet Welsh heroine. Mary Emily Bond (née Jones) from Pontardawe joined the QAs in 1940, serving on hospital ships in Norwegian waters, the south Atlantic and the eastern Mediterranean, in tented hospital units in north Africa and in field and makeshift hospitals in Normandy and Belgium but in May 1945, while her group was celebrating VE Day, Emily received a further posting – to the former concentration camp at Belsen. The suffering she and her colleagues witnessed on their arrival at Belsen took them completely by surprise – the world had not yet been told of the horrors of the camps. As senior sister, Emily was in charge of an area known as Square Eleven, which housed a thousand internees and one of her duties was to write down on a blackboard the number who had died each day. She saw at first hand the full horrors of the Nazi regime and did her utmost to bring relief to the survivors.

Many servicewomen worked very long hours, often under great stress, but others were underutilized. Phyllis Bowen from Pontypridd, a Wren officer, who was posted to Liverpool, enjoyed the grand title of assistant duty commander to the commander-in-chief of Western Approaches but, as she told Fay Swain, 'But I didn't do anything – I've never done less in my life.' Similarly Pamela Barker of Llanelli, who joined the Wrens to 'free a man for the fleet' – as the advertisement urged women to do, was so bored by her first posting to Yeovilton, where she 'spasmodically issued rifles', that she broke out in boils. But of all the women in the services to whom I have spoken over the years, I have no doubt that those who did the hardest physical work were the members of the Women's Land Army.

Technically the Women's Land Army was not a government service, as members were paid by the farmers. Farmers, at first reluctant to take women on, put a low monetary value on their work, but were forced by County Agricultural Wages Boards to ensure that wages did not fall below £1 2s. 6d. for a forty-eight hour week after deductions for board and lodgings. Government demands that farmers expand the amount of land under the plough made them put their misgivings to one side and by the end of 1941 there were 2,000 land girls working in Denbighshire alone. There were many appeals to get Welsh women to join the WLA, in particular to work on farms in Caernarfonshire and Anglesey, where by 1942 some 400 land girls were employed, but many of these came from England, particularly Lancashire. While some lived on the farms, others lodged in hostels and were sent out daily to work on any farm which needed them. By the end of the war in north-east Wales there were hostels at Rhuthun, Gresford, Overton, Wrexham and Abergele. As in the First War, women undertook a wide range of tasks including cultivation (with and without tractors), harvesting and threshing, poultry management, milking and milk delivering, and pest control – killing rabbits, moles and rats. The Women's Timber Corps, set up in 1942, had bases at Brechfa near Carmarthen, Milford Haven, Crickhowell and elsewhere: its members felled trees with axes and cross-saws for use as telegraph poles and pit-props. The need for women on the land did not end with the cessation of hostilities and the WLA was not disbanded until 1950.

Women donned a whole variety of uniforms, from the green coats and hats of the Women's Voluntary Service to the full 'fireman's rig' of the Women's Auxiliary Fire Service, but, as in the First World War, it was the appointment of women police which was to prove the most controversial issue in Wales. There were no women police in Wales, as we have seen, throughout the whole of the inter-war period. The antagonism of Welsh chief constables to the appointment of women was an amazing display of blatant chauvinism, which in several cases continued to be exhibited during the war years. With the outbreak of war, the Home Office was eager to replace men in clerical, telephonist and driving jobs in the police force and so created the Women's Auxiliary Police Corps (WAPC). Some feared that the auxiliaries would be used to replace 'proper', attested, policewomen but in Wales, the creation of the WAPC meant that some authorities employed women for the first time and were thus converted to the cause of women police. Cardiganshire, one of the first counties to take women on, appointed four, one of whom spoke German, which was especially useful in the control and search of enemy aliens: by 1940 the chief constable of Cardiganshire was paying fulsome tribute to them for their good work. Also by 1940, Anglesey had appointed its first three women, followed by another three in 1942. By 1943 Brecon, Glamorgan and Swansea had responded to the Home Office call for WAPCs and at some point Newport and Merthyr Borough also took women on. The Glamorgan Constabulary, which had employed women in a civilian capacity since 1939, formed its WAPC in 1943: Violet Harvey from Barry, who had been employed as a civilian clerk typist since 1939, thought that the WAPC in Glamorgan was established to prevent the women being called up for other war work. This is an interesting and important topic, which requires far more research to establish the chronology of the Welsh authorities bowing to increasing Home Office pressure to take on women. In some Welsh constabularies there was very strong opposition to the employment of women in this traditional role of patriarchal authority. In 1941, for example, despite appeals from the Women's Institute and mounting Home Office pressure, the Merionethshire Joint Police Committee decided to take no action on the matter of WAPCs. Caernarfonshire was distinctly hardline in its opposition: although four WAPCs were appointed to the county's police force late in 1941, their duties were clerical, they were only to work indoors and they were not allowed to wear uniform – only blue overalls. In 1942, the chief constable, who was being pressurized by women's groups and by church bodies to get women police on the streets to deal with immorality and drunkenness, remained adamant. He had, he said, according to the *North Wales Chronicle*, 31 July 1942, consulted with another (unnamed) chief constable who told him that 'the women in his county had not helped him in the least.' In 1944, the Home Office toughened its stance and ordered chief constables, in areas where troops were stationed, to appoint regular women police or WAPCs. Pembrokeshire and Caernarfonshire gave way in that year but Cardiff, under Chief Constable Arthur Wilson resisted: Cardiff did not get women police, despite the agitation of the Cardiff Women's Citizens Association and the Transport and General Workers Union, until Wilson retired in 1946.

Conscientious objectors

Whereas thousands of Welsh women worked in war factories or joined the various uniformed services, yet others could, in conscience, have nothing to do with the war effort. Some women in Wales had been pacifists in the First World War and we have seen the strength of the women's peace movement, particularly in north Wales, in the inter-war years. The Women's Co-operative Guild, which had a substantial membership in the south, was also committed to pacifism: in the 1930s guildswomen bravely wore white poppies on Armistice Day as a demonstration of their commitment to peace. The horrors of the First World War, the influence of Christian teachings and, in some cases, membership of Plaid Genedlaethol Cymru created a significant body of opinion in Wales which was totally opposed to militarism. The role of women pacifists and indeed, after 1941, women conscientious objectors has been neglected in Wales: women were members of all the main pacifist bodies – the Baptist Union of Wales, the Peace Pledge Union (founded in 1936), Cymdeithas Heddychwyr Cymru (1937) – and, in refusing to be conscripted, were subject to the full rigour of the law.

It is, however, one thing to be an apostle of peace in peacetime and quite another to be a pacifist in wartime. By 1940, when France fell and Britain faced the real threat of invasion, there was widespread hostility towards 'conchies'. Houses were daubed, newspapers launched attacks on these 'traitors' and local councils made life difficult for the opponents of the war. Annie Humphreys, one of the founders of Cymdeithas Heddychwyr Cymru, recalled that the Peace Pledge Union was refused the tenancy of the building in King Street, Wrexham, which had formerly been its headquarters, and Rosalind Rusbridge (née Bevan) noted how Swansea City Council rescinded the tenancy of the peace stall in Swansea market. Councils, often coming under pressure from residents, began to sack employees who were conscientious objectors. Among Welsh authorities, Anglesey, Cardiff, Cardiganshire, Flintshire and Swansea dismissed council employees, including teachers. In Swansea, the Swansea League of Loyalists, set up in the spring of 1940, attacked those with 'pacifistic and communist tendencies', and in July pressurized the council into issuing a declaration of loyalty, which all council employees had to sign or lose their posts. It stated:

> I hereby solemnly and sincerely declare that I am not a conscientious objector or a member of the Peace Pledge Union, nor do I hold views which are in conflict with the purpose to which the Nation's effort is directed in the present war. And I further declare that I wholeheartedly support the vigorous prosecution of the war.

Among those who lost their jobs through failure to sign this were Dorothy Walton, a housing officer and chair of the local pacifist group; Miss Phyllis Boycott, a teacher at Delabeche girls' school; and the young Rosalind Bevan, classics mistress at Glanmor School for Girls. Miss Winifred Naylor, the respected head of Delabeche, a supporter of the League of Nations, but not a known pacifist, refused to sign and instead submitted a plea for toleration. She was suspended, but later reinstated by the authority. In all, nineteen people were suspended, ten of them women, before the council, on instruction from the Home Office, rescinded the suspensions in September 1940.

The introduction of conscription for women in December 1941 made it illegal for any woman to refuse to do war work or enter the services. They were, however, allowed to claim exemption as conscientious objectors – though technically it was almost impossible for women to gain this status, as the law permitted conscientious objection only to military (and not civil) service and women were invariably conscripted to the ATS *or* factory work. By the summer of 1942, the first women claiming exemption from war service began to appear before tribunals. In June 1942, as reported by the *South Wales Evening Post*, 9 June, the first joint tribunal for the south Wales area dealt with the cases of six women – all of whom claimed exemption on religious grounds. None of the women succeeded in gaining recognition as conscientious objectors, but were all dealt with sympathetically, and were registered for social, hospital or land work. One of the women was the young Maedwen Daniel (née Davies) of Godre'r-graig, a well known contralto, who had refused to sing in aid of Swansea's Warship Week and had turned down a job, at seven pounds a week, singing for the troops. Her case was heard in Welsh and the verdict was 'registered for full time social work': in practice she was allowed to carry on as a chapel cleaner. The first six women from north Wales appeared at a tribunal in August and the proceedings were reported in the *North Wales Chronicle*, 28 August 1942. Three of the women, all Jehovah's Witnesses, and one of whom had already been imprisoned for her stand, objected to any kind of war work, while the remaining three agreed to non-combatant work. The fact that one of the women, a 22-year-old from Colwyn Bay, had already been in prison indicates that she had already been through a process of interviews and appearances before the magistrates, before her appearance at the Conscientious Objectors Tribunal. In south-east Wales Iris Cooze, an eighteen-year old Jehovah's Witness in Abercarn, Monmouthshire, was directed to war work and, on refusing, made seven appearances before the local magistrate. On her seventh appearance, the magistrate, who explained he was compelled to enforce the law, sentenced her to a month in Cardiff prison. In *Parachutes and Petticoats*, she recalled her grim experience of prison life, of wearing a coarse flannel uniform, and the loneliness of being a young innocent girl amidst a prison population made up largely of prostitutes. 'That month seemed like a year', she wrote. On her release, she returned to her religious work and was frequently verbally abused with taunts of 'conchie'.

The Home Front

The First World War had been a soldiers' war, the Second was a civilian war. As *Woman's Own*, 19 October 1940, put it, 'We all live in the battlefield now.' But how true was that of Wales? Until 1940, people in Wales would feel a certain security that they were tucked away far to the west, beyond the range of the enemy. The main fear in 1939, based on memories of the First World War, was that of gas attacks – a fear reinforced by the issue of gas masks as early as the Munich Crisis of 1938. But gas attacks never came. In fact, all was quiet in the months of 'the phoney war', down to the British evacuation from Dunkirk in June 1940. The fall of Belgium, Holland and France by that date brought the towns and cities of Wales within easy reach of German bombers. The worst of the bombing came in 1941, with the south Wales ports, particularly Swansea, suffering devastating aerial bombardment.

Swansea endured three nights of unsparing horror in the blitz of 19, 20 and 21 February 1941. In all there were forty-four raids on the town between 1940 and 1943. A total of 369 people were killed, including 230 who died in the three night blitz. In Swansea and Cardiff women and children were in the front line. Major English cities had been evacuated, but not Welsh towns: only with 'Swansea aflame', and with Welsh nationalists protesting against 'the neglect of the English government' did any evacuation begin from Swansea. Most people voted with their feet. Despite official government propaganda that the inhabitants of bombed towns were 'keeping a stiff upper lip' and 'smiling-through', people flocked at night to the safety of Gower and the surrounding countryside. Pembroke Dock, another German target, was depopulated at night in May 1941. W. L. Richards, reporter of the *West Wales Guardian* described the exodus, with an endless stream of overloaded buses, lorries, bicycles and horse-drawn carts, weary mothers with children in their arms, young children running behind and 'long after the stars had studded the sky there were stragglers hurrying from the devastated town'. The ports were a legitimate target, but other small communities were hit by the enemy planes dumping their load on the return flight, as in the case of Cwmparc on 30 April 1941, where, within minutes, twenty people were killed and 800 made homeless: 8-year-old Mary Evans survived after being buried for six hours but her 24-year-old aunt, who was to have been married in a few weeks, died as she was lifted out from the rubble.

The war created a world of blackouts, windows criss-crossed with tape and sandbags. Women joined civil defence units and the Marchioness of Anglesey once again organised training in self-defence for the WI members of Llanfairpwll. In 1940 women, queuing for stamps at the post office, could read a leaflet on guerilla warfare. It told them that when the Germans arrived they would confiscate civilian cars and force British women to drive German officers about. Somewhat bizarrely the leaflet advised them,

> If you happen to be standing in a ditch or behind a tree or some other position of safety, and you have some kind of grenade or bomb in your hand, and a car comes along with enemy officers, driven even by your best friend, YOU MUST LET THEM HAVE IT. It is what your friend would want you to do.

Luckily, it never came to that.

Women bore the brunt of wartime shortages. Welsh women, with their long experience of poverty, brought to this challenge a wealth of experience in making a little go a long way, though the war was to tax even their ingenuity. They registered, as required by the government, with the shops of their choice – butcher, grocer and dairy – and eked out the meagre weekly rations, introduced in January 1940, of 4 oz of ham or bacon, 12 oz of sugar, 4 oz of butter and about 1 lb of meat per person. There was a grim quality to the wartime diet – grey, unpalatable bread and, from July 1940, just 2 oz of tea a week. They queued for hours – an impossibility for war workers – for the basics and for any extras which became available, such as offal or fish which were not rationed and tinned goods which were available on a 'points system' from December 1941. Government agencies warned them that 'Food is a Munition of War' and to waste it was tantamount to sinking a merchant vessel, and they were urged, through newspaper 'Food Facts' columns, Kitchen Front wireless broadcasts and local centres, and austerity cookery books to produce tasty and filling meals with unlikely ingredients. Ingenious recipes were published such as Stuffed Ear (pig's presumably), Hash of Calf's Head and even Snoek Piquante (based on a mysterious whale-like fish). Those who had stuck with, or reverted to, the old Welsh diet of *cawl* and oatcakes were better off. Potatoes were served as the chief ingredient of soups, pies, pastry and even some custards. Other foods disappeared entirely. Eggs and onions became treasured luxuries in towns and imported fruit a thing of the past. When the headteacher in Nevern, Pembrokeshire, showed a banana to the infants class, none of them knew what it was and some recoiled in fear. If people were lucky enough to get hold of an orange, they ate the peel too. Those who lived in the countryside, keeping pigs and poultry and growing vegetables, were in a better position. Olwen Hughes Jones, who went as a war worker to Liverpool, used to travel home to Anglesey on her annual leave and take back farm butter and home cured-ham.

In fact, the wartime diet was healthier than that of the previous decade. Rationing ensured equal distribution of food, while price-fixing meant that working-class people could afford it. The unpopular national loaf, which in fact was 85 per cent wholemeal, was more nourishing than pre-war white bread. People also ate less fat and more vegetables and this, together with various schemes providing milk and vitamins, led to a better-nourished population.

There was little that was new for many Welsh women to learn from propaganda campaigns directed at 'Mrs Sew and Sew' to 'Make Do and Mend'. They had been doing that for generations. Clothing was rationed through a points system from 1941, with so many points fixed for each garment. A female black market quickly grew up, with prosecutions taking place throughout Wales both of buyers and sellers of clothing coupons. It was a frustrating state of affairs for Welsh women, who for the first time had money in their pockets, that by the end of 1941 there was almost nothing to buy in the shops. Young women particularly felt the lack of silk stockings and they had no compunction about buying from spivs or going out with an American soldier to get a free pair. Others took to colouring their legs with gravy browning and drawing a seam up the back with an eyebrow pencil.

Thousands of evacuees, women and children from English danger areas, poured into Wales. They came from Liverpool, Bootle, Birkenhead and Wallasey to north Wales – 2,500 to Anglesey, 2000 to Bangor, over 19,000 to Flintshire and 17,000 to Denbighshire – and from London, Birmingham and the Midlands to south Wales: Aberdare took in not only waves of London and Midland evacuees but the whole of Ilford and Essex mixed grammar schools. It fell on women to provide a home and home comforts to the newcomers. It was a culture shock for both sides. Interestingly, London women, used to dressing up for nights out in the pub, were shocked at the harsh existence of Valleys' women, by the lack of fun in their lives and their premature ageing. On the other hand, the *Welsh Nationalist*, December 1941, journal of Plaid Genedlaethol Cymru, deplored 'the questionable moral behaviour of certain English women who have attempted to destroy the pristine Christian way of life in Welsh villages'. It is testimony to the warmth of the Welsh women who acted as foster mothers to the evacuees that in a significant number of cases their young charges stayed with them and did not return home at the war's end. The experiences of the young girls coming in to Wales varied. Beryl Mills, sent from the London area to Pembrokeshire, although billeted first with unsympathetic spinsters, who were unused to children, was later sent to an idyllic village pub, where she was taken to the bosom of her new foster-mother and became quickly absorbed into the Welsh-speaking community. Patricia Parris, on the other hand, was taken into a childless home where her letters and even birthday cards from home were withheld. She was not allowed to go upstairs during the daytime for fear of wearing out the stair carpet and the man of the house attempted to molest her. For Welsh girls, the coming of the evacuees meant the excitement and upheaval of half-time schooling and the making of new friends.

Sexuality

Sexual behaviour could not remain unchanged by the turmoil of wartime. All the women's services were the butt of sexual jokes and innuendo – the ATS was called the 'Groundsheet of the Army', Land Army girls were said to have their 'Backs to the Land' and the saying was, 'Up with the lark and to bed with a Wren'. Such remarks were, at least in part, based on male resentment of seeing women in uniform and were, on the whole, unfair. Young women certainly came under a lot of pressure from men to 'give in'. Two Welsh girls, quoted by Penny Summerfield in *Out of the Cage*, described how they coped with a pair of over-amorous Poles when they worked as student land girls in Devon. Finding it difficult to fend off the unwanted advances,

> We proceeded to speak entirely in Welsh, which neither of us could really speak. We recited the whole of the Lord's Prayer in Welsh to each other, talking a line at a time and various things like the national anthem, so that it sounded like conversation.

It was an interesting use of the language as a moral shield: it worked too, as the baffled Poles eventually gave up. We have also to bear in mind the innocence and inexperience of many women, in an age when there was no sex education in schools and the subject was taboo at home. ATS member Eileen Gilmore and the other occupants of her hut were taken totally by surprise when one of the girls gave birth in the camp ablutions: although they had shared accommodation with her, they had no idea of her condition. Unwanted pregnancies were a real risk as contraceptive advice was not given to single women. Servicewomen were also accused of a lack of femininity and of lesbianism. Unfortunately we do not have the historical sources to study Welsh lesbians in this period, but clearly the war brought some women into contact, for the first time, with this alternative sexuality and may have helped others to define feelings to which hitherto they had been unable even to put a name.

The war caused a tremendous upheaval in the lives of individuals – women worked alongside men, they moved away from home, they were separated from husbands and boyfriends for periods of years, and they socialized with men from outside their immediate small communities, in pubs and dance halls. As in the First World War, they were attacked for enjoying themselves on their wartime wages. The chief constable of Cardiff, commenting in 1943 on the enormous increase in the number of women, especially young women, frequenting the city's public houses, condemned their 'provocative spirit of independence'. In Bridgend, home of the great arsenal, the police superintendent went further and accused the women of turning pubs from reputable places of (male) recreation into 'haunts and hunting grounds of sharks and loose women whose business consists of exploiting the follies and weaknesses of the unsuspecting'. There were other, stronger indictments. An anonymous attack on the morals of women in Cardiff, published by the *South Wales Echo*, 8 September 1943, and written under the pseudonym of 'Woman Who Talks', spoke of 'girls of fourteen and upwards haunting the places where troops are stationed' and of 'professional prostitutes losing trade to the more tempting and successful amateurs'. She wrote of Cardiff in the blackout as full of courting couples having intercourse in the shop doorways of the main streets, on bomb sites and in back alleys. But the main thrust of the attack by 'Woman Who Talks' was against young married women who slept around and were unfaithful to their husbands serving overseas. They were, she wrote, 'anybody's meat'. It is hard to know how much truth there is in this – but there is certainly some. For young women in Wales, there was the chance to meet men, often with different and more romantic attitudes than the home-town boys. With nearly a million and half overseas troops as well as British servicemen encamped in Britain in the run up to D-Day in 1944, they were spoilt for choice. The Americans with their tailored uniforms, charm and sexy accents – not to mention their supplies of cigarettes, chocolates and nylons – bowled the girls over. As poet Gloria Evans Davies put it,

> When the Yanks hit town, the women
> sparkled. To be switched off
> when their husbands came home
> on leave.

Some married their Americans and became GI brides, sailing off to a land they knew only from Hollywood films. Many others, in practically every town in Wales, whether married or single at the time, are still remembered 'for going about with Yanks'. For some young married women, who had rushed into marriage, long separations bred loneliness and gave them a chance to reflect on their hasty decision. In-laws and friends were quick to inform men serving away from home of any infidelity on their wives' part and there were numerous cases of men coming home on leave to discover that their wives were in relationships with other men. 'Woman Who Talks' foresaw the situation, 'when the men come back to many dishonoured and desecrated homes it will be a red mist before their eyes that they will see, not just smoke in them, and they'll take the law into their own hands.' A Newport, Monmouthshire, soldier did just that. Coming home suddenly on leave, he discovered that his wife had taken up with another man. He beat her up, for which he was sentenced to three months hard labour: the wife was awarded a separation order. In fact, the post-war divorce rate shot up, from under 8,000 cases in England and Wales in 1939 to a record 60,000 cases in 1947, a figure which was not to be surpassed until 1971. Whereas, between 1931 and 1935, 55 per cent of divorces were sought by wives and 45 per cent by husbands, the 1940s saw a reversal of the pattern: between 1941 and 1945, 56 per cent of divorces were sought by husbands and 44 per cent by wives and the same male/female breakdown of petitions continued throughout the rest of the 1940s. Illegitimacy rates rose too – doubling for England and Wales between 1939 and 1945 and alarming moralists, but in fact rather than showing a 'moral decline' the figures demonstrate the disruption of life caused by the war. Before the war some 70 per cent of illegitimate conceptions were 'regularized by marriage' but only 37 per cent were in 1945. In pre-war days, women would only have had intercourse with the man they intended to marry, but brief wartime love affairs or the posting away of the men meant that many births could not be regularized. Nor do illegitimacy tables show the numbers of illegitimate children born to married women – in Birmingham where a record was kept, roughly 50 per cent of children born to married women were fathered by men other than the husbands.

Demobilization

Demobilization of women at the end of the Second World War was not an exact rerun of 1918, when women had been dismissed en masse and were expected either to take up low-paid posts as domestics or disappear quietly back into the home. In 1945 demobilization was a slower, more drawn out process with workers in filling factories laid off well before VE Day (8 May 1945) but those in aircraft and other factories continuing in employment, in some cases, into 1946. But the difference between demobilization in the two wars was more than merely one of time scale. In 1918 things were clean-cut – women were expected to leave work immediately to make way for ex-servicemen. In 1945, however, more complex, and indeed contradictory, forces were at work.

There were forces which boded ill for women's continued participation in the waged workforce. Many voices had been raised during the war that 'the world had been turned upside-down' with young girls working and older men unemployed. As the end of the war came closer, opponents of this state of affairs grew even more vociferous. During a parliamentary debate on post-war 'manpower' in 1944, the prejudices of many in Wales were articulated by Professor W. J. Gruffydd, Liberal member representing the University of Wales. He said,

> I should like to warn whoever is concerned with this, there will be great and grave resentment if women are conscripted at the end of the European War for work for which civilians will be clamouring.

It was a remarkable intervention. Apart from the bizarre and inaccurate reference to peacetime conscription of women, the language is revealing. Gruffydd 'warns': he speaks of 'great and grave resentment' if women were to be employed and he uses the word 'civilians' to mean only men – what were women, ex-servicewomen and all the other wartime workers, if not civilians? Many similar demands and pleas were made from public platforms and newspapers in Wales when the war ended, to safeguard the employment of the male breadwinner and hence reinforce his role as head of the family. By early 1946 a columnist in the *South Wales Echo*, 29 January , asked,

> Is it time to cry a halt and to return to the old-fashioned view that it is the man's job to go out to earn the family's income and that the woman's natural sphere is the home, where she must be and is indispensable?

There were anxieties too centring on government plans to create jobs for women in post-war factories which were to be built on the sites of wartime works. Against a background of rising male unemployment in Wales at the end of the war, feelings became heated, as may be seen in the deliberations of one local council, Aberdare, which were reported in the *Aberdare Leader*, 13 October 1945. Against a background of 1,500 people signing on in Aberdare Labour Exchange, concerns were raised both over 'inadequate employment for male labour' at the Hirwaun Trading Estate (the former ROF) and over information received from the Board of Trade that 70 per cent of those to be employed on the new Rhigos Trading Estate would be females. One councillor stated bluntly, 'That was not what our boys fought for: to place the responsibility of earning money on the women while the men are on the dole.' On the other hand, several councillors spoke up for the women. The chairman, D. R. Jones JP, said, 'I don't like this anti-feminist trend in the discussion. What we want is work for everyone,' and Councillor Islwyn Williams pointed out that, 'It was not just a question of married women: single girls had a right to live.'

As to the women themselves, although some, often older married women, were glad to return home, others were happy to continue earning much-needed cash. Chapter 5, which covers the years 1945 to 1970, examines further the clash between the forces of tradition and those of economic progress and charts what, in fact, happened to women's role in the Welsh workforce in the post-war period.

Though there is no doubt that, in the longer term, the war was extremely influential in reshaping the Welsh economy, what broader effects did it have on the lives of women in Wales? Essentially the war did little more than superficially dent the notion of separate spheres. In post-war Wales, men remained the breadwinners and women custodians of the home and family. Nor did the war raise the status of women as workers. Their war work, though well paid, was not rewarded equally with men's work and the perception was, 'if women can do it, it must be easy'. But women's wartime experience of work – whether in a neighbouring munitions factory or in the services in far-flung corners of the earth – enhanced their confidence and raised their expectations. Young women wanted a better, more affluent and more enjoyable life than their mothers before them: they wanted more than heavy domestic drudgery and successive pregnancies and they sought wider horizons than the four walls of their homes. Part-time and shift work, themselves mainly war time developments, would help them achieve this. The era of the self-sacrificing Welsh Mam was drawing quickly to an end. But in essence the post-war world was as male-dominated and as patriarchal as ever. In fact, the absence of prominent Welsh women in key positions of authority in the Second World War stands in contrast to the highly visible and important roles played by women such as Lady Rhondda and Violet Douglas-Pennant in the First World War.

Those two had operated against the background of the strong suffrage movement, but by the Second World War, feminism, or what passed for feminism, had been transmuted and diluted into a movement to improve conditions of women in the home.

~ 5 ~
Jobs, Gadgets and the Pill, 1945–1970

THE years between 1945 and 1970 form one of the most neglected, complex and fascinating periods in twentieth-century Welsh women's history. Neglected, because what few studies there are of women's lives in 'post-war' Wales, although extremely welcome, stretch the term 'post-war' to encompass the period from 1945 to the present day and concentrate almost exclusively on the 1980s and 1990s. The most complex, because powerful contradictory forces were at work in shaping women's lives, pulling them in opposite directions at the same time. And finally, arguably one of the most fascinating, because the period covers such a contrasting range of decades – the austerity years of the late 1940s, which promised the fulfilment of the socialist dream and the building of the new Jerusalem and actually delivered the Welfare State; the prosperous, consumer-orientated 1950s, with their repressive emphasis on sugar-and-spice femininity – a period which most women, who lived through it, regard as best forgotten; and finally the so-called 'Swinging Sixties', the decade of flower-power, the pill and the sexual liberation of women. No groundwork has been done to retrieve the experiences of women in Wales in this whole quarter of a century and a wide field of study awaits detailed research. What follows here are the main developments in Welsh women's lives, as I see them, which further study may confirm or contradict.

The essential starting point must be an examination of the tension caused by the conflicting forces which pulled women in two directions at once. On the one side, there were the powerful agents of conservatism and tradition, which tried to push women in Wales back into the home, after their wartime sortie into the world of paid work. On the other side, there were the forces of economic change, often working in tandem with women's aspirations, which drew them into the waged workforce. Thereafter, this chapter looks in more detail at women's paid work, home life, health, education and at politics and issues affecting the lives of women in Wales.

Patriarchy versus capitalism

The late 1940s, all of the 1950s and much of the 1960s was a profoundly reactionary time, when life, and therefore women's role, was expected to return to normal, after the abnormality of wartime. In Wales, the war's end was greeted with jubilation and street parties and the landslide victory of the Labour party, in the 1945 general election, produced a new mood of optimism. But despite the euphoria, there were fears of a return to the bad old pre-war days and many remembered with foreboding the economic downturn which had followed the end of the First War. There was a desperate desire to prevent a repetition of that and to avoid any return to the dark days of mass unemployment. Agreement was widespread amongst the holders and upholders of patriarchal authority in Wales, that central to the strategy of avoiding a return to past economic misery was the restoration of the old social order. In south Wales, in particular, those who wielded power, an exclusively male group of politicians, trade union leaders and a strongly unionized male workforce, sought a return to the traditional model of family with male breadwinner, doing a man's job in heavy industry and earning a family wage, and of dependent, home-based wife and mother. There is widespread testimony to this viewpoint in local newspapers throughout Wales in the 1940s, as shown at the end of chapter 4, and demands that 'no woman should be given a job in this valley until all the men have work' or 'all married women should leave work to create jobs for the men' were commonplace. This Welsh view coincided with a wider British consensus on the need to ensure stable family units following the dislocating effects of the war, with couples separated for years on end, a rising divorce rate and an alarming fall in the birthrate. Such concerns formed the background for the creation of the Welfare State. The Beveridge Report (1942) and subsequent legislation was posited on the notion that men and women were 'equal but different' and that they had distinct roles to play. Though Beveridge took care to avoid calling married women dependants, the National Insurance Act, passed in 1946 and coming into effect in 1948, ensured that was just what they were. Under the Act, the right of a married woman, whether she had children or not, to benefits was based on her husband's contributions and her entitlement to support was based on his claim. Even married women who did work were not expected to pay National Insurance contributions and hence could make no claim to benefits in their own right. The Women's Co-operative Guild made a request to the Labour government that married women should be made insured workers, but the government ignored this. To this extent the Welfare State enshrined the dependency of married women upon their husbands. But the Welfare State did bring benefits to women. Family allowances (child benefit), which Eleanor Rathbone had been advocating since 1917, were first paid in 1946. These were not exactly as she envisaged them but a rate of five shillings a week for the second and any subsequent child was paid directly to the mother: the ministry originally intended to make these payments to the father, but after a very strong intervention by Eleanor Rathbone and other women MPs, agreed to make the payments directly to the mother. It was not only the Welfare State that classified women as financial dependants. Throughout this whole period 1945–70 a woman, whether married or single, could not apply for a mortgage or even take out a hire purchase agreement to buy a three-piece suite without the signature of a male guarantor on the application form.

Other agencies, from the education system, fashion designers, the advertising industry to psychologists and childcare experts reinforced the role of women as home-makers and mothers. The 1944 Education Act brought in free secondary education for all. Girls and boys who passed the eleven-plus examination went to grammar schools but those who failed, the great majority, had to attend the newly created secondary modern schools. State policy promoted the view that the education of girls in this sector was for 'citizenship'. When used in the context of girls' education, this did not mean an extensive course on the workings of democracy or training on how to stand for the council: from the 1940s to the 1960s, 'citizenship' for girls meant marriage and motherhood. The late 1940s were characterized by austerity and shortages. Many foodstuffs were still rationed – bread rationing was introduced in 1946 – and clothes could only be bought if the purchaser had enough coupons. But, as the 1940s gave way to the 1950s, austerity gave way to affluence. Wales reached a level of prosperity last seen before the First World War and cars, fridges, electric cookers and vacuum cleaners came within the reach of ordinary working people. The functional short skirts and military-style jackets with padded shoulders, which had used as little material as possible, of the war years and the later 1940s were replaced by feminine full skirts and the narrow waistline of Dior's New Look. Though launched on the fashion world in 1947, the New Look took a little longer to filter through to Wales but Welsh girls did their best to keep up. The 1950s saw a media hype of the modern feminine woman. Whereas, in wartime, Welsh women workers on a night out in the cinema watched strong female actresses, like Joan Crawford, Bette Davis and Katherine Hepburn, stride purposefully across the screen, sometimes as a career woman but always as the protagonist, by the 1950s they were served up with Debbie Reynolds and Natalie Wood, sweet girl-next-door-types and definitely the marrying kind, or sexy but invariably mindless stars such as Marilyn Monroe, Jane Mansfield and Anita Ekberg. In Welsh films, or at least films set in Wales, the dominant image of womanhood, the Welsh Mam, as played by Rachel Thomas in *Proud Valley* (1940) and Edith Evans in *The Last Days of Dolwyn* (1949), remained constant. By the 1950s, the advertising industry, fully aware of women's power as consumers and trading on the rising tide of affluence, depicted women as modern feminine housewives, and advertisements featured women in large kitchens, packed with electrical appliances, plastic ware and packaged foods. There was a renewed emphasis on childcare too in the late 1940s and the 1950s. Nurseries had shut down at the end of the war, and women were encouraged to devote themselves to childcare. The ideas of the popular, new childcare expert, Dr Benjamin Spock, marked a radical departure from pre-war advice which had insisted on a disciplinarian approach. Dr Spock told mothers that what a child enjoyed was good for him. If a child enjoyed throwing his food about or dropping his toys, that this was quite alright: mother was left to clean up the mess. The work of psychologist John Bowlby on 'maternal deprivation', which was widely available in popularized editions, was interpreted at the time as meaning that a mother should not leave her child with anyone else at all. Good mothers were afraid to leave their child for an instant, lest it suffer from 'maternal deprivation' and develop mental troubles or turn into a juvenile delinquent.

The forces of patriarchy which combined to ensure the maintenance of the old order of things were powerful indeed and weighed heavily on women's lives. But there were other factors which pulled women in the opposite direction and would in the long run prevail. The two dominant agents of long term change were economic and social.

Economists and the government were agreed that Wales's pre-war economic problems stemmed from an over-reliance on just one industry – coal – and that in order to set the post-war Welsh economy on a sound footing there was a need to diversify. The solution was to attract manufacturing industry but this would take time and initially a great deal of emphasis was placed on developing heavy industry. At the time of coal nationalization in 1947, there were still 222 collieries in south Wales, employing over 115,000 workers. The other heavy industry on which great emphasis was placed was steel – with the opening of the Abbey works at Margam (1951), the largest steel works in Britain, and Llanwern near Newport (1962). But alongside this, diversification proceeded. Wartime factories, warehouses and depots were converted to peacetime use. The munitions works at Bridgend and Hirwaun in south Wales and Marchwiel in north-east Wales became trading estates, and the Trefforest estate was developed further, while a new estate was built at Fforest-fach. In 1945, the south Wales coalfield and parts of Pembrokeshire was scheduled as a development area with incentives to industrialists to set up businesses, with the result that by 1947 more new industry had gone to south Wales than any other part of Britain. Part of the attraction to industrialists was the huge reservoir of female labour. Already by 1948, 8,981 (37 per cent) of the 24,151 total employees at work in surplus government factories in south Wales were women. In the whole of the South Wales Development Area in 1948 there were 105,201 employed females, compared with 54,712 in 1938 – an increase of over 90 per cent. There was a rise too in the numbers of women employed in the professional and service sectors including office work, many of them employed in the new services operated by the Welfare State. All this was to lead to a gradual build-up of women's participation in the Welsh workforce. The rise in women's participation in the workforce in the period covered by this chapter is an indication of things to come and points towards the major reshuffle in the male/female composition of the workforce which became evident in the 1980s and 1990s. The increase in women's activity rates – of almost 4 per cent between 1931 and 1951 – is more significant than it first appears, because this rise reverses the trend of falling Welsh female participation rates which characterized the inter-war years. Undeniably, however, the 1951 figure was still low, with only a quarter of Welsh women engaged in paid work. The more significant rises occurred in the 1950s and 1960s. Another striking feature is the increase in these years of the number of married women working. In 1911, 78.8 per cent of Welsh women in paid work were unmarried, 10.8 per cent were widows and only 10.4 per cent were married. By 1951, 32 per cent of women workers were married and by 1961, almost 50 per cent.

Table 5.1: Female Economic Activity Rates, Wales 1931–1971

	%
1931*	21.00
1951*	24.96
1961*	28.02
1971†	36.07

NB. There was no census in 1941.
* Source: J. Williams, *Digest of Welsh Historical Statistics*.
†Source: T. Rees, *Women and Work: Twenty-Five Years of Gender Equality in Wales*, University of Wales Press.

In addition to the increase in women, especially married women, working, two important social trends began to emerge which militated against a return to the old model of family and the conventional order. Firstly the divorce rate rose.

In 1931 there had been just 628 divorced women living in Wales. In 1951 there were 4,935; in 1961, 7,481 and in 1971 the number had reached 14,365 – a twenty-three-fold increase since 1931. Secondly the illegitimacy rate, which had stood at 7.8 per cent for Wales in the untypical year of 1945 and hovered around 4 per cent in the late 1940s and in the 1950s, began to rise: by 1967, it stood at 6.86 per cent. The dramatic rise in illegitimacy was to come in the 1970s and 1980s, but already the 1960s were showing portents of things to come.

Work

A whole range of jobs in manufacturing was opened up to women in light engineering, textiles, clothing and footwear. On the four south Wales industrial estates (Trefforest, Fforest-fach, Bridgend and Hirwaun) they made everything from lipsticks, zip fasteners and dental equipment to radios. They made teapots in Neath, washing machines and toys in Merthyr, gramophone records in Pontardawe and electricity meters in Bangor. They manufactured rayon at Courtaulds in Flint and Greenfield, spun nylon in Pontypool, made candlewick at Brynmawr and Dowlais, celanese in Wrexham and woollen cloth in Llanrwst and Llandysul. They made woollen coats in Swansea, raincoats in Brynmawr, and fur coats in Gorseinon, shirts in Cardiff, ladies' underwear in Merthyr, Pontardawe and Wrexham, corsets in Ebbw Vale, gloves in Barry, shoes in Bridgend and boots in Nant-y-glo. Other industrial women worked in the food, drink and tobacco sector and, although women continued to work in 'old-type' tinplate works, their number was down to 2,000 in 1954. By 1952 nearly 70,000 women in Wales out of an insured female workforce of 232,000 were engaged in manufacturing.

Employers were pleased with the adaptability of the female workforce. Miss D. Scriven, personnel manager at the Dunlop Rubber Company in Hirwaun, stated confidently in the *Western Mail*, 19 January 1953, 'The fact which our Welsh women have now irrefutably established is their right to take their place in a live industrial society.' Women predominated in some industries, such as clothing, where, in the early 1960s, some 85 per cent of the workforce was female – mainly employed as skilled machinists – but only 15 per cent of managers were women. It was a young workforce with 83 per cent of women aged under forty, and 64 per cent of these under twenty-five: that still left 17 per cent of women workers aged more than forty. Clothing workers were taken on straight from school and trained on the job. Many remained following marriage but left to have children. Changing patterns of marriage and childbirth – with earlier marriages and childbearing reduced to a span of just a few years – meant

Lines Brothers Toy Factory, Merthyr Tydfil, 1951. Women packing a toy milk cart.

that increasingly married women returned to work after their children started school. Women relied on their mothers for childcare. Olive Lee, a textile worker, returned to work at Courtaulds Flint works and left her daughters with her mother: they grew up calling their grandmother 'Mam'. Grandmothers were called into service as childminders in many parts of Wales, particularly in the Valleys, but women who had moved out to new housing estates had to rely on friends and neighbours, usually paid, to look after the children.

Women went out to work, full- or part-time, for the money. They needed it to help their children, by paying for school trips and helping them out in higher education; and they wanted it to improve their standard of living by making hire purchase payments on furniture, televisions and radiograms and, by the 1960s, on cars. They wanted holidays in Mallorca and on the Costa Brava and they did not want to live the hard-pinched lives their mothers had led. Money was the main motive, but the company and contact with other people that going out to work gave, was another attraction. In fact, by the 1960s, when Mavis Jones interviewed women for the *Western Mail*, 13 September 1963, many spoke with

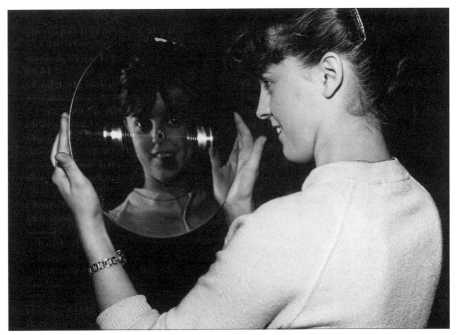

Qualiton Records, Pontardawe, 1951. An employee checks a master disc from which records would be pressed.

disdain of women who did *not* work, saying 'I do not know what they find to do all day. They must be lazy.' But women's low wages, compared with men's, meant that they were emphatically not the breadwinners. Women's wages were just over half those of male workers. In 1948, for example, Welsh women earned £3 18s. a week, compared to £7 3s. earned by men.

The numbers of women in the professions, office work and the distributive trades continued to rise. Teaching remained the main women's profession. Although the 'pledge' system, under which entrants to training colleges and universities had been given grants on condition that they declared in writing that it was their intention to enter the teaching profession, was dropped by the mid-1950s, the main career destination of women graduates remained teaching: in 1965, 40 per cent of women graduating from the University of Wales entered the profession. These women, together with students from Welsh training colleges, meant a glut of Welsh teachers, who were forced to leave Wales to work in Liverpool, Birmingham and London. Hafina Clwyd, an enormously talented and distinguished Welsh woman, on leaving Bangor Normal College in 1957 was turned down by Denbighshire Education Authority and forced to take up a post in London. At that time it is thought that some 70 per cent of London's teachers were Welsh. Only candidates whose fathers 'were somebody' or 'knew somebody', she reflected in her diary at the time, could get a job in their own country. Women teachers were a well-trained, totally unionized, professional body. They achieved two hard-won victories. The 1944 Education Act removed the marriage bar, though it remained almost impossible for years for married women to obtain posts in south Wales: grammar schools remained primarily staffed by single women until the 1960s, but teacher shortages, by this time, meant more and more married women were employed. The second victory was equal pay. After years of pressure by the National Union of Women Teachers and despite niggardly opposition by the National Association of Schoolmasters, the principle of equal pay was effectively achieved in 1954. In fact, it was phased in, through seven increments, with women teachers finally receiving an equal salary with male colleagues in 1961. Few Welsh girls attending grammar schools in the 1950s would have realized that the able and dedicated women who taught them were not being paid on a par with the men in boys' schools.

The Civil Service similarly introduced equal pay, though in reality women were largely confined to the lower, clerical ranks of the service. The expansion of the Welfare State, which spawned a huge bureaucracy, meant an increasing number of clerical jobs for women in government departments. In Cardiff, the Inland Revenue was a major employer of women. In the private sector, too, women confirmed their hold on office work, but as shorthand typists, filing clerks, comptometer (a pre-electronic calculator) operators and secretaries, and not as office managers. Mainly these were dead-end jobs for single and young, childless, married women but increasingly women returned to office work when their children were older. The new National Health Service quickly revealed itself as a major employer of women. Women doctors, nurses, administrative and cleaning staff were employed in ever-growing numbers. Nursing, like teaching, ceased to be a profession where women were forced to 'take the veil': by 1963 without married nurses half the hospital wards in Wales would have had to close. Similarly women doctors returned to work after marriage and when their families were old enough. A Rhondda woman doctor told the *Western Mail*, 1 December 1963,

> Married women like myself have had a training and are anxious to use it again as soon as our families are old enough. This may not be essential to family income but we want to maintain our independence and not have to go cap in hand to our husbands for everything we want.

It was women who filled the lowly jobs of ward orderlies and cleaners. In Cardiff, where an influx of Caribbean families had taken place in the 1950s, it was mainly in these menial jobs that black women were employed.

The most significant single change the Second World War brought about was the end of domestic service. Although this had been the largest single employment sector of Welsh women up till 1939, there was no mass coercion of women back into service in 1945, as there had been in 1918. Domestic work for women however did not disappear, it merely changed its form. Well-off housewives employed working-class women to come on a daily basis to clean their homes. In the 1950s, the trains from Caerphilly to Heath Halt were packed with women each morning setting off to clean, wash and iron in Cardiff's well-to-do Cyncoed area. Domestic service was also relocated from the private to the public sphere, with thousands of women cleaning hospitals and office blocks.

The major changes in women's work between 1945 and 1970 however must not be allowed to obscure the blatant sexism of this period. Women were discriminated against in training and employment. Dr Eurwen Gwynn was shortlisted for an appointment as a science lecturer at a technical college in Rugby but when she turned up for the interview she was sent away: they had not realized 'Eurwen' was a woman's name. Practices such as 'sexual harassment' existed long before they were labelled. Ceridwen Eluned Meese from Bagillt, who worked in offices in north Wales from the 1930s to the 1970s, experienced the 'laying-on of hands' several times, warning the offenders off by squealing and shouting. Finally, in this period of apparent women's gains in the world of work, there was one ominous sign threatening that archetypal female authority figure – the headmistress of a girls' grammar school. The coming of comprehensive schools from the 1960s, together with the practice of amalgamating boys' and girls' schools, was to lead to the end of the one avenue in which intelligent and able women had previously been able to fulfil their ambitions and their potential.

Home life

Housing was a huge problem at the end of the war. There was a chronic shortage and the war meant an even further deterioration of the old housing stock. Newly-weds faced the prospect of setting up home in rented rooms in their parents' or somebody else's house, while others were forced to squat. They took over Nissen huts on former naval bases and army camps from Holyhead to Barry Island, putting up with lack of heating and running water in their desperation for a home.

The Labour government's answer to the problem was rented council housing in both temporary and permanent buildings. Over 7,000 Portal houses, prefabricated, factory-made temporary dwellings, were erected in Wales by

1949, with an intended lifespan of ten years, but many 'pre-fabs' were occupied thirty years later. There were long waiting lists for council houses. In early 1948, Maesteg, for example, had a thousand families on its waiting list. Houses were supposed to be allocated by a points system but accusations were always rife that people were jumping the queue and that councillors pulled strings for their family and friends. For those who were fortunate enough to get a new council house, the benefits were immense. The houses were spacious, three-bedroomed, with bathrooms, separate kitchens and big gardens, while hot water on-tap and separate wash-houses made life easier for the housewife. Some up-market models, built in the 1950s, even had parquet flooring and french windows. Heating was still, of course, mainly by coal fires. But not every council house had all 'mod cons'. In many rural areas there was still no electricity and, in the mid-1950s, council houses in the Flintshire villages around Holywell were not connected to mains water: water had to be carried from standpipes. The downside of moving to a new council house, even with all the facilities, was moving away from a close-knit area, with uncles and aunts and parents all within just a few streets.

Between 1945 and 1951 an average of 8,250 houses was built each year in Wales, 87 per cent of them council houses. But, even in 1951, nearly half the families in Wales had to share a fixed bath with another family or use a tub in front of the fire and one household in seven had no kitchen sink at all. Conservative governments continued the house-building programme. Between 1951 and 1964 an average 13,500 houses a year were built, 63 per cent of them council houses. The percentage of council housing built in Wales was higher than in the rest of Britain and by the end of the 1960s, a quarter of the inhabitants of Wales lived on council estates. Between 1951 and 1971 there was a clearance programme of old houses with whole areas such as Cardiff's Butetown and Caernarfon's old town demolished, while grants improved over 200,000 houses providing their inhabitants with hot water, baths and indoor lavatories. Rural housing in particular was brought up to standard, with modern sanitation and old mud-walls replaced by brick.

Within the home, there were significant changes to the way women carried out their daily tasks. The widespread provision of pithead baths, following the nationalization of the coal industry in 1947, did away with the nightly chore of filling the tin bath with buckets and kettles of hot water, and the wider availability of domestic technology or labour-saving devices took much of the heavy drudgery out of housework.

The new domestic technology depended on a supply of electricity. This was slow to come to Wales. Many south Wales towns were only 'connected-up' in the early 1950s, but at least these had had the benefit of a domestic gas supply for heating and cooking. In rural Wales, the transition was more dramatic – from the open fire and the oil lamp to the benefits of electricity. The process of 'wiring up' farmhouses and cottages took place in the 1950s and in some cases the 1960s. Lighting was widely perceived as the main benefit, even if the average strength of bulbs in use was twenty-five watts, and only gradually did housewives buy electric gadgets. Minwel Tibbott's study of the impact of electricity on Welsh rural kitchens shows that the housewives' first priority was buying an electric iron, followed by vacuum cleaners (a surprising choice given the absence of fitted carpets), a wireless (radio) and an electric cooker. The latter was to change not only the way in which women cooked, but also the actual diet of rural Wales. Until the 1950s, many women continued to cook on the open fire and the iron range, while some of the more adventurous had purchased paraffin stoves, which enabled them to roast joints, bake puddings and produce 'new cakes', like Victoria sponges, queen cakes and maids of honour. Manufacturers emphasized the virtues of the electric cooker – it was clean and it was certain: the thermostatic control took the guesswork out of cookery. Demonstrators extolled the wonders of the Baby Belling or the Jackson Giant and rural housewives gradually shifted from a centuries-old style of cooking, from the pot of *cawl* over the hearth and the bakestone on the fire. Other appliances came later to both urban and rural Wales. Washing machines of the period were in fact far less labour saving than later models: their single tubs had to be both filled and emptied via a hose and the wet clothes emerged in a heavy tangled knot, with which the housewife had to wrestle. Many working-class as well as better-off women continued to use the local laundry, which sent back items washed, neatly ironed and wrapped in brown paper, while thousands of others continued using the wash-tub, the dolly and the mangle. But, by 1971, the majority of Welsh homes had a washing machine. Similarly, refrigerators, which had only been owned by 5 per cent of households in Wales in 1960, were installed in 60 per cent of homes by 1970. By then, a quarter of Welsh homes had central heating.

Domestic technology took the back-breaking element out of many tasks but it did not redistribute responsibility for housework. That remained women's role. Welsh men, many of whom still worked in heavy industry and came home tired out, continued to leave all domestic work to the women. Domestic technology allegedly speeded up housework, allowing women the time to go out to work to earn the money to buy more domestic appliances. But we should not exaggerate the impact of the electric appliances. A survey in 1955 showed that urban housewives spent fifty-six hours a week on domestic duties and that rural women spent fifty-two hours working indoors plus a further twenty-six hours on outside work. Housework expands to fill the time available. But

1950s Hoover washing machine with mangle.

Welsh fashion designer Mary Quant in 1960s mini skirt.

whichever way we view the issue, owning a vacuum cleaner certainly did not give women 'equality'.

Shopping changed too. For most of this period the woman went, with her shopping basket over her arm, often daily, to individual shops – to the grocer, the greengrocer, the butcher, the baker and the ironmonger. In the grocer's, for example, be it a family owned shop or part of a chain like the Sugar King, Home and Colonial or the Co-op, she stood at the counter and asked the shopkeeper for what she wanted. She bought butter from a huge yellow slab, biscuits from jars, loose tea and sugar, weighed out into blue bags, and bacon sliced from the flitch. By the 1960s, the shopping experience was undergoing a revolution as supermarkets, relatively small self-service stores in town centres, began to spring up. Here the housewife pushed her trolley around its cluttered aisles, loading it as she went not only with packaged butter, tea, sugar and bacon, but increasingly with her meat and vegetables too, before queuing to pay at the checkout. She did this 'big shop' weekly. Women saved for larger purchases or bought them on the 'never-never'. They bought clothes in shops, sometimes paid for at stratospheric interest rates by 'checks' issued by check companies, and paid off the debt at a shilling in the pound a week; they bought from 'packmen' coming around the doors, or they sent off for things from booming catalogue companies, again payable, over the odds, in instalments. Larger items, like three-piece suites were bought on hire purchase agreements taken out in the husband's name.

Marriage was more popular than ever in these years and women's age at marriage continued to drop until 1970. By 1975, the average age of marriage was twenty-two. In the 1950s, it was the norm for British women to spend only four years pregnant and nursing: the children were in school by the time women reached their early thirties. The theories of Bowlby (and his popularizers) on maternal deprivation and the preaching of educationalists at mothers to encourage discovery and creativity in their children could lead to an intense and claustrophobic relationship between mothers and children. By the time a woman reached thirty, she was often more than ready to go out to work in a part-time job. Part-time work for women with children was widely accepted by the 1960s, but there was a great media emphasis on 'latch-key' children. Official anxiety over the 'decline' of the family was never far from the surface in this whole period, though Rosser and Harris's study of Swansea, published in 1965, showed that the extended family was still alive and well there. Some 70 per cent of married sons and 80 per cent of married daughters continued to live in either the same part of the town as their parents, or in some other locality of Swansea, and over half the married daughters had seen their mothers in the last twenty-four hours. The mother was the pivot, around which all family life revolved – managing family affairs and demanding family cohesion. Mr Hughes, the first respondent interviewed by Rosser and Harris, shows the mother or 'the Mam' as the key figure: interestingly, he used the word 'Mam' to describe both his own mother and his wife. As the authors commented, 'The Mam is dead, long live the Mam.' Within the marriages of the younger generation, men probably did do a little more in the house, though it was still considered 'cissy' by many to be seen pushing a pram. The social life of the older generation remained segregated, with older men going out to their men-only clubs, but amongst the younger generation this period saw a shift to married couples going out together, to the pictures and, by the 1960s, even out to meals.

Leisure was revolutionized by television: by 1960, 60 per cent of Welsh homes had a television set and by 1969, 92 per cent. At first the only service was the BBC, but by the second half of the 1950s commercial television came to Wales, giving a further boost to consumerism. For women, television meant that they would at least sit down and take it easy – they did not all have labour-saving appliances – and it opened up a wider world to them. Leisure became increasingly secularized, though church and chapel continued to play an important role in the lives of many women and girls. By the 1950s, religious bodies tried to adapt to changing times and provided youth clubs, but the explosion of youth culture was not to be contained. Pop music was central to the new scene, with teenagers (a newly recognized category) rocking and rolling in the aisles to the music of Bill Haley and his Comets, when 'Rock Around the Clock' was shown in Welsh cinemas in 1956, and in the 1960s, getting swept up by Beatlemania. On the Welsh-language scene Parti Sciffl Llandygai and Dafydd Iwan shattered the myth that Welsh was strictly the language of hymns and arias. Young girls stopped dressing like their mothers and began to wear trousers, and even jeans, and the really daring in the 1960s wore Welsh designer Mary Quant's mini skirts. There was a new confidence amongst the young. In Carmarthen in 1962, three hundred teenagers, roughly half girls and half boys, staged a demonstration to press the council for a youth centre. Boys and girls may have looked more alike in their appearance, but strict gender divisions were not challenged. It may have been the 'swinging sixties' with laxer sexual mores, but unmarried mothers were still condemned or pitied in Wales. In asking Welsh women about their experiences of the 1960s, the common response is 'well it wasn't swinging around here. Perhaps in London'. The 1960s was also a time of teenage disillusionment with the establishment and of student revolt. In Wales these energies were chanelled into a variety of left-wing movements challenging the old class system and into the campaign to save the language, which was led by Cymdeithas yr Iaith.

Health

The National Health Service (NHS), established in 1948, brought in free treatment and free medicine: at last, women had the same right to free health care as men. The extent of women's ill health became evident as much untreated chronic illness came to light, notably gynaecological problems, thyroid deficiency, varicose veins and menopausal difficulties. For Welsh women, who had been prepared to soldier on despite ill health, the service was a godsend and they took advantage of it. People in Wales rushed to get free spectacles and false teeth. By June 1954, out of a population of two and a half million, 1,652,000 eye tests were followed by the supply of 1,826,000 pairs of glasses. False teeth were free, so at a time when many working-class people had lost all their own teeth by their twenties, they flocked to get their dentures: conservative dentistry was free only at first to those under sixteen, raised to twenty-one by the early 1950s. Of course, the availability of free medicines and dressings led to some abuses. Some women went to the doctor for free lint and cotton wool for non-medicinal purposes and the NHS Association of Welsh Executive Councils, meeting in Cardiff in 1953, was told, 'In one of the mining valleys, a woman has been hawking dressings, which she kept stored in suitcases, at a cut price.'

Among other important post-war improvements was the use of antibiotics, which almost totally eliminated childbirth fever and meant that tuberculosis (TB) was no longer a killer. In 1948, the number of new cases of TB diagnosed in Wales was 3,255: by 1968, there were just 587. More and more women had their babies in hospitals, now far safer places. In 1949, 50.5 per cent of all births in Wales took place in hospitals and, by 1968, the figure was 88 per cent.

Birth control for married women had become generally accepted by the 1950s, but responsibility for contraception remained largely the province of the man, with the sheath and withdrawal being the most commonly employed methods. The introduction of the contraceptive pill into Britain in 1961 marked a radical departure which gave women control over their own fertility. Birth control advice was only available however, for most of the period 1945–70, to married women, and unmarried women found access to the pill very difficult. Only by saying that they were planning to marry could single women obtain the pill. One male doctor in a Rhondda family planning clinic was aware that younger women who had no intention of marrying were coming in and that they were quite unashamed about coming forward. Only slowly was the principle of giving advice to unmarried women accepted. The Brook Advisory Centres, supported by the Family Planning Association, began giving such advice in England from 1964 and after 1969 advice was available through the National Health Service. But health risks associated with the pill meant that birth control advice could no longer be left to amateurs and in 1970 GPs took over, prescribing contraceptives through the NHS. It is difficult to assess the impact of the pill on female sexuality in Wales in the 1960s. It certainly made life easier for married women and enhanced relationships with their husbands. For single women, who were able to obtain it, the pill undermined the moral imperative of being a virgin on marriage and allowed them the freedom, hitherto a male preserve, to enter more lightly into sexual relationships without having marriage as their goal. On the other hand, the notion that permissiveness enhanced women's lives and 'liberated' them needs to be treated with caution. The removal of the fear of pregnancy put enormous pressure on girls to 'give in' to their boyfriends, who labelled them 'frigid' and 'odd' if they did not. In fact, as Angela Holdsworthy put it, 'what had appeared as a new way of women pleasing themselves had turned out to be yet another way of women pleasing men. All their new found sexual freedom had merely increased the pool of available crumpet.'

Illegitimacy rates were rising in Britain in the early 1960s. In Wales, where the increase in the rate was smallest, the rise was exclusively confined to teenage mothers. There is no reason to suppose that these pregnant Welsh teenagers were deliberately cocking a snook at convention. In fact a Cardiff welfare worker told the *Western Mail*, 2 December 1965, that: 'The greater number of girls are still terrifically shocked at finding they are pregnant. Only a very small percentage are the blasé, what-about-it sort. Their greatest concern is to shield their parents from it.' But it is against the background of rising illegitimacy rates and fears of a world population explosion (which had replaced the immediate post-war fears of falling population) that we must view changes in the law on abortion.

Abortion was illegal until 1967 but there were loopholes in the law and a legal judgement in 1938 had indicated that it was lawful to terminate a pregnancy to safeguard a woman's health and to prevent her becoming 'a physical or mental wreck'. In essence, before 1967, a woman could obtain an abortion if she could afford to pay for it. Peta Riley, a journalist writing in the *Western Mail*, 15 July 1966, looked at the cases of three Welsh women who sought abortions. One, apparently a single woman, had an abortion in distressing circumstances in a London flat, which cost 250 guineas. The second, a well-off married woman, who found she was pregnant just three months after the birth of her second child, was referred by her doctor to a private specialist: she had the abortion the next day in a comfortable private clinic, also at a cost of 250 guineas. The third woman, who was already the mother of three, suffered badly from arthritis and two slipped disks. Her own GP, anxious for her welfare, referred her to an NHS specialist in Cardiff. Here, not only was she refused an abortion, but she said, 'I was treated like dirt and spoken to like a criminal.' She was well aware that had she had the money, there would have been no problem: 'What makes it worse is the knowledge that if I had £300 to spare there would have been an entirely different attitude and the operation would have been done for the asking.' The Abortion Act of 1967, which came into force in 1968, allowed termination up to twenty-eight weeks, if two registered doctors agreed that were the pregnancy allowed to continue it would damage the mental and physical health of the mother or any existing children. Environmental and social factors could be taken into account to assess the health risk. Termination was also permitted if there was a substantial risk of physical or mental handicap in the unborn child. In Wales the inadequacy of the service meant that women had in some cases to travel to London or Birmingham for an abortion. The Act caused great controversy, and there were later moves to dilute it, but it was certainly not abortion on demand.

Education

The 1944 Education Act heralded in a new era. It provided secondary education for all, which was free from 1945, and raised the school leaving age to fifteen, a clause which was implemented in 1947. The new system was based on a rigid division between 'the able' and the 'less able' pupils. The able, those who passed the eleven-plus examination ('the scholarship', as it was widely known), went to grammar schools, while those who failed attended the newly created secondary modern schools, housed mainly in the old senior elementary schools which had been built as nineteenth-century board schools. In Wales a higher proportion of pupils went to grammar schools than in England. Central to the 1944 Act was the principle of equal opportunities, which meant allowing the ablest children, from whatever social class they came, to benefit from a grammar school education. But in the 1940s, in the absence of a strong feminist movement, equal opportunities took no account of gender. Detailed research is required to establish to what degree the selection process admitting girls and boys to grammar schools in the years after 1944 was gender-biased. In some areas of Wales there were more places available for boys than for girls and, if the evidence drawn from several English counties holds good for Wales, then it suggests that girls had to score higher marks in the eleven-plus examination than boys in order to win a place.

Girls' grammar schools in Wales offered a good academic education. Working-class girls were introduced to the world of the classics, foreign languages, literature, history, science and mathematics and they studied for O- and A-levels, which in the 1950s replaced the old matriculation exams. Modelled on minor public schools, the grammar schools (the old county schools renamed) were a world of gowned mistresses, prefects, the house system, rules, school uniforms – box-pleated gymslips, house girdles, shirts and ties, Burberries and school hats, hockey, lacrosse and netball and strict discipline, enforced by detention and 'lines'. The 1944 Act, and the Norwood Report (1943) on which it was based, made no distinctions on grounds of sex in the education offered to 'the able'. But in fact girls' grammar schools had inferior facilities to boys' schools, notably fewer and less well-equipped laboratories and not all girls' schools were able to offer physics as a subject. At O-level, by 1969–70, girls held their own with boys, but by A-level they lagged behind them, not because they had a higher failure rate, but because they entered for fewer subjects.

When it came to the 'less able', it was a very different story. The Norwood Report thought in terms of education for boys as future breadwinners and for girls as future wives and mothers. Later influential education reports carried on in the same vein. The Crowther Report of 1959 stated:

The incentive for girls to equip themselves for marriage and home making is genetic . . . her interest in dress, personal appearance and problems of human relations should be given a central place in her education.

The Newsom Report (1963), which was concerned with the needs of pupils of 'average and less than average ability', was couched in terms of educating girls to meet their 'main social function – which is to make for themselves, their children and their husbands a secure and suitable home and to be mothers'. The Report advocated, in addition to lessons in cooking, sewing and cleaning that each girl should run a flat (provided by the school) for a week and that children should be imported from infant schools for them to look after. This report could have been written in 1910. It contained no recognition that their childbearing role had been kaleidoscoped to a few years and that they would be available for paid work by their early thirties. Girls in many secondary modern schools were given no careers advice, and apart from domestic subjects, the only vocational training they were given was basic typing. Small wonder that the better-off sent their daughters to commercial colleges instead of secondary modern schools.

In 1969–70, only 19 per cent of boys and 23 per cent of girls in Britain went on to full-time further and higher education, but there was a marked difference in the kind of educational courses pursued by girls and boys. In further education more than half the girls did relatively low-level subjects such as shorthand and typing or hairdressing and in higher education more than half the girls went to teacher training colleges (colleges of education), compared with only one in six of the boys. In British universities in 1970, 30 per cent of undergraduates were female, against 70 per cent male.

Teacher training colleges in Wales provided a sound academic and pro-fessional training for young women. In the 1950s, students were allowed the opportunity to study one subject in depth and the two-year course was extended to three. In addition to their theoretical education studies, students 'practised' as teachers in local schools. In some respects colleges were run very like schools. Principal Ellen Evans at Barry, for example, regarded herself as *in loco parentis,* and regularly lectured her charges on behaviour: students wore college uniform with its brown and cream blazer and there was a system of college 'mothers', whereby a senior student looked after a junior. Rules were strict: in the early 1950s students had to be in by 8 p.m. on weekdays and 10 p.m. on weekends. All the women's training colleges in Wales fostered a camaraderie and an *esprit de corps,* which old students remembered with affection. Though, sadly, as has already been pointed out, English schools were to be the main beneficiaries of these women's expertise.

The University of Wales and its halls of residence continued to run a strict regime with regard to women students, only gradually relaxing rules in the 1960s. Men students far outnumbered women, though the number of women students rose significantly (Table 5.2). As postgraduates women fared worse (Table 5.3).

Table 5.2: University of Wales, full-time undergraduates

	Males	Females		Total
	No.	No.	%	No.
1947	3544	1218	25.6	4762
1957	3261	1436	30.6	4697
1967	6984	3655	34.4	10639

Table 5.3: University of Wales, full-time postgraduate students

	Males	Females		Total
	No.	No.	%	No.
1947	108	22	17.0	130
1957	562	179	24.0	741
1967	1421	519	26.7	1940

Girls opted mainly for Arts subjects, though there was some increase in their entering the sciences in the 1960s. It was far easier to get a university place with science A-levels but girls seemed less aware of future careers than boys when making A-level choices. The University of Wales remained male-dominated throughout the period 1945–70, both in terms of staff and students. Nor did women have much say in student politics in these years. It was extremely difficult for young women to gain places at Oxford or Cambridge, with only the small women's colleges admitting them. Medical schools continued to take only small quotas of women students.

Girls and women made some good progress in these years but they were clearly discriminated against at every level of education. Yet there was no clear understanding of the process of discrimination or even a language to express it in. In Wales we had to wait until the women's movement of the 1970s to appreciate the effects of 'sexism' in school textbooks and readers and to see how teachers and the system perpetuated gender-stereotyping.

Politics and issues

The 1950s marked the nadir of British feminism. In fact, what passed for 'feminism' then – not that they used the word – was a woolly set of aspirations based on women's 'special values', namely the promotion of world peace, democracy, good citizenship and partnership within marriage. The aim of the older generation of feminists to win equal rights was written off as old-fashioned, aggressive and irrelevant. As the old campaigners in Wales died off – Mary Collin in 1955, Lady Rhondda and Professor Barbara Foxley in 1958, and Edith Picton-Turbervill in 1960, there was no one to take their place. In terms of Welsh feminism, there was a vacuum between the end of the war and the early 1970s, when the Women's Liberation Movement, the second great feminist wave of the twentieth century, burst onto the scene (see chapter 6).

Throughout the period covered by this chapter, women's organizations promoted good citizenship and concentrated primarily on women's special domain of the home. Branches of the Electrical Association of Women and the Women's Gas Federation, both essentially organizations to promote the utilities, opened throughout Wales. When, in 1952, the upper Rhondda branch of the Gas Federation opened, its chairman [*sic*], Mrs Evans, pointed out that domestic appliances had freed women to 'take their rightful place in civic affairs' (*Rhondda Leader*, 16 February 1952), but attending talks and cookery demonstrations run by the gas board can hardly be classed as participating in civic affairs. The WI continued to raise issues affecting rural women's lives from cuts in rail services, the slow process of electrification and road safety to cervical cancer screening. The minute books of the Pembrokeshire Federation show members actively concerned with farming issues, particularly the control of Foot and Mouth Disease in 1967 and the eradication of brucellosis. Organizations like the WI and the Townswomen's Guild (TG) performed social, fund-raising and educational functions, but avoided narrowly political issues, this despite the fact that the TG was founded in 1928 out of the old National Union of Women's Suffrage Societies with the express purpose of politically educating women. One campaign which both organizations supported in the early 1960s, was that to remove turnstiles – a real obstacle to large ladies – from women's public lavatories. As Mary Stott commented, 'this battle may have a faintly comic ring now but the campaign did show how much persistence is needed to remove a grievance which affects only the female sex'. The Women's Co-operative Guild, which had campaigned against the dependent status of women as built into the legislation of the Welfare State, also advocated divorce law reform, but by the 1950s the guild was dwindling in numbers and its membership ageing. Of the political parties in Wales, the

Labour Party had the largest women's organization, with a network of women's sections, but by the 1950s these were in decline. In east Denbighshire, for example, there had been twenty-two women's sections in 1945 but by 1961 there were only ten. But, if the 1950s and much of the 1960s marked a low ebb in feminism, by the late 1960s clearly feminist issues were again beginning to emerge. The issue of equal pay, highlighted by the strike of women workers at Ford's Dagenham plant in 1968, meant renewed political involvement by women and was to tie in with the demands of the new Women's Liberation Movement, which was emerging in England.

The pioneers would have been disappointed at the slow progress of Welsh women in parliament. Megan Lloyd George held Anglesey from 1929 to 1951 as an independent-minded Liberal. In the 1950s she campaigned actively for a parliament for Wales and regained her place at Westminster when, standing for Labour, she won Carmarthen in a by-election in 1957. She held the seat in three further elections until her death in 1966. Eirene Lloyd Jones was another daughter of a famous political father, Thomas Jones, former cabinet secretary. She stood unsuccessfully as Labour candidate for Flint in 1945. In 1950 however, now married, Eirene White was elected for East Flint, which she held until 1970, before going to the House of Lords. A well-educated woman and with experience in journalism, she worked hard to represent this industrial seat. Though always denying that she ever encountered discrimination, she followed a feminist agenda. On entering parliament in 1950 she won fifth place in the private members ballot and took up a bill to liberalize the divorce laws. She came under pressure from the Labour Party hierarchy to drop this contentious measure, and withdrew the bill when the government offered a Royal Commission on Divorce. Also in 1950, another woman was elected as a Labour MP. Unlike Megan Lloyd George or Eirene White, she was not the daughter of a famous man. Dorothy Rees was a docker's daughter, who had won a scholarship to Barry County School and then trained as a teacher at the local training college. She was elected as MP for Barry in a three-cornered fight in 1950. She had been elected to Glamorgan County Council in 1934 and, though sadly she lost her parliamentary seat in a straight fight with the Conservatives in 1951, she returned to Glamorgan Council. She was a great advocate of the education of girls and Glamorgan benefited from her experience. For a period of just one year Wales had had three women MPs. But after the defeat of Dorothy Rees in 1951, and the death of Lady Megan in 1966, by the late 1960s Wales once again only had one woman MP. The House of Lords finally admitted women peers in 1958 but it came too late for Lady Rhondda.

The women MPs, while no longer a novelty, were still regarded as exceptional. None of them had children. The more normal role women played in mixed organizations, from chapels to political parties, was that of subordinates: men still made the decisions, while women still made the tea.

Women in Plaid Cymru, as in the other political parties, were the organizers of jumble sales and coffee mornings, but, perhaps surprisingly, it was Welsh-speaking women who were the first to appear in the vanguard of political activity in the 1960s. By the early 1960s, the fate of the language was balanced on a knife-edge. The 1961 Census showed that only 20.9 per cent of the people of Wales could speak Welsh. Welsh had virtually no public status. Road signs were in English; the Post Office, local government and the utilities produced only monoglot forms and bills and there were just a few hours of Welsh on television each week; the only public buildings with notices in Welsh outside were Welsh churches and chapels. Wales was being treated with contempt as was shown by the decision to flood Tryweryn to provide water for Liverpool. Saunders Lewis in a ground-breaking radio lecture, 'Tynged yr Iaith' ('Fate of the Language'), drew attention to the plight of the language and this, in turn, led to the formation of Cymdeithas yr Iaith (The Language Society). Women, many very young, played an important and active part in the non-violent direct action campaigning of the society from the 1960s onwards. Gwyneth Wiliam was the first of many women to be imprisoned and Eileen Beasley, together with her husband, had inspired the movement. Women formed an integral part of the Society. As Angharad Tomos stated,

> Take the women from Cymdeithas, and it wouldn't be the same movement at all. That's why, come to think of it, we've never had a 'women's section' in Cymdeithas. Because if we did form such a group, what would you call the rest?

Although women in the early years did not hold 'high office' in Cymdeithas yr Iaith, the ratio of men to women in the executive committee was balanced and women had a record equal to the men in terms of direct action. It was the language that politicized these women. Nor was it only young women who were stirred to action. In 1967 Zonia Bowen left the WI to form the Welsh-speaking organization, Merched y Wawr, with its first branch at Y Parc, Bala.

Conclusion

The years 1945–70, taken as a whole, formed an oppressive period in women's history. There was a great emphasis on women's role as the housewife and, as housewives, women were told that they were equal and free from drudgery, thanks to electrical appliances. Liberation in the 1950s, meant owning a vacuum cleaner. Alongside the domestic emphasis, the 1960s brought a new dimension to women's oppression. The 'swinging sixties', while admittedly removing the fear of unwanted pregnancy from sexual relations and enabling some heterosexual women uninhibitedly to enjoy their sexuality, had a downside too. Not only were young women subjected to increased pressure to go 'the whole way', but the sexual revolution of that decade both objectified and trivialized women. Women publicly became sex objects. In addition to television and magazine advertisements featuring Katie, the Oxo housewife, and Persil Mums, there were other advertisements displaying the bodies of scantily clad women, which were used to sell everything from underwear to tyres and cars. With their glossy lips, long stockinged legs and floating shining hair, women had become an advertiser's gimmick and an emblem of male status and spending power. But neither the perfect housewife nor the sex symbol were real women. In fact, both left real women ill at ease, but only in the period covered by the next chapter of this book did women begin to understand their feelings of unease and to articulate what was going wrong. How could anything have gone wrong? They were free and equal weren't they? Only in the 1970s in Britain did women begin to grapple with what American writer Betty Frieden called the 'problem with no name'. In the 1960s all women's problems remained nameless and no one spoke about battered women, discrimination at work or in the legal and tax systems, sexism in education or sex stereotyping. In Britain, a growing feminist consciousness and influences from the USA, together with a rising tide of anger about equal pay, would turn vague stirrings of discontent into a new mass feminist movement in the 1970s.

~ 6 ~
Sisterhood is Powerful,
1970–1999

THE last thirty years of the twentieth century witnessed more radical and sweeping changes in the lives of women in Wales than did the previous seventy years put together. Many of the seeds of change had already been sown by 1970, but the process was rapidly accelerated both by the transformation of Wales itself from an industrial to a post-industrial economy and by women's own demands and actions. Wales has changed out of all recognition. Gone are the old heavy industries. Steel plants closed down, Ebbw Vale and East Moors in Cardiff in 1978 and Shotton in 1980, the last named marking the single biggest job loss Europe had ever seen, while other works were severely trimmed back. Coal-mining, the core activity of old industrial Wales, went the same way. Pits were closed throughout the 1970s but even so, in 1984, there were still 20,000 miners employed in twenty-eight collieries in south Wales. It was the bitter miners' strike of 1984–5 and its vindictive crushing by politically-motivated Prime Minister Margaret Thatcher that spelt the demise of coal-mining in south Wales. By the end of the 1980s, there were just seven deep pits in the south Wales coalfield, and by 1999 just one, the worker-owned Tower Colliery. Similarly, north Wales saw the closure of its coalfield and the rundown of the slate industry. Old industrial Wales, with its jobs for men in heavy industry and the most macho perception of what constituted 'work' of any area of Britain, was dismantled. The new Welsh post-industrial economy, with its growing service sector, created the conditions for women's rapidly increasing participation in the workforce.

But women were not merely the passive beneficiaries of changes in the economic structure of Wales. Women were themselves the agents of change. In the early 1970s, in Wales as in England, women rose up and spoke out against the whole male-dominated edifice of society and culture and challenged the sexist assumptions on which they were based. Feminism, long thought to be dead and buried, re-emerged in the second great twentieth-century wave of women's protest, the Women's Liberation Movement (WLM). The movement exposed and brought to public attention the existence of widespead dis-crimination against women and made vociferous demands for fundamental change. Though feminist activists in the 1970s and 1980s constituted only a small minority of women in Wales, just as they had in the first wave of the women's movement before the First World War, their actions would lead to changes which would have a profound influence on the lives of almost all women in Wales. We cannot begin to understand our history over the last thirty years unless we look first at the part played by the women's movement.

Women's movements

In the early 1970s, the growing frustration of women in Wales against their powerlessness in a particularly male and macho society found an outlet in the WLM. The women's protest, which had erupted in America and England in the late 1960s, was taken up in Wales at first by a relatively small group of women who began to organize local groups. 'Consciousness-raising' and action groups were formed in Cardiff, Swansea, Aberystwyth, Pontypridd, Newport, Bangor, Lampeter, Harlech, Abergavenny and elsewhere. Welsh feminists read the new wave of revolutionary women's magazines and seminal texts such as Kate Millet's *Sexual Politics* (1969) and Shulamith Firestone's *Dialectic of Sex* (1970). They also read Elaine Morgan's, from Mountain Ash, feminist bible, *The Descent of Woman* (1972). The publication of this key text, which questions male-centred theories of evolution, made this Pontypridd- and Oxford-educated Welsh woman one of the stars of international feminism, but it was through her television dramatizations of the lives of Vera Brittain and Marie Curie that she brought feminist role models into millions of homes. The WLM sought to remove the barriers to full participation and success in education, at work and in public life. In Wales women had their work cut out. Writing in 1972 in *Planet*, Beata Lipman noted that in Wales everything functions 'on the fundamental premise that the men and the boys do the leading and most of the thinking, the women bring up the supportive tea-making rear.'

Welsh women campaigned on the four initial demands of the WLM (i.e. equal pay; equal education and opportunity; twenty-four-hour nurseries; free contraception and abortion on demand) and on a whole range of other issues. In Cardiff, for example, abortion was high on the agenda and members of Cardiff Women's Action Group (CWAG) focused on the fact that although a 'lunch-time abortion centre' had been opened at the Heath Hospital in 1973, it was scarcely used; there were demonstrations and marches in 1975, 1979 and 1981 against various parliamentary attempts to dilute the 1967 Abortion Act. CWAG was also active in promoting the issue of equal pay and campaigning against discrimination in the workplace: following a major conference

Women's Rights Committee for Wales march against women's unemployment, 1982. *Left to right*: Oonagh Hartnett, Gwen Awbery, Gertie Tuck, Stella Garrett Jones, Charles Jackson.

Swansea Women's Aid members taking part in a demonstration in Birmingham in support of refuges for battered women, 1976. *Front*: Jenny Lynn (standing) and Rose Barnes (in wheelchair).

organized by CWAG and the National Council for Civil Liberties in Cardiff in 1974, the Women's Rights Committee for Wales (WRCW) was set up to act as a pressure group and a source of information on both the Equal Pay Act (1970) and Sex Discrimination Act (1975). The WRCW, which attracted many older members as well as women in their twenties and thirties, also organized high-profile events, including the March Against Women's Unemployment, which set out from Pontypridd in September 1982, after a rousing speech by veteran 1930s hunger marcher Dora Cox, to Cardiff. Nurseries were urgently needed and there were campaigns in Aberystwyth and Swansea to establish them. The contribution of Mudiad Ysgolion Meithrin, the Welsh Language Nursery School Movement, set up in 1971 to provide Welsh-language education to young children, is usually assessed only in terms of its promotion of the Welsh language, but it played a vital role too in actually providing nurseries: by the mid 1990s, there were over a thousand nursery groups operating under its umbrella. As the 1970s progressed, the WLM in Wales took on an ever broadening range of issues. One of the most important of these was 'batteredwomen'. It was the Women's Aid movement in Wales that brought the age-old problem of wife-beating out into the open. Cardiff Women's Aid was founded in 1974 and by 1975 had set up its first refuge. In 1977, Swansea women opened the city's first refuge in Morriston and in the same year the national organization Welsh Women's Aid was created: by 1992, there were thirty-five refuges and thirteen information centres throughout Wales. Women's Aid is one of the greatest legacies of the Welsh women's movement. By the late 1970s, women's centres, which acted as meeting places and became focal points for a wide range of operations, had been set up: the Swansea Women's Centre, which is still running, opened in 1979 and the Cardiff Women's Centre in 1981. By the early 1980s, groups in Wales were focusing on such matters as rape, pornography and other aspects of violence against women, but one issue above all was to predominate, the campaign against nuclear weapons. But before turning to the protest at Greenham Common, we need to assess how widely the WLM was taken up by women across Wales.

Just like the early suffrage movement, the WLM was strongest in urbanized south-east Wales and its members were primarily young, educated middle-class women. But there are dangers in generalizing: in Swansea, for example, there was a strong working-class presence. Women who had moved into Wales and made their homes here played a leading role, such as Gill Boden, Jane Hutt and Oonagh Hartnett in Cardiff, but other CWAG members were Welsh-born and some were Welsh speakers. CWAG attracted women from Barry and Cowbridge as well as Pontypridd and the Valleys. There were groups throughout Wales, particularly in university towns. By 1984, Bangor Women's

Enterprise Bureau could produce the *Wales Women's Directory*, with sixty-one pages of listings of women's groups, organizations and businesses throughout the country. Nor was feminist literature an exclusively English-language affair. In 1975, Gwasg Gomer, a traditionalist Welsh publisher, produced *Asen Adda* (Adam's Rib), edited by Ruth Stephens, a collection of feminist sociological essays which urged readers to take matters into their own hands since 'this was our battle about our rights'. The magazine *Rhiannon*, which first appeared in 1977, was a feminist publication produced by and for women in Wales and contained Welsh as well as English-language articles.

Belonging to the WLM – though there were no membership cards and lists in this informal milieu – gave women a sense of solidarity and of confidence. As the badges worn at the time said, 'Sisterhood is Powerful' and 'The Future is Female'. In this supportive setting lesbian women in Wales felt comfortable about 'coming out' and some became involved in gay liberation campaigns. Again such activity was not confined to south-east Wales: CYLCH (Cymdeithas y Lesbiaid a Hoywon Cymraeg eu Hiaith/Society of Welsh-Speaking Lesbians and Gay Men) was set up in Aberystwyth and Border Women/Merched y Ffin in Ludlow, as a contact point for rural gay women. There have always been lesbians in Wales: the WLM enabled them to become visible.

Feminism took a new direction in the early 1980s. Welsh women, young and old, had long been active in the Campaign for Nuclear Disarmament (CND), but against the background of the WLM, a new women's peace movement, Women For Life on Earth (WFLOE), was born. It was the decision in 1979 to site cruise missiles at Greenham Common airbase in Berkshire – which galvanized women into action. Ann Pettit from Llanpumsaint organized a march from Cardiff to Greenham in August 1981. The thirty-six women, four men and a few children arrived at Greenham Common on 5 September. When they arrived, several women chained themselves to the fence and from this action grew the notion of a women's peace camp. Though widely attacked by the press as unwashed, unfeminine women, who had abandoned their children, the Greenham Common camp caught the imagination of women throughout Britain and the world. Actions such as 'Embracing the Base', December 1982, attracted 30,000 women, many of them older and many from Wales, who surrounded the perimeter fence, pinning to it family photographs and babies' clothes as symbols of life: Thalia Campbell of Borth produced a series of exquisite women's peace banners for use at this and other demonstrations. Greenham was a focal point for Welsh women, both Welsh and English speaking, and many were imprisoned for their actions there. Angharad Tomos's *Yma o Hyd* (1985) is a powerful account, based on personal experience, of a young Welsh woman imprisoned in an English jail. Helen Thomas, a 23-year-old woman

'Babies against the Bomb' demonstration, 1982.

from Newcastle Emlyn, and a dedicated Welsh-language activist as well as a peace campaigner, was killed at Greenham in 1989 by a police vehicle. There were women's peace actions in Wales too. Susan Lamb and four other local women set up a 'peace camp' in Porth, chaining themselves to railings on the town square in November 1981 and the nuclear-submarine tracking base at Brawdy in Pembrokeshire became the focus of marches and the site of a peace camp. Similarly the ROF in Llanishen, Cardiff, was the site of a peace vigil and demonstrations.

The next mass protest by Welsh women took place in the Valleys of south Wales, in support of the miners' strike against pit closures in 1984–5. Fear and anger that the Conservative government's policy would lead to the destruction of their communities, impelled women to action. Though there was a long tradition of women supporting the men in industrial action, which included not only running soup kitchens but attacking 'scabs' and 'blacklegs' and getting arrested by the police, this time the women went further. They organized, as never before. They set up a network of women's support groups throughout the coalfield. They raised funds, ran food centres and soup kitchens, addressed public meetings throughout Britain and stood alongside

Maerdy, Rhondda, women's support group in the strike of 1984–5.

the men on picket lines. On the western side of the south Wales coalfield, women from Onllwyn and Seven Sisters were involved in running nine food distribution centres in the Neath, Dulais and Swansea valleys, where they distributed 1,100 food parcels a week. They rose at 4 a.m. to picket coal mines, steelworks and power stations and at Cynheidre they occupied the pit-head baths. In some areas there was initial reluctance by the men to accept the women. In Abertillery, the first barrier women had to break down was to gain entry to the men-only miners' institute. As one local woman wrote in Jill Miller's *You Can't Kill the Spirit* (1986), 'What a breakthrough it was getting into that institute. People were amazed. They thought we were bloody wonderful just getting our feet through the door.' The Abertillery women went on to set up a soup kitchen, a welfare group to advise on financial problems, and to join the picket lines. In many valleys the strike brought a new respect for women. In other places men felt threatened by this new demonstration of women's power. At Markham in the Sirhowy Valley, the men refused to allow women onto picket lines, so the women split off and continued raising funds and collecting food. As Hilary Rowlands told Glenys Kinnock:

> I never really got to find out why they resented us doing our own thing but they may have thought we were going to take their power away . . . I think they were afraid of our growing power and influence.

Protest by Cymdeithas yr Iaith in London.

The strike gave women confidence in themselves. Some went on to set up co-operative businesses and others, like Hilary Rowlands, went to University; yet others trained at the Dove Workshop in Banwen, which was set up following the strike. Shortly after the miners' strike ended, women in Blaenau Ffestiniog formed a support group and played a prominent role in the Slate Quarry Dispute of 1985–6.

Meanwhile the women activists in Cymdeithas yr Iaith (CyI) continued with direct action and gained a growing prominence in the movement. In 1981 Meri Huws became the first woman chair and by 1988, Rosanne Reeves commented that the society 'had been virtually taken over by women'. There are strong similarities between the experiences of the women of CyI and the Greenham women. Indeed some women were involved in both groups and women were imprisoned for both causes. For some, imprisonment in the cause of the language raised consciousness of a broader oppression of all women. Menna Elfyn wrote:

A law breaking dreamer, I eventually went to prison myself as a language activist, but came out a feminist. Imprisonment brought home to me the existence of another silenced war, waged this time against women.

Public demonstrations had made women visible: in the 1980s they also 'found a voice' through film-making and publishing. Red Flannel, a women's collective, was set up. It showed feminist films and videos to women in Valleys' towns as a stimulus to discussion and also produced its own works. Their best-known film is *Mam* (1988), which examined the role of that stereotypical icon 'Mam', and disentangled myth from reality. Boadicea Films, another all-women group, produced *I'll Be Here for All Time* (1985) showing women's involvement in protest from food riots in 1790s Pembrokeshire to Greenham Common. Running a publishing house, like film-making, had hitherto been a male preserve but in the 1980s two Welsh feminist imprints were launched. Women-write Press was short-lived but produced the useful *Women in Wales: A Documentary History of Our Times* (1987), a snapshot of women's contemporary activities. Honno has proved more enduring and is committed to publishing books by and about women in Wales. Beginning with the publication of the autobiography of Crimean-war nurse Betsi Cadwaladr, and Hafina Clwyd's autobiographical *Buwch ar y Lein*, both in 1987, Honno has gone on to publish novels and short stories by contemporary women writers, autobiographical accounts by 'ordinary' Welsh women and reprints of long out-of-print Welsh- and English-language classics.

Many of the women's actions, particularly in the 1970s, had been on the radical fringe, but, by the mid 1980s, women were gaining a toe-, if not a foot-, hold in more mainstream organizations. The Wales TUC Women's Advisory Committee was set up in 1984 and South Glamorgan Women's Committee, the only local government body of its kind in Wales, in 1985. The activist 'cells' of the 1970s gave way to more 'respectable' organizations such as the Wales Assembly of Women, founded in 1984, to report on the United Nations' Conference on Women held in Nairobi in 1985 and to provide a Welsh perspective. Women's Studies courses (see section on education below) began to come in from the cold and were offered in universities and colleges in Wales. Other bastions of male authority began to crack in the 1990s. The struggle for women to be admitted to the priesthood in Wales was long and hard. Whereas in England, the measure for the ordination of women was passed in 1992 and the first women priests were ordained in 1994, in Wales a small number of priests prevented women's admission to the priesthood in the vote on the issue in 1994. The measure permitting Welsh women to become priests was eventually passed in 1996. By the late 1990s, when respectable organizations and pressure groups represented the public face of feminism in Wales, women made a major breakthrough in another jealously guarded male arena, politics.

The law and politics

The 1970s saw the passage of two important Acts which were to benefit women. The first was the Equal Pay Act (EPA), 1970. This was an essential piece of legislation to comply with European law, if Britain was to enter the European Economic Community (EEC). Britain joined the EEC in 1973 and the EPA came into force in 1975. It provided for equal pay for the same or similar work or work which had been rated as equal by an evaluation scheme. This Act was amended in 1984 to include work of equal value, again to bring Britain in line with Europe. The Sex Discrimination Act (SDA) of 1975 made discrimination on the grounds of sex illegal in the areas of employment, education, advertising or when providing housing, goods, services or facilities. This Act also made it unlawful to discriminate in employment and in advertising jobs against people because they were married. Under the terms of the SDA, the Equal Opportunities Commission (EOC) was set up to oversee the implementation and workings of the SDA itself and the EPA; to promote equal opportunities; and to fight cases of discrimination. Various other Acts and European Community (EC) Directives from the 1970s to the 1990s sought to improve the position of part-time workers and to mitigate the effects of pregnancy and childbearing on women's working lives.

It is impossible to bring about fundamental social change by legislation alone but major changes have taken place since the early 1970s. In those days, employers advertised for barmen, waiters and *male* accountants and journalists, while a man and a woman serving in the same shop were paid different rates for exactly the same work. Although the SDA was widely ridiculed at first, employers came to recognize that they had to comply with the law and there is now widespread disapproval of those who blatantly discriminate against women. Some traditionally male-dominated organizations, such as the police, have found it difficult to adapt and the employment of women officers, in, for example, the South Wales Police, remains below the British average. The EOC in Wales has to confront an old-fashioned culture. Fewer discrimination cases are brought by women in Wales and fewer are won than in other parts of Britain. Industrial tribunals here may decide that an employer has acted 'reasonably' in dismissing a pregnant woman without, as Teresa Rees, EOC commissioner for Wales, pointed out, 'understanding the complexity of the concept of discrimination especially indirect discrimination'. Equal opportunities still have a long way to go in Wales.

Women are the majority sex in Wales – a fact that has not been reflected in their political representation. From 1970, when Eirene White, MP for East Flintshire, was elevated to the House of Lords, until 1984, when Ann Clwyd won a by-election in the Cynon Valley, not a single woman represented a Welsh constituency. From 1984 to 1997, Ann Clwyd remained the sole female representative from Wales in the House of Commons: in those years she was, in effect, MP for women in Wales. Beata Lipman, writing in 1972, said:

> In politics the situation is bathetic: Labour without a single woman Member of the House representing Wales, the Blaid feebly forming a woman's committee to

try and repair huge gaping omissions. Both Tory and Labour are well beyond their first, able suffragettes who decided that the only way to have a career was to give up children or a husband; it seems to me that the feminist position in both parties has been steadily eroding ever since, in Wales at any rate.

Two factors, however, were to bring about change, albeit slowly, notably the rise of the WLM and the reaction of political parties in Wales to successive Conservative governments, from 1979–97. In its early days the radical, anti-establishment WLM had not placed a high priority on the representation of women in government, either local or national. From the late 1970s, things began to change as feminists sought a political base in both Plaid Cymru and the Labour Party. The apparently unassailable position of the Tory government, winning victory after victory under Margaret Thatcher, made these parties more open to women's ideas in an attempt to broaden their appeal. In Plaid Cymru, feminists from south-east Wales transformed the role of the party's women's section and secured extra representation on its working party from 1981–6. In the Labour Party too, women's sections grew. But none of this resulted in the increased representation of women at Westminster. Male-dominated selection committees in all parties simply did not select women. It was not until 1997 that a significant advance came, when the Labour Party introduced positive discrimination in the form of women only shortlists in half the party's winnable and safe seats. This enabled Labour to increase its representation from one woman MP to four, with the election of Julie Morgan in Cardiff North, Jackie Lawrence in Preseli and Betty Williams in Conwy. While this increase was dramatic, in 1997 women still only held four out of forty Welsh parliamentary seats.

Women have done better in getting selected for and elected to the European Parliament, perhaps because all political parties have regarded Strasbourg as less important than Westminster. Beata Brookes won the North Wales seat in 1979 for the Conservatives and held it until 1989. Ann Clwyd served her apprenticeship in Strasbourg, where she sat as MEP for Mid and West Wales 1979–84. Glenys Kinnock has been MEP for South Wales East and Eluned Morgan for Mid and West Wales since 1994. Jill Evans, one of Plaid Cymru's first two MEPs, was elected in 1999.

In local government women remain grossly under-represented. In 1998 just 25 per cent of local authority members were women. Only Torfaen (39 per cent), Cardiff (36 per cent) and Wrexham (31 per cent) had a female membership of over 30 per cent, while at the other end of the scale, Ceredigion and Ynys Môn had just 5 per cent and Newport 8.5 per cent. Such under-representation means that issues of concern to women are simply not raised.

The picture is similar for non-elected public bodies, the quangos, where, in 1997 women made up 25 per cent of board members and held only 14 per cent of 'chairs'.

The real breakthrough did not come until 1999, the very last year of the century, with the first elections to the new National Assembly for Wales. Women won twenty-four (40 per cent) of the sixty seats. Fifteen are held by Labour women, who make up just over half their party's twenty-eight Assembly members, six by Plaid Cymru women, or a third of their party's seventeen places; three, or half, of the Liberal Democrats' six seats are held by women. The Conservative Party has no female Assembly members. The gender-mix of the Assembly means that for the first time women have a strong and visible presence in the Welsh political arena. This is due mainly to the large female Labour Party contingent. Labour women, including the four MPs, fought, against strong opposition, for the policy of 'twinning', whereby adjacent constituencies are twinned and one is required to select a woman. It was this process that laid the ground for their success. It is a particularly noteworthy achievement that women were appointed to fill half the seats in Wales's first cabinet with Christine Gwyther as secretary for agriculture; Edwina Hart, finance; Jane Hutt, health; and Rosemary Butler, education and children. Other women hold high office in the minority Labour administration, notably Jane Davidson and Val Feld.

Education

At the beginning of the 1970s boys outperformed girls in attaining educational qualifications. It was widely presumed by those whose thinking was stuck in the mid-nineteenth century that this was the result of superior male intelligence. Feminists, however, identified a quite different reason for this state of affairs – sexism. A series of studies in the 1970s clearly demonstrated widespread sex-role stereotyping in children's books and showed that teachers had different behavioural expectations of boys and girls. In readers for the very young, John dug the garden and helped Daddy wash the car, while Janet helped Mummy dust and vacuum. Illustrations in science textbooks depicted boys actively carrying out experiments, while girls looked on admiringly. Hidden cameras showed teachers giving far more time to boys than to girls, and allowing, and even encouraging, boys to be assertive, while girls behaving in the same way were reprimanded and punished. There were boys' and girls' subjects in both primary and secondary schools. Boys did woodwork, metal-work and technical drawing: girls did needlework and domestic science.

Mathematics, physics and chemistry, the hard sciences, were similarly viewed as boys' subjects, whereas biology, languages and the arts were for girls. It is scarcely surprising that girls did badly in the areas of mathematics, science and technology. The evidence for this all-pervasive gender-stereotyping was overwhelming and the SDA (1975) made it illegal to offer separate girls' and boys' subjects. Though many schools in Wales were slow to adapt, the old system, where all girls compulsorily sewed peg-bags and all boys hacked out pipe-racks, became a thing of the past. Efforts were made to encourage girls into the sciences and other traditional 'boys' subjects'. Although many girls still opt for arts subjects, the improvement in their achievements has been remarkable. By 1991, girls in Wales achieved a higher success rate in forty-six (out of sixty) GCSE subjects than boys. In Gwynedd, in the same year, 54 per cent of pupils going on to A-level were girls and, in turn, 57 per cent of all A-level students going on to higher education were girls. Young women have taken increasing advantage of higher education. By the mid-1990s, the numbers of male and female undergraduates in the University of Wales, in stark contrast to the immediate post-war period, were roughly equal and by the end of the 1990s women undergraduates actually outnumbered men: at postgraduate level women form 47 per cent of students. Mature students have also benefited. The development of access courses has opened the doors of higher education to many women. One interesting development is Women's Studies. From small beginnings in the 1970s, by the 1980s Women's Studies courses, which challenged the male-centred learning of the traditional curriculum, began to appear as options on degree courses in higher educational establishments in Wales: by 1988 University College, Cardiff launched its pioneering master's degree in Women's Studies and other courses have followed.

However, women's educational success has not been reflected in the job market. Although this is in part the result of the male culture of the workplace, it is also a function of women's subject choices. Women tend still, despite initiatives to encourage them into science, technology and engineering, to choose arts-based academic subjects, which are non-vocational, though the numbers of women following courses in law, business studies and medicine has greatly increased in the past two decades. In further education, girls are far less likely than boys to be sponsored by employers in day-release schemes and to obtain apprenticeships. This also hinders them in the job market and means that many are employed below their potential. At the very bottom of the pile are the girls (and boys) who leave school with no educational qualifications at all. In 1995–6, 9 per cent of girls and 12 per cent of boys entered the job market with no leaving qualification.

Employment

Women's participation in the Welsh workforce increased rapidly over the whole period 1970–99, despite the recession of the early 1980s, which led to a rise in women's unemployment. Table 6.1 shows women's rising economic activity rates from the 1970s to the 1990s. The table shows not only the rise of the female rate but the decline of the male rate. In the 1980s, these developments led to much anxious talk of the feminization of the Welsh workforce, and to fears that traditional gender roles would be reversed with women as breadwinners and men as homemakers. Professor Gwyn Williams predicted that by 1990 women would make up the majority of the Welsh workforce. Though this has not yet happened, women have certainly entered employment in unprecedented numbers and now form an integral part of the workforce. The disappearance of the old heavy industries, and with them the archetypal Welsh male worker, has been a profound culture shock for many. But an analysis of the changing composition of the Welsh labour force calls for caution and perspective. Despite the rapid increase in women's participation rates, Wales still lags behind the rest of the UK, with only Northern Ireland having a lower female economic activity rate. Women, though many are sole earners in a family, have not replaced men as 'breadwinners', in the sense that men were paid a wage intended to be sufficient to keep a wife and family. Nor has women's increasing participation in employment led to a wholesale reassignment of domestic responsibilities between the genders. Along with recognizing how far women have progressed in the last half century, we should be aware of how far there is still to go.

Table 6.1 Economic activity rates in Wales, by sex 1971–1994

	Females %	Males %
1971	36.7	78.4
1981	42.9	73.3
1991	48.1	69.0
1994	48.9	68.7

Source: T. Rees *Women and Work: Twenty-Five Years of Gender Equality in Wales.*

Changes in the industrial structure of Wales between the mid-1970s and the 1990s have meant job losses for men in the extractive industries, manufacturing and the energy and water supply industries. The growth of banking, finance and insurance over this period created jobs for both men and women, but the growth of jobs in distribution, hotels and catering and in services has mainly benefited women workers.

The Welsh labour force remains highly segregated. Men and women do different jobs: they work in different industries and are employed in different occupations within those industries. In 1981, the five main industrial sectors employing women in order of size were 'other services' (an inadequately named sector for the largest single employer of women, which covers both local government and personal services); followed by distribution, hotels and catering; manufacturing; public administration and transport, banking and finance. By 1991, other services remained in first place (with an increase of over 50,000 full- and part-time women employees), distribution in second place and manufacturing (with only a small increase) in third. The transport, banking and finance sector took over fourth place in 1991, while public administration slipped to fifth place. Women are not only concentrated in certain industrial sectors, but also in certain occupations. By 1994, for example, four main occupational groups accounted for 62.5 per cent of employed women in Wales i.e. 23.8 per cent in clerical and secretarial occupations, 15.3 per cent in personal and protective services, 11.9 per cent in 'other occupations' and 11.5 per cent in sales. By contrast, the four chief occupational groups of male workers were craft and related skills (23.2 per cent), managerial and administrative posts (17.9 per cent) and plant and machine operatives (15.3 per cent): together these account for 56.4 per cent of the male workforce. As Teresa Rees points out, 'These are for the most part better-paid jobs, which are more likely to offer training and promotion opportunities.'

Another distinctive feature of women's work from the 1970s to the 1990s has been the rise in the numbers who work part-time. Whereas in 1975, 36.7 per cent of female employees were part-timers, by 1994 the figure had risen to 49.6 per cent. A lack of childcare provision, coupled with the long hours' culture of work of the 1980s and 1990s, goes some way to account for this striking rise. Women are also less likely than men to acquire permanent, as opposed to temporary, contracts of employment. At the very end of the century, in 1999, only 25 per cent of female academics at Cardiff University were on permanent contracts, compared with 51 per cent of their male colleagues.

Women still earn less than men. This is in large part because they do not do the same jobs, though until the 1970 Equal Pay Act, which came into force in 1975, it was perfectly legal for employers to pay men and women different rates for exactly the same work and many did so. In 1975 the weekly earnings of all full-time female employees in Wales represented just 60 per cent of male earnings. By 1994 women's average weekly earnings had risen to 74.4 per cent of male earnings, and by 1999, 75 per cent. Although this represents an improvement, it also clearly shows that there is some way to go before equal pay between the sexes becomes a reality. It ought also to be noted that part of the narrowing of the gap between 1975 and 1994 has come about because male rates of pay in Wales have fallen in comparison with that of the UK male average.

Top jobs in Wales have remained throughout the period covered by this chapter an almost exclusively male preserve. As late as 1991, only 3 per cent of women were employed in civil service grades 1–4, 3.5 per cent had achieved principal officer status in local government, 1.3 per cent were professors in higher education and only 6.9 per cent of secondary school heads were female. In the case of the latter group, the headmistresses of secondary schools, this figure represents a significant drop from the early days of the century. Women have done rather better in the public sector than in the private: by 1997, only fourteen women occupied senior posts in Wales's top 300 companies compared with almost 1,500 men. There remains a long way for women to go in attaining top jobs, although the late 1990s have seen the appointment of a small number of women to highly visible and prestigious posts. By 1999 the director of the University of Wales Press, the controller of BBC Wales, the chair of S4C, the chief executive of the Arts Council of Wales, the director of the National Museum of Wales, the British Telecom national manager for Wales and the director of the CBI in Wales are all women.

Ethnicity and locality also have a bearing on women's role in the workforce. Wales has only a small non-white ethnic minority population: in 1991, 98 per cent of the population was white and born in the UK. The ethnic minority population is largely based in urban south-east Wales, including Cardiff's old mixed community of Butetown. Afro-Caribbean women have the highest economic activity rate of any group, including white women, whereas Pakistani and Bangladeshi women have the lowest. Black and ethnic minority women are twice as likely to be unemployed as white women. They also face the additional barriers of racial discrimination, the non-recognition of overseas qualifications and the lack of suitable education and training provision. Location also affects both job opportunities and wages for all Welsh women. In south-west Wales women manual workers receive the lowest pay. In rural Wales women have always contributed to the domestic economy and successive agricultural crises, such as the cutting of milk quotas in the 1980s and the beef crisis of the 1990s, have increased the burden on them. Shan Ashton's study of farmwives in north-west Wales shows the women working long days; taking total responsibility for the domestic work of the farm and often for the accounts and paperwork generated in a modern agricultural business; undertaking manual work, such as livestock feeding, shepherding, silage harvesting and haymaking; working off the farm, in the low-paid tourist sector or in professions, according to their qualifications, and in some cases operating on-farm diversified businesses such as running a bed-and-breakfast or a caravan site. Officialdom does not recognize the key role women play in agriculture, though women's voices are increasingly being heard in the protests of the late 1990s against the deepening agricultural crisis.

The history of women in the trade union movement in Wales has been totally neglected. Its recovery is both an urgent and major task. Although some sectors of Welsh women workers, such as teachers and some shop assistants, had been unionized from very early in the century, and both World Wars brought about huge rises in female membership, it was not until after the Second World War that they began to join trade unions in significant numbers in peacetime. The boost to their membership came as a result of their entry into the manufacturing industry and the large growth in the numbers of female employees in the public sector. In the 1960s and 1970s the numbers employed in the civil service, local government, the health service, teaching and social work rose rapidly and, with this, the numbers of women trade union members. Unions were keen to recruit women, but beyond negotiating a minimum women's rate ignored their needs. They remained monoliths of male power, conducting their business in arcane ways, as set out in rule books and standing orders, and in a language incomprehensible to the uninitiated. Some unions were overtly hostile to women. In the 1970s, male unions fought to maintain single-sex monopolies, such as those held by bus drivers and postmen, and in 1980–1 the AEUW at Hoover in Merthyr reached an agreement with the management which would have made women workers redundant, despite their seniority. Women successfully challenged this. Women also participated in a number of industrial actions in the 1970s and 1980s, notably NHS workers in 1979 and 1982, workers at Lefray Toys in 1984, and teachers and civil servants throughout the period.

The women's movement encouraged unions to take women's issues more seriously but the process has been slow. The Wales TUC was established in 1973 but only in 1984 did it set up a Women's Advisory Committee (WAC). One of the earliest acts of this committee was to conduct a survey which showed women's low level of participation in union affairs, with only 6 per cent of paid officials, 20 per cent of members of district and regional committees and 10 per cent of delegates to the Wales TUC being women. Since then, women-only day schools and courses have been provided to encourage more women to participate in union affairs. Some individual Welsh women have made great contributions to the trade union movement, but barriers discouraging wider participation by women remained. In 1993, for example, women constituted 68 per cent of the membership of Unison but only 42 per cent of its National Executive Committee (NEC) and 20 per cent of its national full-time officers. In the same year, women made up 74 per cent of the membership of the National Union of Teachers, but only 27 per cent of its NEC and 30 per cent of its national full-time officers. Dedicated women activists have struggled to bring about change in the male culture of trade unions in Wales and by the late 1990s some change was apparent. The main incentive for change however lies in the fact that the survival of the whole movement in Wales may well, given the changing structure of the workforce, depend increasingly on women.

The changing family and home life

There have been enormous changes in the Welsh family since the beginning of the century and the pace of change has accelerated in the last thirty years. In 1970 the small nuclear family with breadwinning husband, home-based wife (perhaps with a part-time job) and dependent children was still the norm. Since then, the structure and composition of family life in Wales has undergone radical change and this has had a fundamental bearing on women's lives. Marriage has declined in popularity: in 1990, 13,600 single women in Wales got married, compared with 18,000 in 1961, though there has been an increase in the number of people remarrying after divorce. As the marriage rate fell, that for cohabitation (living together before marriage) rose, so that by 1991 some 5.8 per cent of all families in Wales were cohabiting couples. The divorce rate has risen too, partly as a result of legal changes which make divorces easier to obtain: by 1991, the divorce rate per thousand marriages in Wales stood at 10.8. The birthrate has fallen since 1961: in 1991 it stood at 64.3 per thousand women aged between fifteen and forty-four. The proportion of illegitimate, or extra-marital births, on the other hand, has increased dramatically: by 1986, it stood at 21 per cent and has continued to rise. Childbirth, such a dangerous activity for women in the first half of the century, continued to become safer. All these changes have resulted in 'the family' becoming a far more diverse and complex entity than in the past. Household composition reflects this diversity: evidence drawn from a sample of the 1991 census shows that 58 per cent of households in Wales were occupied by married couples, 9 per cent by lone parents, 25 per cent by one person and 8 per cent by other groupings.

These are the bald statistics of change, but what lies behind them? It would be premature to write the obituary of the Welsh family. In fact, the family has shown itself to be a remarkably adaptable concept. Young couples living together are no longer scorned as 'living in sin', but are generally accepted: there is a broad consensus that cohabiting is a sensible option for many as compared with entering the legal union of marriage, which might later have to be dissolved by divorce. Single women who bear children are no longer drummed out of the chapel or cast out by their families. Divorce, once such a shocking thing in Wales, too has lost its stigma. These changes have come about in large part because of women's greater financial independence and their wider presence outside the home in such places as pubs, which, in small communities, even in the 1960s, was still considered inappropriate. The weakening of the code of gender-appropriate behaviour means that hypocrisy and moral disapproval are now far less frequently used against women to make them toe the line. The decline of religion has been another factor in shaping changing social attitudes: by the early 1980s, only a fifth of the people in Wales were members of a Christian church and the numbers have since fallen further. This has meant that the chapel no longer exerts such great influence over the local community and has lost much of its old power as an agency of the social control of women.

In 1991, lone-parent families constituted 13 per cent of all families in Wales, the great majority of them (93 per cent) headed by single mothers. The lot of lone mothers and their children depends greatly on their economic circumstances. Whereas, from the 1970s onwards, some professional single women actively chose to have a child without marrying or having a permanent male partner, and were well able to afford childcare, the majority of single mothers find life a struggle. Few single mothers are in employment. In 1994 only 16 per cent of this group (the same percentage as for married women with dependent children) worked full-time and only 23.4 per cent worked part-time, compared with nearly 60 per cent of married women with children. Part-time work renders women particularly vulnerable to the poverty trap, with loss of state benefits and the high cost of childcare acting as disincentives to working in low-paid jobs. In 1999 the New Labour government targeted women in its Welfare to Work programme, but it is too early to tell the impact that this will have on the incomes and living standards of lone-parent families. Many single-parent families have been created by divorce or the breakdown of other long standing partnerships, but in Wales, in particular, we have seen increases in teenage pregnancies. Whereas the rate for teenage pregnancies in England, given in figures published in 1999, stood at forty-four per thousand, the Welsh rate was fifty-one. In certain economically deprived areas, the rate was far higher than in more affluent parts of Wales. In Rhondda Cynon Taff, for example, it was sixty-five, while that for Monmouthshire was twenty-eight.

With low aspirations and lack of opportunities very young women drift into motherhood without thought for the consequences for their own lives.

Within the home, although late twentieth-century women no longer waited hand, foot and finger on their husbands and sons as their mothers had done, there has been no fundamental redistribution of domestic tasks between men and women. A tiny minority of men have opted to be house-husbands, in cases where the wife is the higher earner, and this has become socially acceptable. More generally, despite women's increased participation in the workforce, everyday household tasks – cooking, cleaning, washing and ironing and child-care – remain women's responsibility. Men 'help' with these. Male responsib-ilities usually lie in the field of household repairs and in some, but not all, cases, decorating. Young women have greater expectations than their mothers and far greater than their grandmothers, that men will share tasks equally but this remains to be seen. The ageing of the population has also in recent decades added the further burden of care of the elderly on women.

Conclusion

There can be no doubt that the last thirty years have seen substantial gains for women, but on the other hand, in the year 2000 it is certainly premature to talk of equality between the sexes in Wales. The old gender hierarchy remains – with men on top. In order to best assess the significance of changes which have affected women between 1970 and 1999, it is useful to set developments in these years within the broader context of the whole of the twentieth century. The conclusion, which follows, attempts to measure change from 1900 to 2000.

Conclusion

RESEARCHING and writing this book has been an absorbing and, indeed, compelling project. As I worked through the sources for each period covered by this book, it was exciting to see an overall picture of women's lives in twentieth-century Wales emerge, though, as I have frequently pointed out, a lot more research remains to be done. In this final section I attempt to answer just two questions. Firstly, does the evidence presented in *Out of the Shadows* show that there is a distinctive Welsh women's history, as opposed to a general British women's history? Secondly, and finally, how far have Welsh women come over the last hundred years and how far is there still to go?

Every nation has its own history: that can be taken as given. But does the experience of women in Wales differ substantially from that of women in other parts of Britain and does this justify the idea of a separate Welsh women's history? Of course, women in Wales have much in common with women in other parts of Britain. Not only do they share 'the female condition' but, just like women in England, Scotland and Northern Ireland, much of their lives has been determined by the British state, with its monopoly of law and war making. The new wave of feminist history-writing, which began in the 1970s, has led to the production of many books which purport to cover the history of women in Britain but in fact concentrate exclusively on the lives of women in England. Yet the English experience is not a universal one and fails to take account of the major differences which determine the life-choices and everyday existence of women in Wales, Scotland or Ireland.

Clearly the lives of women in Wales have been shaped by a distinctive Welsh culture, which has itself largely been defined by Nonconformity. The response of nineteenth-century Welsh cultural leaders to the attack on their religion, language and the morality of their women folk in the 1847 *Report into the State of Education in Wales*, was to adopt the doctrine of separate spheres with an outstanding fervour. In defence of their religion and the nation's good name (but with little regard for the Welsh language), ministers of religion, politicians and other male public figures zealously promoted the domestic ideology and the role of women as a civilizing force within the home. This, in turn, imposed on women in Wales a whole set of prescriptive rules: they were to be 'respectable', with all that word entails. The chapel policed their behaviour: women were cast out of chapels as late as the 1950s, and possibly the 1960s, for becoming pregnant while unmarried or on reports of adulterous behaviour. Purity was a moral imperative. In other ways, such as secondary and university education, Welsh girls enjoyed advantages over those in England. The 1889 Intermediate Education Act and the admissions policies of the University of Wales were influenced by pioneering Welsh women advocates of education, though the belief that the education of women would make better wives and mothers and contribute to the stability of the Welsh family played a part too in this advance. In terms of women's paid employment, there has also been a distinctive Welsh dimension. Female participation rates in Wales lagged behind England throughout the century. In the inter-war years the women's rate in Wales actually fell, going against the rising British trend. In the 1920s and 1930s an army of domestic servants was compelled to leave Wales and seek work in more prosperous areas of England: in this, and in other respects, ours is a colonial history. The nature of industrialization in Wales meant that there was very little paid work for women in the mining valleys of south Wales before 1939. The Second World War was to have a tremendous impact on women's participation rates in Wales, which rose by a staggering 134 per cent, compared to the average increase of just 30 per cent for the whole of Britain. The war identified factory work as women's work and post-war opportunities meant that women began to enter the workforce in increasing numbers, despite a great deal of male hostility. The last thirty years of the century saw the speed-up of this process, as men's jobs disappeared with the dismantling of the old, staple, heavy industries. Between 1971 and 1994 women's economic activity rates in Wales rose more rapidly than those in England, while at the same time the Welsh male rate dropped more sharply. There have been distinct Welsh dimensions to other aspects of women's history. Maternal mortality in Wales in the inter-war years rose significantly over the average for England and Wales. Wales remains a nation in poor health. The 1991 Census shows that while in Britain as a whole 13.9 per cent of women suffer from a debilitating illness, in Wales the figure was 17.4 per cent.

It can be argued too that Welsh women were subjected to a particularly 'virulent strain' of patriarchy. The nature of men's work in Wales, in heavy, dirty and dangerous jobs in extractive industries, meant not only that women's unpaid work was essential in the home, but that in Wales, work itself was defined in exclusively macho terms: only men's work was real work. Men were disparaging about the new post-war light industries, which employed large numbers of women: the *Welsh Nationalist*, August 1946, called the new factories 'doll's eye' industries. In Wales there was a particular male pride in being able to support a 'non-working' wife. The legacy of the nineteenth-century notion of separate spheres lingered longer in Wales, keeping women, with few exceptions, out of the public sphere. Women were excluded from power and policy making. Scottish feminist historians lament the fact that only eight women MPs were returned from Scotland between 1918 and 1945: the comparable figure for Wales was one. Only in the last decade of the century did women in Wales make a real breakthrough into the world of politics. In short, the lives of women in Wales were determined by a particular set of cultural values and by specific economic circumstances, which in turn has produced a distinct Welsh women's history.

The Wales of the year 2000 has changed out of all recognition from the Wales of 1900. In many respects, so too has the position and status of women. But how far have we come and how far is there still to go?

Legal changes throughout the century, won only by long, hard campaigning by feminists, have enfranchised women; removed legal barriers to entry to the professions; allowed women the right to custody of their children; and, through the Equal Opportunities legislation of the 1970s, outlawed discrimination against women, though the burden of proof still lies with the victim and, in Wales, women still have a harder time proving discrimination than women in other areas of the UK.

Nineteenth-century pioneers fought for women's entry into higher education, and Welsh girls, as well as boys, benefited from the Intermediate Education Act of 1889, the generous provision of free places in county schools by Labour local authorities and, since the 1940s, universal free secondary education. Since the 1970s, schoolgirls in Wales have improved their performance dramatically and in very recent years women actually outnumber men as undergraduates in our national university. But the twentieth century has not been a success story for women teachers. The age of the great headmistresses of single sex girls' schools was over by the 1960s and the status of the profession has declined. Although women have always been employed in large numbers in education, they have had little say in policy making and running the education service in Wales. At the end of the twentieth century Wales still had no female director of education.

The twentieth century saw huge changes in Welsh women's role in paid employment. The rise in women's participation since 1900 has been astounding, in large part because we started from such a low base. The rise has been particularly marked since the 1970s, but, even so, Welsh female rates lag behind England and Scotland. The existence of even a small group of women who held top positions in 1999 would have been unthinkable in 1900. Yet much of women's work remains low paid and without prospects, and there is no sign that the unpaid domestic workload has diminished; indeed care of the elderly and disabled may have increased the burden. There is a clear difference between educated, professional women whose work gives them economic independence and personal fulfilment, and low-paid women workers, who work solely from economic necessity and survive in some cases through a complex packaging of benefits and wages.

Measured over the whole century, and with the pace rapidly accelerated in the last thirty years, there have also been enormous social changes. Women have a far greater degree of control over their own bodies: they are no longer worn out by successive years of childbearing and contraception has given them a far greater degree of sexual freedom. Divorce has become commonplace and we are far more tolerant of a wide variety of personal relationships and living arrangements. The phenomenal rise in illegitimacy in the last thirty years may only in part be regarded as a demonstration of 'female power', in as much as some women positively chose to have a child outside of marriage and others, who in the past would have been forced to give up their babies for adoption, are now able to keep them. The very high figures for teenage pregnancy in Wales at the end of the twentieth century, however, have more to do with lack of prospects and the low aspirations of girls in deprived communities, and represent for some their only route to adulthood and 'independence', which is, in fact, achieved only through dependence on the state and the benefits system. Divorce and the rise in illegitimacy has resulted in an increase in single-parent families, over 90 per cent of these headed by women. This, in turn, has produced a huge increase in female and child poverty.

In 1900 women's place was in the home. Domestic work – washing, ironing, and cleaning – was hard and heavy and, in the absence of hot water on tap, electricity and modern appliances, meant that women worked long days to keep their homes free of dirt and disease. The new post-war domestic technology certainly removed some of the heavy drudgery from housework, but as married women increasingly went out to work in post-war Wales (in part to pay for the new gadgets), women found themselves shouldering the double burden of housework and a job. In families where both partners are in paid work, the major responsibility for domestic tasks still rests primarily on women, despite women's rising expectations that men will share the load. The great majority of women at the beginning of the century saw themselves purely in terms of their domestic role. By the end of the century, far fewer women would identify themselves exclusively in this way.

At the beginning of the twentieth century women were excluded from the public sphere and the realm of politics and decision-making. Despite the victory of the suffrage movement and the passage of the 1918 Eligibility of Women Act, Welsh women have been grossly under-represented at Westminster and at the very end of the century only one-tenth of Welsh MPs were women. The breakthrough has come only with the election of members of the National Assembly for Wales in 1999. Given our past history, this is a truly staggering departure. Women figured prominently in the Assembly's first cabinet under Alun Michael, but Rhodri Morgan's cabinet has gone one step further and at the beginning of the year 2000 there is actually a majority of women in the cabinet. This is believed to be the first cabinet in western Europe with a majority of women. As such it is a splendid chance for Welsh women to do some much needed catching up. Enormous hopes ride on the women in the Welsh Assembly but we should be cautious too. The election of the largest group, Labour women, owes much to 'twinning': there is no guarantee that this arrangement will continue, so women's current position in the Assembly, while opening up exciting prospects for change, remains fragile.

From the standpoint of the year 2000, it would seem to be a fair assessment of women's progress in twentieth-century Wales to say that we have come a long way, but there remains a long way still to go.

Bibliography

Newspapers

Aberdare Leader; Caerphilly Journal; Carmarthen Times; County Herald (Flintshire); Cambrian News; Daily Post; Denbighshire Free Post; Flintshire Leader; Glamorgan Gazette; North Wales Daily Chronicle; Rhondda Leader; Rhondda Socialist; South Wales Daily News; South Wales Daily Post; South Wales Echo; Western Mail.

Periodicals

Birth Control News; The Colliery Workers' Magazine; Common Cause; Y Frythones; Y Gymraes; Labour Gazette; Labour Woman; The New Generation; Peg's Paper; School World; The Suffragette; Swansea and District Workers Journal; Time and Tide; Y Traethodydd; The Vote; Votes for Women; The Welsh Nation; Welsh Nationalist; Welsh Outlook; Woman; Woman's Dreadnought; Woman's Own; Worker's Dreadnought; Young Wales.

Selected Primary Sources, *arranged by chapter*

Abbreviations	GRO	Glamorgan Record Office, Cardiff
	IWM	Imperial War Museum, London
	NLW	National Library of Wales, Aberystwyth
	PP	Parliamentary Papers
	PRO	Public Record Office, Kew

Chapter 1

GRO: records of Cardiff and District Women's Suffrage Society (CDWSS), D/DX/158; school log books (various); Cardiff School Board, minutes of Cookery Schools committee, 1890–1904 E/SB/68; rough book of Emma Edmunds, D/DX fq 25.

Flintshire Record Office, Hawarden: school log book, council girls' school, Mold.

NLW: medical officer of health annual reports, Caernarfonshire, Cardiganshire, Carmarthenshire, Flintshire, Rhondda.

Museum of Welsh Life, St Fagans: transcripts of interviews with outdoor farm servants, tapes 4187–8, 4189.

Official Reports: PP, 1893–4 (C 6894 XXIII) XXXVII, pt 1: *Royal Commission on Labour. Reports from the Lady Commissioners, Miss Eliza Orme, 'Employment for Women in Wales'*, 233–66.

Board of Education, *Special Report on the Teaching of Cookery to Public Elementary School Children in England and Wales*, HMSO, 1907.

See also *Project Grace* Unit 5, 'Women in Public Life in Nineteenth Century Wales' and Unit 6, 'Women and Politics in Wales 1880–1920', both compiled by Neil Evans.

Chapter 2

Sources include:

GRO: records of CDWSS, op. cit.

NLW: CDWSS printed annual reports, 1914–16 (XHQ 1221. C27); minute book of Llangollen NUWSS, 1914–18 (NLW MS 22636B); correspondence of Catherine Powell Evans in 'War Book: Collected by Catherine Powell Evans and Her Only Surviving Brother, George Eyre Evans, Penparcau', a bound collection of press cuttings, letters and notes (XD 523. E90); as examples of many thousands of wartime reports and pamphlets, see also *Report of the Work of the Glamorgan VADs During the Great War* (Barry, Barry Dock News, 1919) (XD 629. G7 G54); *Gwaith i Ferched Trysorfa'r Frenhines*, (XD 1); and National Union of Women Workers, *An Appeal to the Women of Wales* (1918/19) (XHD 6079. N17).

IWM holds a large collection of material on women, including reports of welfare officers in National factories; for diary of Policewoman West, Pembrey, see DD 77/156/1.

Swansea Museum: holds papers of Mrs Ross, NUWSS police 'patrol'.

Butetown History Centre, Cardiff: correspondence concerning recruitment of women to the WAAC, 1917.

For further documentary sources see *Project Grace* Unit 7, 'Women in the First World War', compiled by Pamela Michael. Note also the contemporary account of Wales in the war by Nicolson and Williams and Hay's study of Queensferry (see bibliography below).

Chapter 3

National Library of Women, (formerly Fawcett Library), Guildhall University, London: holds records of the National Vigilance Association, including annual reports, daily reports by workers and letters from mothers of Welsh girls in service in London.

PRO: for information on training schemes in domestic service run by the Central Committee on Women's Training and Employment see LAB/2.

NLW: for records and printed reports of many local societies set up to rescue 'fallen women', see, for example, Ladies Association for the Care of Friendless Girls, Caernarfon (Box XHV 1438 C and Box XHV 1431–47); Lletty Cranogwen, Tonypandy (Box XHV 1429 LL); and Barry Purity and Protective Society (Box XHV 1429 B).

Official Reports: Ministry of Reconstruction, *Report of the Women's Advisory Committee on the Domestic Service Problem*, Cmd 67 (1919); Ministry of Reconstruction, *Report of the Women's Employment Committee*, Cmd 9239 (1919); *Report and Minutes of the Royal Commission on the Coal Industry* (Sankey), Cmd 359, 360 (1919). *First Report of the Commission for the Special Areas*, Cmd 4957 (1934–5); *Second Report of the Commission for the Special Areas*, Cmd 5090 (1935–6); *Third Report of the Commission for the Special Areas*, Cmd 5303 (1936–7); *Fourth Report of the Commission for the Special Areas*, Cmd 5595 (1937–8); *Fifth Report of the Commission for the Special Areas*, Cmd 5896 (1938–9); Ministry of Health, *Report on Maternal Mortality in Wales*, Cmd 5423 (HMSO, 1937); Ministry of Health, *Report of the Committee of Inquiry into the Anti-Tuberculosis Service in Wales and Monmouthshire* (HMSO, 1939).

For the Women's Health Inquiry of 1939 see M. Spring Rice in bibliography below.

See also *Welsh Housing and Development Association Yearbooks*.

For further sources see *Project Grace* Unit 8, 'Women and Welfare', and Unit 9, 'Women in Inter-War Wales', both compiled by Pamela Michael.

Chapter 4

PRO holds records on women's war-work, LAB 8/ to LAB 26/. Note LAB/10/367, chief conciliation and industrial relations officer, Wales division weekly reports; LAB 26/4 enquiry into absence from work, 1943–4; LAB 26/60 shop hours for war workers 1940–8; LAB 26/61 shopping difficulties 1941–3.

NLW and *IWM* both hold original manuscripts submitted to the editors of *Parachutes and Petticoats* (L. Verrill-Rhys and the author), including many unpublished pieces.

Chapter 5

Official Reports: Ministry of Reconstruction, *Welsh Reconstruction Advisory Council; First Interim Report* (HMSO, 1944); Board of Trade, *Distribution of Industry*, Cmd 7540 (HMSO, 1948); *Occupational Survey of Manufacturing Industries in Wales*, 3rd report (Cardiff, Welsh College of Advanced Technology, 1964); *Occupational Survey of Manufacturing Industries in Wales: Statistical Abstract* (Cardiff, Welsh College of Advanced Technology, 1964); *Report by Sir William Beveridge on Social Insurance and Allied Services*, Cmd 6404, 1942–3; The Welsh Regional Hospital Board, *Annual Reports*, 1949–73; National Health Service, Association of Welsh executive councils, *Proceedings of Annual Meetings*, 1952–55; Health Services Wales, 1975, *Report of the Chief Medical Officer* (Cardiff, Welsh Office, 1975); *Digest of Welsh Statistics* (HMSO, 1954–).

Chapter 6

For material on the women's movement and other protests see:

GRO: Gertrude Tuck/Women's Rights Collection D/D/WRC.

Bristol Feminist Archive: Local Newsletters Collection.

NLW: Political Archive, MS Collection.

Other assorted papers are held in the South Wales Miners Library, Swansea, and the

National Library of Women, London. Many other papers are held in private collections.

The Equal Opportunities Commission Library, Cardiff, holds press-cuttings from the 1990s.

Secondary Works

Reference

Jones, B., *Etholiadau'r Ganrif/Welsh Elections*, 1885–1997 (Talybont, Y Lolfa, 1999).

The Suffragette Annual and Women's Who's Who (London, Stanley Paul and Co., 1913).

Town Directories.

Wales Trades Directory, 1903.

Who's Who in Wales (Cardiff, 1st edn., 1920; 2nd edn., 1933; 3rd edn., 1937).

Williams, J., *Digest of Welsh Historical Statistics*, 2 vols. (Cardiff, Welsh Office, 1985).

Databases

Masson, U. and Rolph, A., *Guide to Sources for the Women's Liberation Movement in South Wales. Database and Booklets: part 1, Events; Part 2, Media; Part 3, Newsletters* (Pontypridd, University of Glamorgan, 1997).

Thomas, D., and Jones, D., *Welsh Economy and Society Post 1945: A Database of Statistical and Documentary Material* (Cardiff, University of Wales Press, 1996).

General histories of Wales

Davies, J., *A History of Wales* (Harmondsworth, Penguin, 1993).

Morgan, K. O., *Rebirth of a Nation: Wales 1880–1980* (Oxford University Press and University of Wales Press, 1981).

Williams, G. A., *When Was Wales?* (Harmondsworth, Penguin, 1985).

Collections of essays and writings on Welsh women

Aaron, J., Rees, T., Betts, S. and Vincentelli, M. (eds.), *Our Sisters' Land: The Changing Identities of Women in Wales* (Cardiff, University of Wales Press, 1994).

John, A. V. (ed.), *Our Mothers' Land: Chapters in Welsh Women's History, 1830–1939* (Cardiff, University of Wales Press, 1991).

Project Grace, Welsh Women's History. Teaching Materials, consisting of ten units of text and documents compiled by Neil Evans, Pamela Michael and Sydna A. Williams. Photocopied units (University of Wales, Bangor, 1994).

Verrill-Rhys, L., and Beddoe, D., *Parachutes and Petticoats: Welsh Women Writing on the Second World War* (Dinas Powys, Honno, 1992).

White, C., and Williams, S. R., *Struggle or Starve: Women's Lives in the South Wales Valleys between the Wars* (Dinas Powys, Honno, 1997).

Other secondary works
Abbreviations OML   (*Our Mothers' Land: Chapters in Welsh Women's History,*
                             1830–1939
                 OSL   (*Our Sister's Land: The Changing Identities of Women in*
                             Wales)
                 Project Grace (*Project Grace, Welsh Women's History*)

Aaron, J., 'Finding a voice in two tongues: gender and colonization', in *OSL*,
     183–98.
Andrews, E., *A Woman's Work is Never Done* (Ystrad Rhondda, Cymric Democratic
     Publishing Co., 1956).
Ashton, S., 'The farmer needs a wife: farm women in Wales', in *OSL*, 122–39.
Baker, E., *'Yan Boogie': the Autobiography of a Swansea Valley Girl* (Pretoria, 1992).
Beddoe, D., *Back to Home and Duty: Women between the Wars 1918–1939* (London,
     Pandora, 1989).
Beddoe, D., 'Women between the wars', in T. Herbert and G. E. Jones (eds.), *Wales
     Between the Wars* (Cardiff, University of Wales Press, 1990), 129–60.
Beddoe, D., 'Munitionettes, maids and mams: women in Wales, 1914–39', in *OML*,
     189–209.
Benn, C., *Keir Hardie* (London, Richard Cohen Books, 1997).
Betts, S., 'The changing family in Wales', in *OSL*, 17–30.
Bondfield, M., *A Life's Work* (London, 1948).
Boston, S., *Women Workers and the Trade Unions* (London, Lawrence and Wishart, 1987).
Braybon, G., *Women Workers in the First World War* (London, Routledge, 1981).
Braybon, G., and Summerfield, P., *Out of the Cage: Women's Experiences in Two World
     Wars* (London, Pandora, 1987).
Bullock-Davies, C., *A Grain of Mustard Seed: An Account of the Founding of the First
     Women's Institute in Great Britain with extracts from its Minute Books* (Bangor, Jarvis
     and Foster, 1954).
Bussey, G. and Timms, M., *Pioneers for Peace: Women's International League for Peace
     and Freedom* (London, WILPF, 1980).
Carr, C., *The Spinning Wheel: City of Cardiff High School for Girls 1895–1955* (Cardiff,
     Western Mail and Echo, 1955).
Charles, N., 'The refuge movement and domestic violence', in *OSL*, 48–60.
Clwyd-Denbigh Federation of Women's Institutes 1933–1983 (St. Asaph, 1983).
Clwyd, H., *Buwch ar y Lein: Detholiad o Ddyddiaduron Llundain, 1957–64* (Dinas
     Powys, Honno, 1987).
Coleman, D. C., *Courtaulds: an Economic and Social History, 1940–65*, III (Oxford,
     Clarendon Press, 1980).
Crook, R., '"Tidy women": women in the Rhondda between the wars', *Oral History
     Journal*, 10 No. 2 (1982), 40–6.
Crwyden, R., 'Welsh lesbian feminist: a contradiction in terms', in *OSL*, 294–300.
Davies, C. Aull, 'Women, nationalism and feminism', in *OSL*, 242–58.
Davies, G. Alban, 'Y got ffwr', *Taliesin*, 75 (1991), 28–35.
Davies, J., *The Welsh Language* (Cardiff, University of Wales Press, 1993).

Davies, M. Llewelyn (ed.), *Maternity: Letters from Working Women* (1915) (London, Virago, 1978).

Davies, M. Llewelyn (ed.), *Life as We Have Known It by Co-operative Working Women* (1931) (London, Virago, 1977).

Davies, R., 'Inside the "House of the Mad". The social context of mental illness, suicide and the pressure of rural life in South West Wales *c.* 1860–1920', *Llafur*, 4 No. 2 (1985), 20–35.

Davies, W., *The Organization of the Curriculum in the County Intermediate Schools 1880–1926* (Cardiff, University of Wales Press, 1989).

Dee, L. and Keineg, K., *Women in Wales: A Documentary of our Recent History* vol 1, (Cardiff, Womenwrite Press, 1991).

Douglas, M., 'Women, God and birth control: the first hospital birth control clinic, Abertillery, 1925', *Llafur*, 6 No. 4 (1995), 110–22.

Dyhouse, C., *No Distinction of Sex? Women in British Universities, 1870–1939* (London, UCL Press, 1995).

Eckley, S., and Bearcroft, D., *Voices of Abertillery, Aberbeeg and Llanhilleth* (Stroud, Chalford, 1996).

Elfyn, M., 'Writing is a bird in hand', in *OSL*, 280–6.

Ellis-Jones, P., 'The women's suffrage movement in Caernarfonshire', *Caernarfonshire Historical Society Transactions*, 48 (1987), 75–112.

Evans, C., *My People* (1915) (Bridgend, Seren, 1987).

Evans, N., and Cook, K., '"The Petty Antics of the Bell-Ringing Boisterous Band": The women's suffrage movement in Wales, 1890–1918', in *OML*, 159–88.

Evans, N., and Jones, D., '"A Blessing for the Miner's Wife": the campaign for pithead baths in the south Wales coalfield, 1908–1950', *Llafur* 6 No. 3 (1994), 5–28.

Evans, N., and Jones, D., '"To help forward the great work of humanity": women in the Labour party in Wales, 1900–2000', in D. Hopkin, D. Tanner and C. Williams (eds.), *A Centenary History of the Labour Party in Wales* (Cardiff, University of Wales Press, 2000).

Evans, W. Gareth, *Education and Female Emancipation: The Welsh Experience* (Cardiff, University of Wales Press, 1990).

Fisher, K., '"Clearing up misconceptions": the campaign to set up birth control clinics in south Wales between the wars', *Welsh History Review*, 19 No. 1 (1998), 103–29.

Francis, H. and Smith, D., *The Fed: A History of the South Wales Miners in the Twentieth Century* (London, Lawrence and Wishart, 1980).

Francis, H., *Miners Against Fascism: Wales and the Spanish Civil War* (London, Lawrence and Wishart, 1994).

Gaffney, A., *Aftermath: Remembering the Great War in Wales* (Cardiff, University of Wales Press, 1998).

Gittins, D., *Family Size and Structure, 1900–39* (London, Hutchinson, 1982).

Ginzberg, E., *A World Without Work: The Story of the Welsh Miners* (1942) (USA, Transaction Publishers, 1990).

Grenfell-Hill, J., *Growing Up in Wales: Collected Memories of Childhood in Wales, 1895–1939* (Llandysul, Gomer, 1996).

Hall, R., *Dear Dr Stopes: Sex in the 1920s* (Harmondsworth, Penguin, 1981).

Hannington, W., *Unemployed Struggles, 1919–36* (1936) (London, Lawrence and Wishart, 1977).

Hay, I., *HM Factory Queensferry: 1915–1918* (Queensferry, Factory Press, 1948).

Holdsworthy, A., *Out of the Doll's House* (London, BBC, 1988).

Horn, P., *Women in the 1920s* (Stroud, Allen Sutton, 1995).

Hughes, H., *An Uprooted Community: A History of Epynt* (Llandysul, Gomer, 1998).

Hughes, O. Wynne, *Everyday was Summer* (Llandysul, Gomer, 1989).

Inman, P., *Labour in the Munitions Factories* (London, HMSO, 1957).

Jenkins, D., *The Agricultural Community in South-West Wales at the turn of the Twentieth Century* (Cardiff, University of Wales Press, 1971).

Jennings, H., *Brynmawr: A Study of a Distressed Area* (London, Allenson, 1934).

John, A.V., '"Run like blazes": The suffragettes and Welshness', *Llafur*, 6 No. 3 (1994), 29–43.

Jones, D., 'Counting the cost of coal: women's lives in the Rhondda, 1881–1911', in *OML*, 109–33.

Jones, D., 'Serfdom and slavery: women's work in Wales, 1890–1930', in D. R. Hopkin and G. S. Kealey (eds.) *Class, Community and the Labour Movement in Wales and Canada, 1850–1930* (Aberystwyth, Llafur/CCLH, 1989).

Jones, E. Vernon, 'A champion of women's rights', *Carmarthenshire Historian*, XX (1985), 5–25.

Jones, E., *A History of GKN: Innovation and Response 1795–1918*, vol. 1 (Basingstoke, Macmillan, 1987).

Jones, G. Orlando, *A Mid-Wales Family* (Llanidloes, Great Oak Bookshop, 1994).

Jones, M., *A Radical Life: The Biography of Megan Lloyd George* (London, Hutchinson, 1991).

Jones, M., *Perlau'r Wawr: Merched Y Wawr, 1967–1997* (Y Bala, Merched y Wawr, 1998).

Jones, R. Chambers, *Bless 'Em All: Aspects of the War in North-West Wales* (Wrexham, Bridge Books, 1995).

Jones, S. Owen, 'Women in the tinplate industry in Llanelli 1930–50', *Oral History Journal* 15 No. 1 (1987), 72–90.

Kinnock, G, and Millar, F., *By Faith and Daring: Interviews with Remarkable Women* (London, Virago, 1993).

Lieven, M., *Senghennydd: The Universal Pit Village, 1890–1930* (Llandysul, Gomer, 1994).

Lipman, B., 'Diary of a Welsh Liberationist', *Planet*, 15 (1973), 33–36.

Lloyd-Morgan, C., 'From temperance to suffrage', in *OML*, 135–158.

Lock, J., *The British Policewoman: Her Story* (London, Robert Hale, 1979).

Marwick, A., *Women at War 1914–18* (London, Fontana, 1977).

Marquand, H. A., *The Second Industrial Survey of South Wales* (London, HMSO, 1932).

Marquand, H. A., 'Industry in Wales', *Welsh Anvil*, 1 (1949), 71–80.

Masson, U., 'Loyalty and dissent: wartime Wales in 1940', *Radical Wales* (Spring 1991), 16–19.

Masson, U., 'Votes for women; the campaign in Swansea, *Minerva: The Transactions of the Royal Institute of South Wales*, 1 (1993), 34–9.

Meese, C. E., *The Life and Times of Ceridwen Eluned Meese* (Bagillt, Gwasg Cartref, 1998).

Miller, J., *You Can't Kill The Spirit* (London, Women's Press, 1986).

Minns, R., *Bombers and Mash: The Domestic Front 1939–45* (London, Virago, 1980).

Morgan, D., 'The changing face of South Wales', *Wales* II No.27, (1947) 364–75.

Morris, D., '"Merched y screch a'r twrw": yr WSPU yn Llanystumdwy, 1912', *Caernarfonshire Historical Society Transactions*, 46 (1985), 115–32.

Nicolson, I., and Williams, L., *Wales: Its Part in the War* (London, Hodder and Stoughton, 1919).

Painting, D., *Amy Dillwyn* (Cardiff, University of Wales Press, 1987).

Parnell, M. Davies, *Snobs and Sardines: Rhondda Schooldays* (Bridgend, Seren 1993).

Parry-Jones, D., *Welsh Country Upbringing* (Upton, Ffynnon Press, 1974).

Phillips, M., *Women and the Miners' Lock Out* (London, Labour Publishing Co., 1927).

Picton-Turbervill, E., *Life Is Good: An Autobiography* (London, Muller, 1939).

Pilgrim Trust, *Men Without Work* (Cambridge, Cambridge University Press, 1938).

Price, H., 'Experiences in World War II', *Llafur*, 6 No. 1 (1992), 110–13.

Raine, A., *Torn Sails* (London, Hutchinson, 1898).

Rees, A. D., *Life in a Welsh Countryside: A Social Study of Llanfihangel yng Ngwynfa* (1948) (Cardiff, University of Wales Press, 1996).

Rees, T., *Women and Work: Twenty-Five Years of Gender Equality in Wales* (Cardiff, University of Wales Press, 1999).

Reeves, R., 'Welsh patchwork', in A. Sebestyen (ed.) *'67, '78, '88: From Women's Liberation to Feminism* (London, Prism, 1988).

Rhondda, Viscountess, *This was My World* (London, Macmillan, 1933).

Rice, M. Spring, *Working Class Wives* (1939) (London, Virago, 1981).

Richards, W. L., *Pembrokeshire Under Fire: The Story of the Air-Raids of 1940–1* (Haverfordwest, J. W. Hammond, 1965).

Roberts, B., 'A mining town in wartime: fears for the future', *Llafur*, 6 No. 1 (1992), 82–95.

Roberts, Ff., *Mae Bod yn Fyw yn Fawr Ryfeddod* (Denbigh, Gwasg Gee, 1996).

Roberts, K., *Traed Mewn Cyffion* (first edn. 1936) (Llandysul, Gomer, 1988).

Rosser, C. and Harris, C., *The Family and Social Change: A Study of Family and Kinship in a South Wales Town* (London, Routledge and Kegan Paul, 1965).

Ruck, B., *A Story-Teller Tells The Truth* (London, Hutchinson, 1935).

Spiers, J., *Minute by Minute: Seventy Years of Pembrokeshire Federation of Women's Institutes* (Haverfordwest, Pembroke Federation of Women's Institutes, 1991).

Stephens, R. (ed.), *Asen Adda* (Llandysul, Gomer, 1975).

Stott, M., *Organization Women* (London, Heinemann, 1978).

Swain, F., *Women: Wales and the Second World War* (Mid-Glamorgan County Council Education Authority, 1989).

Thomas, D. A., 'War and the economy: the south Wales experience', in C. Baber and J. Williams (eds.), *Modern South Wales: Essays in Economic History* (Cardiff, University of Wales Press, 1986).

Tibbott, S. Minwel, 'Going electric: the changing face of the rural kitchen in Wales, 1945–55', *Folk Life*, 28 (1989), 63–74.

Tibbott, S. Minwel and Thomas, B. *O'r Gwaith i'r Gwely: Cadw tŷ 1890–1960 / A Woman's Work: Housework* (Cardiff, National Museum of Wales, 1994).

Tomos, A., 'A Welsh Lady', in *OSL*, 259–66.

Tudur, G., *Wyt Ti'n Cofio? Chwarter Ganrif o Frwydr yr Iaith* (Llandysul, Y Lolfa, 1989).

Veysey, A. G., *Clwyd a'r Rhyfel / Clwyd at War, 1939–45* (Hawarden, Clwyd Record Office, 1989).

Wallace, R., *Organize! Organize! Organize! A Study of Reform Agitations in Wales 1840–86* (Cardiff, University of Wales Press, 1991).

Webb, R. A., *From Caerau to the Southern Cross* (Port Talbot, Alun Books, 1987).

Webb, R. A., *Sirens Over the Valley* (Port Talbot, Alun Books, 1988).

Webb, R. A., *A Tree Grew in Caerau* (Port Talbot, Alun Books, 1990).

Welsby, C., '"Warning her as to her future behaviour": the lives of the widows of the Senghenydd Mining Disaster of 1913', *Llafur*, 6, No. 4 (1995), 93–109.

White, E., *The Ladies of Gregynog* (Cardiff, University of Wales Press, 1985).

Williams, C., *Capitalism, Community and Conflict: The South Wales Coalfield 1898–1947* (Cardiff, University of Wales Press, 1998).

Williams, C., 'Work, sex and rugby', in G. E. Jones and D. Smith (eds.), *The People of Wales* (Llandysul, Gomer, 1999).

Williams, G. A., 'Women workers in Wales, 1968–1982', *Welsh History Review*, II No. 4 (1983), 530–48.

Williams, L. J., and Jones, D., 'Women at work in the nineteenth century', *Llafur* 3, No. 3 (1983), 20–9.

Williams, M. A., '"Where is Mrs Jones Going?": Women and the Second World War in Wales'* (Aberystwyth, Centre for Advanced Welsh and Celtic Studies, 1995).

Williams, M. A., 'Yr ymgyrch i "Achub y Mamau" yng nghymoedd diwydiannol de Cymru, 1918–1939', in Geraint H. Jenkins (ed.) *Cof Cenedl* XI (Llandysul, Gomer, 1996).

Williams, Lady Juliet, 'Malnutrition as a cause of maternal mortality', *Public Health*, 50 (1936), 11–19.

Williams, S, A., 'Law not war: hedd nid cledd: women and the peace movement in north Wales, 1926–1945', *Welsh History Review* 18 No. 1 (1996), 63–91.

Wiltsher, A., *Most Dangerous Women: Feminist Peace Campaigners in the Great War* (London, Pandora, 1985).

Winckler, V., 'Women in post war Wales', *Llafur*, 4 No. 4 (1987), 69–77.

Wood, B., *Wednesday's Child* (Port Talbot, Alun Books, 1989).

Woollacott, A., *On Her Their Lives Depend: Munition Workers in the Great War* (Berkeley, University of California Press, 1994).

Index

36377